Routledge Library Editions

MONETARY THEORY
AND PUBLIC POLICY

ECONOMICS

Routledge Library Editions – Economics

KEYNESIAN &
POST-KEYNESIAN ECONOMICS
In 11 Volumes

MONETARY THEORY
AND PUBLIC POLICY

KENNETH K KURIHARA

Routledge
Taylor & Francis Group

LONDON AND NEW YORK

First published in 1951

Reprinted in 2003 by
Routledge
2 Park Square, Milton Park, Abingdon, Oxon, OX14 4RN
or
270 Madison Avenue, New York, NY 10016

First issued in paperback 2010

Routledge is an imprint of the Taylor & Francis Group

British Library Cataloguing in Publication Data
A CIP catalogue record for this book
is available from the British Library

Monetary Theory and Public Policy
ISBN 978-0-415-31374-2 (hbk)
ISBN 978-0-415-60783-4 (pbk)
ISBN 978-0-415-31367-4 (set)

Miniset: Keynesian & Post-Keynesian Economics

Series: Routledge Library Editions – Economics

Monetary Theory and Public Policy

By KENNETH K. KURIHARA

Rutgers University

Routledge
Taylor & Francis Group

LONDON AND NEW YORK

FIRST PUBLISHED IN GREAT BRITAIN
IN 1951

SECOND IMPRESSION 1956
THIRD IMPRESSION 1958

Preface

JOHN MAYNARD KEYNES' *General Theory of Employ-ment, Interest, and Money* has had a revolutionary impact on monetary theory and policy as well as on other fields of economics. His monetary theories and policy recommendations have proved most helpful in the solution of major economic problems associated with the Great Depression, the war economy, and the immediate postwar transition, and will doubtless continue to be helpful in meeting our future economic problems. The details of policy must necessarily differ from place to place and from time to time, but Keynes' diagnosis of the fundamental economic problems of our times has provided us with an objective technique of thinking which transcends any partisan policy discussions—particularly in a free society. If we are to minimize the harmful effects of fluctuations in effective demand and to maintain continuous full employment and output within the framework of the democratic traditions, it will be necessary for us to investigate the "endogenous" and "exogenous" determinants of the parameters of the Keynesian functions; namely, the positions and shapes of the liquidity, consumption, savings, and investment functions.

This volume is an attempt to present in systematic form the latest developments in monetary theory and the implications of such developments for public policy. It also attempts to fill the gap between the esoteric literature and the standard text. As such, this book might be used as a supplement to the text on business cycles, money and banking, economic theory, and other related fields. Primary emphasis has been placed upon the tools of analysis, for I am firmly convinced that no amount of information will solve major economic problems without the theory to interpret it correctly. Nor, for that matter, is it possible for "tool users" to make correct policy decisions without the theory to guide policy. Following the late Lord Keynes' realistic interest in the "cure" as well as in the "diagnosis," policy discussions have been included in this book. The relevant policy alternatives are evaluated as to their theoretical soundness and practical wisdom.

Part I of this book deals with money and general prices. For the first time, I believe, two full chapters are devoted to inflation in a text on monetary economics. Inflation is discussed in terms of modern monetary theory rather than in terms of the traditional quantity theory, that is, as an integral part of the general theory of effective demand. Part II may be regarded as the heart of the book, dealing as it does with interest, the consumption function, the savings-investment equilibrium, and related policy discussions. The Keynesian and non-Keynesian contributions are examined in some detail, to facilitate later policy considerations. Particular care has been taken to clarify the common confusion concerning the definitional and determinate equality of savings and investment. Part III is an application of the Keynesian "income-expenditure" approach to an "open system" with foreign economic relations. Various theories of the determination of the external value of money, the roles of the International Monetary Fund and the International Bank, the problem of a "chronic dollar shortage," the international aspect of depression, and other international currency and financial problems are considered against the background of a changing international setting.

The reader will find the footnote references useful in suggesting readings for further study on particular points.

I wish to record my gratitude to those persons who have been associated with the development and preparation of this book. Dean C. A. Phillips of the University of Iowa and Professor Elmer Wood of the University of Missouri must be mentioned as responsible for my initial interest in monetary and banking theories. My former colleagues, Professors F. D. Graham, F. A. Lutz, and J. Viner of Princeton University, have given me the benefit of their suggestions on questions of international finance. Professor A. H. Hansen of Harvard University and Professor P. A. Samuelson of the Massachusetts Institute of Technology have extended to me stimulating suggestions on some theoretical and methodological points. I owe much to the encouragement and stimulation of Professors Eugene E. Agger, Max Gideonse, Anatol Murad, Broadus Mitchell, and Messrs. Seymour M. Miller and Robert J. Alexander of Rutgers University. I also wish to express my appreciation to Professor Arthur D. Gayer and Mr. Charles Hoffmann of Queens College for many helpful comments toward the improvement of the content of this book. Above all, my greatest debt of gratitude is due to Dean Howard R. Bowen of the University of Illinois for his constant encouragement and guidance all through my creative ventures. I alone, however, am responsible for any defects of analysis or errors of fact in this book.

The editors of the *Journal of Political Economy* have kindly granted me permission to reproduce substantial parts of my articles (Chapters 20 and 21).

Kenneth K. Kurihara

Contents

Part III. Domestic vs. International Equilibrium

Figures

Tables

Monetary Theory and Public Policy

1

Introduction: The Significance of Monetary Analysis and Policy

MONETARY THEORY, like all theories, changes and should change with the changing problems of the actual world. Classical economists had a common tendency to regard monetary phenomena as rather misleading reflections of real phenomena, on the ground that money obscured the otherwise transparent exchange relations. They therefore placed major emphasis on the production, exchange, and consumption of goods. They precluded the possibility that money might distort the smooth operation of the "natural" laws of supply and demand. They were of course right in asserting that monetary phenomena do not vitiate the fundamental laws that govern economic behavior, for it remains true that the physical law of diminishing returns and the psychological law of diminishing utility, to mention only the most familiar, had existed even before the advent of money and will probably exist even after money is demonetized out of existence. They were amiss, however, in supposing that monetary phenomena could not be a cause of change in real phenomena. Why did classical economists deny monetary phenomena as independent variables

3

capable of disturbing the functioning of the entire economy? The answer is that they tacitly assumed the stability of the value of money.

On this assumption one could cogently argue that money could never be a disequilibrating factor and therefore could dismiss it as irrelevant. With the general price level and therefore the purchasing power of money assumed to be constant, one could indeed concentrate on the determination of prices and quantities of individual commodities. This is precisely what the traditional individual-firm analysis does. Accordingly, there was no need for a special theory of money to explain fluctuations in the value of money and their effects on economic activity. Even when economists finally recognized the disturbing influence of monetary phenomena, they were inclined to view it merely as a deviation from the "norm." They therefore relegated a theory of money to the background of the value theory. This tendency to regard monetary disturbances as incidental is still reflected, e.g., in the view that relative prices are more relevant to policy than the general price level. Nevertheless, a theory of money and general prices found a respectable, though subordinate, place in economic theory. To "neutralize" the disquieting effects of money became the favorite pastime of "purely monetary" economists, and the quantity theory of money was its theoretical expression.

By contrast, the starting point of modern monetary theory is that money is inherently unstable. Keynes is credited with having developed a general theory of monetary equilibrium in which such monetary variables as income, consumption, savings, and investment play major roles. His earlier works (e.g., *Monetary Reform*, 1923, and *A Treatise on Money*, 1930) bore imprints of the traditional theory of money, but with the publication of his *General Theory of Employment, Interest, and Money* (1936), monetary theory definitely shifted its center of gravity from an explanation of the effects of changes in the value of money on the distribution of wealth to an explanation of the effects of changes in aggregate income and expenditure on general economic stability, including the stability of the value of money. Thus the modern theory of money is almost the reverse of the traditional theory. The stability of money is no longer taken for granted, and yet the stabilization of the value of money is brought into direct relation with the stabilization of the levels of income and employment.

Keynes and others emphasize the monetary approach to the problem of economic stabilization for the following reasons.

1. Money is the most dynamic element in a modern economy—"a link between the present and the future." As long as monetary expectations are capable of influencing our present economic activities, so long will money remain a device to link the present and the future. Money as such can take the form of any durable asset capable of performing the store-of-value function. Largely through this function money influences the cyclical behavior of consumption, savings, investment, and employment.

2. In the end the volume of employment is increased and recovery effected through monetary adjustments. It is an increase in monetary outlays for consumption and investment that gives rise to increased output and employment, regardless of whether these outlays are private or public. It is, in other words, the manipulation of income and expenditure (i.e., effective demand) that "does the trick." High levels of output and employment are found in the flow of income rather than in the accumulation of wealth. As far as advanced economies are concerned, spending is more conducive to the stability of income and employment than saving, particularly in conditions of less than full employment.

3. Monetary adjustments are publicly controllable. To the extent that the monetary-fiscal authorities exercise an appreciable influence over the flow of income or, what amounts

to the same thing, total expenditure, economic activity is freed from the erratic fluctuations to which it is otherwise exposed. More important still, monetary-fiscal policy is an alternative to an "authoritarian" policy of achieving full employment "at the expense of efficiency and of freedom." [1] The monetary-fiscal control of aggregate income and expenditure is a substitute for the regimentation of the market.[2] It is typically an attempt to maintain "full employment in a free society." Monetary adjustments considered as a matter of public policy rescue the economy from the dictates of "blind forces" and at the same time render both deflation and inflation definitely dispensable.

Monetary theory is essentially a short-run analysis, for it is in short periods that monetary factors make their influence felt most and the value of money and the flow of income fluctuate significantly. As such, monetary theory is an indispensable supplement to the traditional long-run analysis, but it is obviously inadequate in explaining the long-run behavior of the economy based largely on such "real" factors as technological, institutional, and structural changes. Keynes' oft-quoted dictum that "in the long run we are all dead" [3] epitomizes the above strength and weakness of monetary analysis.

Although monetary theory is inseparably linked up with public policy, it must not be supposed that theory is immediately or perfectly applicable to policy. Like all tools of analysis, monetary theory is primarily a technique of thinking for drawing correct conclusions.[4] To the extent, however, that monetary theory is conceived broadly and realistically it is also a fruitful guide to policy. A monetary policy which is based on a realistic theory goes a long way toward economic

[1] Keynes, *General Theory*, p. 381.

[2] A. H. Hansen, *Economic Policy and Full Employment* (Whittlesey, New York, 1947), p. 293.

[3] *Monetary Reform* (Harcourt, New York, 1924), p. 88.

[4] Keynes' preface to D. H. Robertson, *Money* (Harcourt, New York, 1929).

stability, but it must be broadly interpreted so as to include fiscal and other measures. Monetary-fiscal policy should be supplemented by nonmonetary policies, if we are to overcome "the real economic evils of society—inadequate production and inequitable distribution" which "lie too deep for any purely monetary ointment to cure." [5] With these possibilities and limitations of monetary analysis and policy in mind, we shall be able to proceed without illusions.

[5] Robertson, *ibid.*, p. 194.

PART I

Money and General Prices

2

The Internal Value of Money

A NATIONAL currency has internal and external value. The internal value of a currency refers to the purchasing power of that currency in terms of domestic goods and services, while its external value is its foreign exchange rate, that is, the domestic price of a foreign currency. For purposes of analysis it is convenient to treat these two aspects of a currency separately. In this chapter we shall assume a closed system without foreign economic relations.

The Quantity Theory of Money

The value of money differs from the value of other objects in one fundamental respect, namely, the fact that the value of money represents *general* purchasing power or command over "things in general." This means that a change in the value of money affects our general ability to command goods and services in exchange. Thus high prices of other things are reflected in the low exchange value of money, and low prices of other things are reflected in the high exchange value of money. The value of money is therefore the reciprocal of the general price level, and can be expressed as $1/P$. Changes in the value of money affect not only individual owners of given units of currency but the entire economy which is carried on in terms of money. These changes affect different groups of individuals differently, as will be shown later. Above all, changes in the value of money inject an element of instability into the economy as a whole. It is for these reasons that the investigation of the forces which alter the value of money is of such theoretical and practical importance.

One of the oldest explanations of the value of money is the quantity theory of money. In its crude form the theory states that the purchasing power of money depends directly on the quantity of money. This may be expressed as $M = kP$ or $P = 1/kM$, where M stands for the quantity of money, P for the general price level, and k for constant proportionality. If, for example, k is 3, M is three times the price level. As long as k is a constant, M and P will be proportional. The validity of this simple quantity formulation depends on the tacit assumptions that (a) the velocity of money is stable, and (b) that the volume of goods and services to be bought with money remains constant.

The quantity theorists neglected the velocity of money because they were preoccupied with what Keynes calls "transaction" and "precautionary" motives for holding money. For as long as we are interested in holding money just to effect ordinary transactions or for "the rainy day," the amount of money held against total expenditure remains rather stable. But as soon as we take into account the "speculative" motive (i.e., the desire for cash for uncertain future price or interest changes), we must admit the possibility of a change in the velocity of money. The speculative motive is facilitated by the "store-of-value" function of money. As we shall see more clearly later, this last motive for holding money is capable of causing volatile fluctuations not only in the value of money but also in general economic activity. If a part of a given quantity of money fails to appear in the income or spending stream, then the demand for money to hold must have increased and therefore the velocity of money must have decreased. And as long as money is capable of serving as a store of value for speculative purposes, there is always the possibility that more money may be held than is required to satisfy the transaction and precautionary motives and thus decrease the velocity of money. Similarly, an increase in the velocity of money may be caused by a decrease in the demand for money to hold, if, for example, lending or investing is considered as a better alternative to holding money. The main point is that an increase (or a decrease) in the quantity of money may be offset by a decrease (or an increase) in the velocity of money, so that the general price level remains unaffected.

The assumption that the volume of goods and services remains constant is implicit in another assumption—namely, that full employment exists. Full employment implies that no idle resources are available to increase the production of goods and services to be bought with money. Hence on this assumption the quantity of goods and services can be taken as fixed relatively to the quantity of money. But if an increase in the quantity of money is offset by an increase in the quantity of goods and services, as is possible at less than full employment, then the general price level may not rise and therefore the value of money may not fall.

If the crude quantity theory of money had its way, the stabilization of general prices and therefore of the value of money would be a simple matter of manipulating the quantity of money, increasing the latter if prices are too low and decreasing it if prices are too high. Many monetary experiments were made and are occasionally proposed even today on the notion that there is a simple, mechanical relation between the general price level and the quantity of money. We have suggested that to achieve the desired level of general prices we need take into account not only the quantity of money but its velocity and the state of employment. But this is not to imply that economic stability is only a matter of price stabilization.

Criticisms of the unrealism of the underlying assumptions of the crude quantity theory of money have led to its refinement. The *transaction* equation of exchange is the best known of the refined forms of the quantity theory of money. In contrast to the crude exchange equation $M = kP$, the transaction version has new variables, i.e., V for the velocity of money and T for the volume of trade. The transaction equation is generally expressed as $MV = PT$, which can be transposed into $P = MV/T$, where P stands for the general price level (i.e., the average price of those goods and services which enter T), M for the quantity of money, V for the velocity of circulation of money, and T for the volume of trade. The equation $MV = PT$ is merely the shorthand expression of the truism that the total amount of money paid by buyers equals the total amount of money received by sellers. For the quantity of money times its velocity, MV, is aggregate expenditure, and the volume of trade times the average price, PT, aggregate receipt. The transposed equation $P = MV/T$ means that the general price level varies directly with the quantity of money times its velocity and inversely with the volume of trade. Thus, if the value of M is 100, that of V 3, and that of T 50, the value of P must be 6 ($= 300/50$). If MV is 600, T being 50, P must be 12 ($= 600/50$). If MV is 300 and T 100, P will be 3 ($= 300/100$).

Determinants of Transaction Variables

Changes in MV and T lead to a change in the general price level and in the value of money, but it is necessary to investigate the behavior of M, V, T, and P separately in order to have a clear understanding of their interrelationships. The behavior of the variables of the transaction equation depends on a multiplicity of factors—economic, institutional, technological, psychological, and political.

DETERMINANTS OF M

M of the transaction equation refers to the total quantity of money, consisting of currency and demand deposits. Excluded from this definition are money in bank tills or vaults, time deposits, and reserves at the Treasury. These latter types of money have no influence on the general price level unless they appear in the form of hand-to-hand cash or of demand deposits. The quantity of money as such is determined by (a) the monetary base, consisting of gold holdings, government-issued money, and central bank credit, (b) the proportion between demand deposits and cash in the hands of the general public, and (c) the ratio between reserves and demand deposits. Each requires elucidation.

In a managed paper-standard country like the United States monetary gold is used to support central bank note issues and deposits. The law requires 25 per cent gold reserves (in gold certificates) to support a given supply of Federal Reserve notes and deposits. Thus $1 gold reserves can support $4 of Federal Reserve notes or of Federal Reserve credit. However, Federal Reserve notes *outstanding* (in circulation) vary with public demand, once so much has been issued on a 25 per cent gold-reserve basis or so much more gold (certificates) has been acquired by the Federal Reserve banks (in exchange for demand deposits to the Treasury) to warrant new note issues. As for Treasury currency (e.g., coins, silver certificates, and United States notes), the amount of coins varies with business needs as indicated by the willingness of banks and businesses to buy them from the government at their face value, and that of silver certificates may be increased against the silver purchased until the Treasury holds $1 in silver for each $3 of gold. Federal Reserve credit may be increased via an expansion of loans and investments, depending on legal reserves, the prevailing Federal Reserve credit policy, member banks' liquidity positions, the financial needs of the government and businesses, and the general business outlook. Federal Reserve credit affects the money supply via its effect on member banks' reserves.

The community's choice between demand deposits and cash, in part determines the quantity of money. Though $1 of hand-to-hand cash can support only $1, $1 of cash deposited in the bank as a checking account is capable of increasing the total money supply by $5, given a 20 per cent reserve ratio. People's choice between demand deposits and cash in turn depends on such objective factors as banking facilities, service charges, the general acceptability of checks, and perhaps many others. Given these objective factors, the larger the proportion of money held in the form of demand deposits, the greater will be the bank reserves for credit expansion.

Under modern conditions demand deposits are by far the most important part of the money supply (about 75 per cent of the total money supply in the United States at any given moment). The members of the Federal Reserve System are required by law to maintain a certain fixed amount of reserves in cash or its equivalent (e.g., demand deposits with Federal Reserve banks) against net demand deposits in the hands of the general public. With a 10 per cent reserve ratio, $1 will support $10 demand deposits. If the reserve ratio were 100 per cent, $1 could support only $1 demand deposits. Thus changes in the legal reserve requirements make a significant difference to the money supply.

DETERMINANTS OF V

The velocity of circulation of money, or V of the equation, is the average number of money transfers among individual spenders during a given period. It includes monetary expenditures for all transactions. In practice, however, V is usually measured by a change in the volume of bank debits representing the dollar value of checks drawn by individuals and businesses against their deposits (after allowing for changes in the value of money and seasonal variations). This practice is justified, at least in the United States, by the fact that about 90 per cent of all goods and services purchased in the United States are paid for by check. The velocity of money is influenced by individual spending habits, expectations, and whims, as well as by a host of objective conditions.

Highly developed banking and financial institutions are a presumption in favor of a high velocity of money, since lending, borrowing, and spending are thereby facilitated. The installment payment system is another institutional factor favoring a high rate of spending. The community's methods of income payment also affect the turnover of money. In general, the greater the frequency of payment, the higher the velocity of money. Technological changes, population growth, the composition of population, the government's fiscal policy with respect to taxes and expenditures, central-bank credit policy, corporate-dividend distribution policies, stock-market activity, the amount and forms of liquid assets—in short, all these and other variables affecting business cycles—exert their due influence on the velocity of money via their influence on consumption, savings, and investment, as will be shown in detail later.

People's habits as to consumption and saving affect the velocity of money. Since people save at the expense of consumption, the velocity of money decreases to the extent that consumption expenditures decline. The velocity of money is influenced not only by people's saving habits but by their ability to invest savings. This ability in turn depends on profit expectations, investment opportunities, interest rates, public policy, and many other factors. People's expectations as to changes in future prices and income exert a considerable influence on the velocity of money. These expectations vary with business cycles. During prosperity people spend more, buy more goods and securities, and thus increase V, for in such a period they are generally optimistic about future prices and

c

income. It is well known that a hyperinflation greatly accelerates the rate of spending, since people are anxious to convert "worthless" money into goods and other stable assets. During depression people tend to spend less, sell securities, and hold on to cash, because they expect prices and incomes to fall further, thereby decreasing V.

DETERMINANTS OF T

The transaction approach to T includes all goods, services, and securities which are sold for money as often as they move toward final consumption. Thus a total output of 100 units sold and bought five times would give 500 units as the value of T. The volume of trade as such is influenced by (a) the quantity and quality of productive factors, (b) the level of employment, and (c) labor specialization and business organization, to mention only the basic factors.

Abundant means of production are a presumption in favor of a large volume of trade. Not only the absolute amount of productive factors but their proportion is important, for a community with more capital relative to land and labor is obviously capable of producing more goods and services than one without much capital. Of all the qualitative properties of productive factors, technical knowledge is perhaps the most decisive. Abundant resources without "know-how" are not very helpful. In the long run the quantity and quality of productive factors influence the volume of trade through their influence on the community's capacity to produce. The actual level of production, however, does not always reflect the potential capacity to produce. Given the state of technology, the actual volume of production varies with the level of employment of available resources. At full employment production cannot be increased materially for lack of idle resources to be utilized, and therefore the volume of trade will be smaller than at less than full employment. Even if large money income is generated by conditions of full employment, there will not be sufficient goods and services on which to spend that money income and thereby increase the volume of trade. Thus if full employment is assumed tacitly or otherwise, T is synonymous with the *fixed* volume of production.

Specialization or the division of labor has the effect of increasing productivity and therefore the volume of trade. Division of producers into manufacturers, wholesalers, and retailers, for example, leads to a larger turnover of goods and services than if one firm combines all these functions under a single management. It must be added, however, that risk and uncertainties attendant on specialization inhibit production and trade, and thus may offset in some measure the favorable effect of specialization on T.[1] To the extent that business is organized along vertical or integrated lines, the volume of trade will be small, since the otherwise manifold productive functions are performed by a single firm and the product stays within the firm from the raw material stage to the finished stage. In general, the larger the number of independent, competitive firms or industries, the larger the total volume of trade.

DETERMINANTS OF P

The interacting behavior of M, V, and T determines the behavior of P. In the actual world M, V, and T do not change in the same direction or in the same proportion. M may increase without an increase in V, and T may remain unchanged while MV increases. And so on. These possibilities affect P differently. It is necessary to emphasize that we must investigate M and V together in order to know the effect of changing expenditures on the general price level. What is relevant is a net increase in MV, for an increase in M may be offset by a decrease in V. An increase in MV, however, has no effect on P, if T can be increased proportionally. In other

[1] On this point see Keynes, *Monetary Reform*, p. 39.

words, we must assume full employment in discussing the effects of MV on P, since full employment implies constant T. Moreover, it should be remembered that M affects P only if V and T remain constant.

A clear understanding of these interactions among P, M, V, and T is essential to an effective monetary policy of stabilizing the general price level. It is generally agreed that MV should be increased with increased T due to increased productivity, since P can thereby be kept down and money income to productive factors raised simultaneously. Such a policy is believed to have the effect of avoiding, in the long run, the extremes of inflation and deflation.

P has a peculiar bearing on the value of money in that it measures general purchasing power. It is this peculiar relation of P to the value of money that makes that variable so unique—so much so that a fetish is often made of it. The view that the stabilization of general prices is the most important goal of monetary policy reflects such a fetishism. This view is just as one-sided as the crude emphasis on the quantity of money at the expense of other variables. These views are likely to lead to a general policy of expanding credit and currency up to the general price level. Others consider relative prices of commodities and factors more important for policy purposes than the general price level. They therefore favor the downward adjustment of monopoly prices to the level of purchasing power. We cannot now enter this controversy, but it may be suggested in passing that the stabilization of money income (or expenditure) rather than that of prices is of crucial importance to monetary policy, for reasons to be explained later.

An Evaluation of the Transaction Theory

The limitations of the transaction theory are largely a matter of its assumptions, especially regarding V and T. V is defined in terms of the "transaction" velocity of money, including all kinds of spending, whether by producers or by consumers, and T as the volume of trade involving both final and intermediate transactions. As such, V and T do not throw much light on the level of national income, which measures aggregate expenditure on "end products" only, and which is crucial in estimating the expected level of employment. This criticism will be elucidated in connection with other types of the quantity theory of money.

The basic determinants of M, V, P, and T are mostly applicable to other types of the quantity theory in so far as they run in psychological, institutional, and technological terms. Yet the usual emphasis on secular determinants injects an air of finality which is often fatal to dynamic monetary policy. For it is like saying that human nature, social institutions, and technological laws being what they are, M, V, P, and T must of necessity behave as they do. Even when short-run influences are admitted, the impression is frequently given that they are too ephemeral and weak to make a significant difference in the general price level or in the value of money. For example, T is assumed to be based on natural resources and technical conditions, independent of the quantity of money, but T will be affected by a change in the quantity of money via the latter's effect on general prices.

The equation $MV = PT$ suffers from the disadvantage that it is unrelated to the more common-sense view of price determination: namely, the determination of the value of money by the demand for and supply of money relatively to the volume of production. Thus the theory of money is artificially divorced from the general theory of value.[2] This is a false dichotomy which only obscures the proper dichotomy between the theory of the behavior of individual firms and the theory of the economy as a whole.

The equation $MV = PT$ or $P = MV/T$ is primarily a frame

[2] *Cf.* Keynes, *General Theory of Employment, Interest, and Money* (Harcourt, New York), pp. 292–293.

of reference for analyzing the quantitative relations that determine the general price level or the "transaction" value of money. The equation is a truism in the *ex post* sense, for what was spent must have become income. But in order to have practical significance the variables of the equation should be interpreted in the *ex ante* sense or in the causal sense. The practical question is: What must and can be done to change any of the variables involved in order to achieve the desired level of prices or the desired change in the value of money? A satisfactory answer would require an estimate of *future* changes in the basic determinants of M, V, and T.

The Income–Flow Equation of Exchange

Another variant of the quantity theory is known as the "income-flow" equation of exchange. In contradistinction to the transaction equation, the income-flow equation may be expressed as $MV_y = P_yT_y$ or $P_y = MV_y/T_y$, where M stands for the quantity of money, V_y for the "*income* velocity of money*," [3] T_y for *final* goods and services, and P_y for the average price of all that enters into T_y. Spelled out, this means that national income is equal to total expenditure on final or "end products."

M is the same as in the transaction equation, but V_y is smaller than V of the transaction equation. V_y excludes derived spending of manufacturers, which is included in the transaction velocity of money, such as expenditures on raw materials and intermediate goods and services. In other words, V_y includes the turnover of money spent on final output only (or final consumption, as some prefer to call it). V_y may be defined as the average time duration of the flow of money among final income recipients. Suppose, for example, that the money supply in a given period is equal to

---

[3] Some writers call it the *circuit* velocity of money. On this concept see D. H. Robertson, *Money* (Harcourt, New York, 1929); also J. W. Angell, *The Behavior of Money* (McGraw–Hill, New York, 1936).

$180 billion. Suppose, further, that total expenditure on final output amounts to $200 billion in the same period. Then the income velocity of money can be obtained by dividing total expenditure by the total quantity of money, that is, $V_y = P_y T_y/M$. Hence the value of V_y is $1.11 per year or about $.09 per month.

T_y of the income-flow equation consists in real national income, that is, the flow of finished goods and services over a period of time (excluding intermediate goods on the way to the ultimate buyers' market). Given the average price of all final goods and services that enter into T_y, $P_y T_y$ is equal to money national income (i.e., the dollar value of output). Since T_y includes only *final* output, it is necessarily smaller than T of the transaction equation. P_y is not so inclusive as P of the transaction equation, since it is the average price of only those goods and services which enter into "ordinary consumption," that is, the ultimate buyers' market. The income-flow equation $P_y = MV_y/T_y$ is a way to measure the *"income-value"* of money, while the transaction equation $P = MV/T$ gives us the *"transaction-value"* of money. The former is perhaps more appropriate for testing the purchasing power of the consumer dollar than the latter, since the cost of living index is a good first approximation to P_y.

The restricted assumptions regarding the variables of the income-flow equation are much more realistic than the catchall assumptions concerning the strategic variables of the transaction equation—namely, V and T. To limit the velocity of money and the volume of trade only to *final* output is to avoid the familiar criticism of the transaction equation that its variables are such as to lead to a "hotchpotch" price level. Furthermore, V_y and T_y clarify the static relation between the general price level and the national income, for the national income, MV_y, can be seen as the resultant of all the expenditures on current output, $P_y T_y$, or as the chief demand factor pitted against supply to determine the general level of prices. However, income-flow variables V_y and T_y suffer from the same disadvantage as transaction variables V and T, in that they are "blanket" variables which fail to distinguish between consumer and business outlays and between consumer goods and capital goods. They therefore fall short of strategically useful variables, for it is extremely important for countercyclical policy to recognize the strategic significance of investment outlays and of activity in the capital-goods industries. It is for this reason that today the more realistic "income-expenditure" equation $Y = C + I$ (where Y stands for national income, C for consumption expenditures, and I for investment outlays) is more widely used for national income analysis. Nevertheless, the income-flow equation has given us the notion, however vague, that the general price level is perhaps influenced more significantly by the flow of income than by the quantity of money.

The Cash–Balance Equation of Exchange

The cash-balance or "Cambridge" equation of exchange $M = PKT$ expresses that type of the quantity theory of money which was initiated and popularized by such Cambridge economists as Marshall, Pigou, Robertson, and Keynes, and which centers on *the demand for money* as the strategic explanatory variable. The Cambridge equation is identical with the income-flow equation except with respect to K. It tells us that total cash balances are equal to real national income over whose purchases cash balances are held in a given period. M stands for total cash balances, that is, hand-to-hand currency plus demand deposits; K for the average length of time for which cash balances are held idle against total expenditure; T for real national income; and P for the average unit price of T.

Interaction of these variables may be illustrated by a simple example. If M is equal to $100 billion, T 500, and P $1, K must be 0.2 ($K = M/PT$). Let P increase to $2. M will then be $200 billion, other things being equal (0.2 × 500 × 2). If T increases to 1,000, M will be $400 billion (T = M/PK). If K increases to 0.4, M will be $800 billion. In reality K, T, and P do not change either simultaneously or in the same direction. Nor does M necessarily change in an equal proportion to changes in K, T, and P. For example, M will remain unchanged, if an increase in T is offset by a decrease in K. That is to say, if T increases to 1,000 and K decreases to 0.1, P remaining equal, M will be $200 billion instead of $400 billion.

Of all the variables of the cash-balance equation, K remains to be explained in some detail. K is usually expressed as a fraction of a definite period of time, such as a year or a month. If K is one month of a year, it is 1/12. If the fraction is two months of a year, K is 1/6. This means that the community holds cash balances sufficient to purchase goods and services for two months. In other words, the community's cash balances should be the monetary equivalent of 1/6 of the real national income. Thus the greater the value of K, the larger the total amount of cash balances to be held by the community. Since V = PT/M and K = M/PT, K is obviously the reciprocal of V, or 1/V. This suggests that whatever influences V also influences K, though inversely. Where V is large, K is small, and vice versa. If circumstances are such as to increase V, the need for money to hold is small and therefore the average length of time for which purchasing power must be held in the form of money is correspondingly short. This is merely another way of saying that the demand for money as a store of value decreases as the demand for money as a medium of exchange increases. Thus K is an index of the demand for money as a store of value. To say that the demand for money as a store of value increases is to say that the velocity of circulation of money decreases, since the money held idle against total expenditure is obviously not in circulation.

Thus the cash-balance equation brings to the fore the

demand for money to hold. This emphasis on the demand side is in sharp contrast with traditional emphasis on the supply side. It is also consistent with modern emphasis on aggregate demand for stabilizing the levels of income and employment. The cash-balance approach links itself up with the general value theory, since it explains the value of money in terms of the demand for and supply of money. Once again the value of money is seen as the resultant of "homely but intelligible" market forces of supply and demand. The transposed equation $P = M/KT$ is perhaps a more useful device than the transaction equation $P = MV/T$ to explain the value of money, since it is more convenient to know how large cash balances individuals hold—or wish to hold relative to total expenditure—than to know how much they spend for all kinds of transactions. The cash-balance approach has in fact given rise to the famous liquidity-preference theory which will play an important part in our discussion of income and employment later.

As long as we are concerned with the general price level or with the value of money, $M = PKT$, along with $MV = PT$, is a useful tool of analysis. But when we move on to the determination of aggregate output and employment, we shall find the "income-expenditure" equation $Y = C + I$ (or some variant of it) to be a much more useful and more powerful tool of analysis. In fact much of modern discussion of changes in the general price level (e.g., inflation) runs in terms of the influences which change people's choice between liquid and nonliquid assets, their disposition to consume or to save out of a given income, and their willingness or ability to invest. In other words, $MV = PT$ or $M = PKT$ is no longer considered indispensable even to general price analysis. Our discussion of the quantity theory of money may, however, lay a basis for a better understanding of the possibilities and limitations of monetary policy for price stabilization and therefore for the protection of the purchasing power of money.

It may be stated parenthetically that the quantity theory of money at its best represents a great advance in economic methodology over the orthodox value theory, since the former is an attempt to explain the behavior of the economy as a whole rather than the behavior of individual prices and quantities on the tacit assumption of the stability of the value of money or on the unrealistic assumptions of full output and full employment.

3

Creation and Destruction of Money

MONEY CAN be created or destroyed in the sense that the money supply is increased or decreased by the government or by the commercial banking system. In this chapter we are primarily concerned to show the mechanisms and processes involved in the creation and destruction of money in the above sense.

Creation of Bank Credit

Demand deposits are by far the most important constituent of the total money supply in modern conditions. Demand deposits arise principally from (a) cash deposits and (b) bank loans and investments.[1] The former are called "primary deposits" and the latter "derivative deposits." In the case of primary deposits there is no net increase in the money supply, since there is merely a shift from cash to demand deposits. Primary deposits, however, are capable of serving as

[1] Strictly speaking, demand deposits arise also from gold inflow and central bank acquisition of assets, since individual sellers of gold or securities are likely to deposit the proceeds (checks) at their own banks.

a basis for credit expansion and therefore for increased money supplies. It is derivative deposits which result in a net increase in the money supply, since bank credit is thereby "created" out of thin air, so to speak. The process involved in the creation of bank credit can be illustrated by a simple model. Let the initial statement of a commercial bank be:

Cash	20	Demand deposits	100
Loans	20	Others	100
Investments	60		
Others	100		
	200		200

Assuming the legal reserve ratio of 20 per cent, the bank has no "excess reserves" over and above the legal minimum (20) to support demand deposits of 100. Now suppose primary deposits of 10 have resulted from customers' cash deposits. The relevant changes in the bank statement are as follows:

(1) After Primary Deposits of 10

Cash 20 + 10   Demand deposits 100 + 10

(Excess reserves = 8)

Since 22 is required to support demand deposits of 110, the bank now has excess reserves of 8 ($= 30 - 22$). But the public has gained no net increase in M, since what was lost to the bank has merely reappeared as demand deposits; the money supply will increase only if the bank decides to use the excess reserves for making additional loans or investments. Although the presence of excess reserves is a presumption in favor of credit expansion, it is not the same thing as an actual increase in the money supply. Whether the bank can make use of its excess reserves for lending or investment purposes depends on a number of factors, e.g., general business conditions, interest rates, borrowers' willingness to borrow, the bank's liquidity position, etc.

Suppose, further, that entire excess reserves of 8 are lent out in cash. The resulting bank statement reads as follows:

(2) After Lending Out the Excess Reserves in Cash

Cash 20 + 2 (10 − 8)   Demand deposits 100 + 10

Loans 20 + 8

(Excess reserves = O; increase in M = 8)

Demand deposits remain unchanged, since the borrowers have left nothing in the form of checking accounts. The bank's cash is now 22 instead of 30, since 8 out of cash deposits of 10 has been taken out by the borrowers. Excess reserves are zero (22 − 22), the minimum legal reserves necessary to support demand deposits of 110 being 22. But the volume of money in the hands of the general public has increased by the amount of the loans taken out in cash, or by 8.

Now consider the case of derivative deposits of 40. The bank statement changes as follows:

(3) After Derivative Deposits of 40

Cash 20   Demand deposits 100 + 40

Loans 20 + 40

(Excess reserves = −8; increase in M = 40)

In order to support demand deposits of 140 the bank must have legal reserves of 28. Yet the bank's cash amounts to 20, and hence excess reserves of −8 are one result of the lending operations. Actually the bank is unlikely, except under unusual circumstances (e.g., an acute postwar demand for bank credit), to lend out to the full extent of its excess reserves; it would make certain that at least excess reserves of 8 are in its possession or obtainable before granting new loans of 40. The other result of the lending operations is a net increase in M, or 40. It is this type of deposit which causes a significant change in the total supply of money. The same principle applies to those derivative deposits which arise from bank purchases of securities. In this case investments of 40 would be substituted for loans of 40 on the asset side. The bank gives the sellers of the securities demand deposits, which increase by the amount of the investments.

Finally, consider a case in which loans of 10 are granted, of which 2 is taken in cash and 8 left in demand deposits. The following changes occur:

(4) After Loans of 10 Part of Which is Taken in Cash

Cash 20 + 8 (10 − 2)   Demand deposits 100 + 10 + 8
Loans 20 + 10

(Excess reserves = 4.40; increase in M = 10)

The legal minimum necessary to support demand deposits of 118 being 23.60, the bank has excess reserves of 4.40 (= 28 − 23.60). The public has acquired a net increase in M, or 10, 8 of which consists in demand deposits created and 2 in cash paid from reserves.

Multiple Credit Expansion by the Banking System

We have seen that each individual bank is able to expand credit only up to its excess reserves, first because it loses cash to other banks through the borrowers' check payments, and secondly because it loses cash to the public (i.e., the borrowers) who may take out a part, if not all, of the loans in cash. But the commercial banking system as a whole can expand credit many times the initial excess reserves.[2]

Suppose bank A lends out 100 on the basis of excess reserves of 100, thus creating derivative deposits of 100. Bank A's borrowers' check payments of 100 to customers of bank B lead to primary deposits of 100 in the latter bank. With a 10 per cent reserve ratio, bank B can create derivative deposits of 90, and so on—until the original excess reserves of 100 are distributed among many banks as a 10 per cent reserve basis for about 1,000 derivative deposits. The process involved is illustrated below.

[2] For an original contribution on this subject, see C. A. Phillips, *Bank Credit* (Macmillan, New York, 1926).

Bank A	Bank B	Bank C
Excess reserves 100	Primary deposits	Primary deposits 90
Derivative deposits	100	Excess reserves 81
100	Excess reserves 90	$(90-9)$
	$(100-10)$	Derivative deposits 81
	Derivative deposits	
	90	

(Derivative deposits $= 100 + 90 + 81 \ldots + n = 1{,}000$, or 10 times the original excess reserves of 100, given a 10 per cent reserve ratio)

It is convenient to compare a multiple expansion of loans by the banking system to credit expansion by the one and only (hypothetical) bank in the community. Given a 10 per cent reserve ratio, such a bank could lend out 10 times the initial excess reserves (e.g., loans of $1,000 against reserves of $100). For the one-bank system does not lose cash to itself; it loses cash only to the public. By contrast, an individual bank in the banking system must be prepared to lose the full amount of the loans to other banks (unless the recipients of the checks happen to bank at the same bank). Since what one bank in the system loses is a gain to another, no loss of reserves is involved for the banking system as a whole. The formula for discovering the extent of credit expansion by the banking system is: Excess reserves/Legal reserve ratio. For example, let the excess reserves be $10 million and the reserve ratio 10 per cent, or 0.1. Then the banking system can expand demand deposits by $100 million (10/0.1).

The Destruction of Bank Credit

Bank credit can be "destroyed" through a reduction in bank loans and investment, the extent of the destruction depending on the prevailing reserve ratio. A reduction of cash below the legally required reserves to support demand deposits leads to a multiple contraction of bank credit throughout the banking system and therefore to a decline in the total supply of money. Suppose that a depositor permanently withdraws $100 from his checking account, that is, not to spend but to keep the money in the mattress. The bank in question loses $100 of cash and $100 of demand deposits. Suppose, further, that the prevailing reserve ratio is 10 per cent. The bank presumably had $10 against the $100 of demand deposits withdrawn, but it had to pay out $100, not $10. The bank had to use $90 of its legal reserves held against *other* depositors' demand deposits in order to meet the original depositor's demand for $100. This means that the bank's legal reserves have fallen below the required minimum and that the bank will have to take some action to improve its impaired reserve position. This is where a 10:1 contraction of bank credit begins! For the bank must call in loans or sell securities to the amount of $90, thus involving other banks in the process of the 10:1 contraction of credit. If, however, the bank could acquire additional cash by borrowing from the Federal Reserve bank, it would not take deflationary action. Barring this possibility, a multiple contraction of credit is inevitable, as shown in the following models.

Bank A				Bank B		
Cash	—$10	Deposits	—$100	Cash	—$9	Deposits	—$90
Loans & investments	$—90			Loans & investments	—$81		
	—$100		—$100		—$90		—$90

As Bank A requires its borrowers to repay their loans or sells securities or does both, Bank B's customers are thereby compelled to withdraw $90, thus causing Bank B to call in loans or sell securities to make good the $81 which it had paid out of reserves held against other customers' deposits. Bank B's action will in turn cause other banks to take similar action. The result is a 10:1 contraction of bank credit. Thus a reduction of cash reserves below the legal minimum, whether due to a cash withdrawal, a repayment of loans, gold

D

outflow, or Federal Reserve sale of government securities, leads to a magnified decline in total demand deposits and therefore to a sharp reduction in the total money supply. The inverse correlation between reserve ratios and the magnified decline in bank credit can be seen in the following model.

Reserve ratio	Initial loss of cash	Magnified decline in total deposits
10% (10:1)	$100	$1,000
25% (4:1)	$100	$400
50% (2:1)	$100	$200
100% (1:1)	$100	$100

It is not difficult to understand why some economists favor a 100 per cent reserve ratio. For with a 100 per cent ratio, a withdrawal of $1 or repayment of a $1 debt would lead to a $1 contraction of loans and investments and therefore of demand deposits, that is, a dollar-for-dollar decline in the money supply. A system of 100 per cent reserves, it is believed, would stabilize the price system, since it would prevent an otherwise inevitable multiple contraction of bank credit. Apart from the merits or demerits of such a proposal, it is a fair question to ask whether it would be wise to allow the quantity of money in general and bank credit in particular to be mainly determined by profit-motivated capricious lending and investment operations of the private banking system. A consideration like this has given rise to various theories of monetary management.

The Creation and Destruction of Money by the State

Under normal circumstances there is no need for government interference with the private creation and destruction of money (i.e., by commercial banks). In the United States, for instance, privately created bank deposits and Federal Reserve notes are sufficient to meet ordinary business and individual requirements. But we have noted that the value of money is inherently unstable when its creation and destruction is left largely to profit-motivated private lending and investment operations (i.e., demand deposits created or destroyed by commercial banks). This fact already anticipates some government interference. The more positive justification for the government assumption of monetary management lies in the possibility that the government may create or destroy money in the overall interest of economic stability, that is, to avoid both inflation and deflation. It is in this sense that money is considered as "a creature of the State." [3]

How can the government create or destroy enough money to affect the national economy? In the first place, the government has the sole authority to create or destroy "legal tender," that is, money which is made legally acceptable in payment of taxes and private money obligations. Although legal tenders are not necessarily acceptable from the standpoint of the general public, as during a hyperinflation which causes the value of money to depreciate dramatically, they can be made acceptable by making other kinds of money unavailable. Besides its power to create or destroy money by fiat, the government can do so through its power to tax the people. Thus viewed, the potential power of the State to create or destroy money is as great as monetary-fiscal policy makes it.

Governments may manufacture money by resorting to the printing press under such extraordinary circumstances as war, inflation, and depression.[4] As long as the cost of war, for example, can be met by taxes and borrowing, the printing press is unnecessary and perhaps undesirable. Most governments avoid the printing press even during a costly war—largely for

---

[3] *Cf.* A. P. Lerner, "Money as a Creature of the State," *American Economic Review*, May, 1947, pp. 312–317.

[4] See J. M. Keynes, *How to Pay for the War* (Harcourt, New York, 1940); also A. H. Hansen, "Defense Financing and Inflation Potentialities," *Review of Economic Statistics*, February, 1941. For an exceptional case see my "Postwar Inflation and Fiscal–Monetary Policy in Japan," *American Economic Review*, December, 1946.

fear of inflationary consequences. As far as its effect on the money supply is concerned, the printing press is exactly the same as bank credit manufactured for the government in exchange for the latter's "IOU's," that is, a net increase in M. Superficially the printing press may be criticized as too easy and too simple, but a more serious criticism is that it tends to overstress quantitative monetary management.[5]

The printing press is rendered almost obsolete by the fact that governments can nowadays borrow from the central banks at practically no cost. For example, a government may directly or indirectly sell government securities to the central bank to obtain the necessary amount of credit, and pay interest on those securities held by the bank out of the bank's own profits, part or all of which ultimately go to the government. Thus the government can get central bank credit in exchange for its promise to pay, virtually free of interest cost. Apart from the question of cost, the most practical way for the government to create new money is to borrow from the banking system (commercial banks as well as the Federal Reserve banks) and to spend the proceeds. This method is usually defended on the ground that taxes and other alternatives are politically less expedient and economically less desirable. This is a rather controversial point. For the moment we are interested only in the process involved. Public borrowing from the banking system leads to the creation of demand deposits in favor of the government in exchange for government securities. Since government deposits are not included in the money supply, an increase in M must be sought in the spending of those deposits by the government.

---

[5] For pro and con arguments about "interest-free financing," see Hansen, *Economic Policy and Full Employment* (Whittlesey, New York, 1947), pp. 202–221; P. Wernette, *Financing Full Employment* (Cambridge, 1945); H. G. Simon, *A Positive Program for Laissez–Faire* (Chicago, 1934); F. D. Graham, in *Planning and Paying for Full Employment*, eds. Lerner and Graham (Princeton, 1946), pp. 40–66; H. G. Hayes, *Spending, Saving, and Employment* (Knopf, New York, 1947), pp. 213–214.

Since the government spends the deposits, the individual recipients of government checks get either cash or demand deposits at their own banks. Demand deposits in favor of the general public increase to the precise extent that government deposits decrease—a shift of money from the government to the public.[6] Commercial banks get additional reserves for further credit expansion, and the general public has additional purchasing power in the shape of demand deposits. Thus public borrowing leads to the creation of new money.

The Treasury can also control the money supply through open-market operations, gold sterilization, and debt management, while the Federal Reserve authorities can do so through open-market operations, reserve requirements, rediscount policy, and other traditional control devices. Since most of these controls are discussed, and can be discussed more fruitfully, in connection with countercyclical policies,[7] it is sufficient here to indicate some of the more novel and daring methods of demonetizing money out of existence.

Perhaps the most dramatic example of demonetization is to introduce a new currency to be exchanged for the old at certain fixed exchange rates and during a specified period, e.g., one new note for several old notes of the same denomination. This method proved to be rather successful where it was tried to combat a hyperinflation which arose from an excessive note issue.[8] A less drastic but nevertheless effective way to extinguish money during a definite period is to block or freeze part of deposit money. Moreover, the government may require holders of liquid funds to make long-term "forced

---

[6] The money supply increased in the United States from $36.6 billion in 1940 to $103.5 billion in 1945 largely because of wartime government borrowing and spending.

[7] For detail see Chapters 5, 14, and 15; also Board of Governors of the Federal Reserve· System, *Public Finance and Full Employment* (Postwar Economic Studies, No. 3, Washington, December, 1945), and *Federal Reserve Policy* (Postwar Economic Studies, No. 8, 1947).

[8] *Cf.* J. E. Meade, *Planning and the Price Mechanism* (London, George Allen & Unwin Ltd., 1948), p. 25; also my " Postwar Inflation and Fiscal–Monetary Policy in Japan."

loans" of part of these assets to the government, that is, to hold the frozen or blocked funds in the form of long-term government securities.[9] The government may, in some cases, find it expedient to introduce additional taxes (e.g., a capital levy and "luxury" taxes) or drastically increase tax rates (e.g., both personal and corporation income taxes) to reduce excess cash balances in the hands of the general public. Under normal circumstances, however, the conventional methods mentioned above may suffice.

A fanciful method of demonetizing money is envisaged by some of the 100 per cent reserve planners as a part of the general scheme to control the money-creating or -destroying power of the private banking system. The method consists in the elimination of otherwise monetizable public debt held by commercial banks. On the assumption that a 100 per cent reserve ratio is already in effect, the Treasury is to provide banks with new reserves for credit expansion by issuing non-interest-bearing paper money in exchange for bank-held interest-bearing public debt. Suppose, for example, that total demand deposits in the commercial banks amount to $100 billion, total cash reserves of the banks being equal to $20 billion and government securities held by them $80 billion. In order to support $100 billion deposits the banks will need $100 billion of *cash* reserves, or $80 billion more than they now have, according to the 100 per cent reserve requirement. The Treasury is supposed to provide $80 billion in cash (paper money) in exchange for the $80 billion government securities owned by the banks. The result is the extinction of potential money (monetizable public debt amounting to $80 billion) "at one stroke," so to speak. The greater the amount of public debt owned by commercial banks, the greater would be the impact of such a method of demonetization on the money supply, not to mention its income effect on those banks.

[9] See R. G. Hawtrey, "Monetary Aspects of the Economic Situation," *American Economic Review*, March, 1948.

Whether this kind of demonetization would have a stabilizing effect on the general price level is certainly open to question, but its theoretical possibility cannot be ignored, especially when the public debt is large and growing.

Thus the government has at its disposal various tools to "create" or "destroy" a significant portion of currency and deposit money, the choice of any particular tools depending on the nature of the given situation that calls for their use. How effective any particular tool is in achieving a given objective cannot be determined on any *a priori* grounds; it depends on a variety of factors, such as the presence or absence of offsetting measures, the gravity of the situation in question, conflicting objectives of monetary and fiscal policies, the prevailing political climate, monetary and banking conventions, and many others. One thing, however, seems fairly clear: namely, that the creation or destruction of money by the State is generally more effective than similar action by the banking system in arresting monetary expansion, but no more effective by itself than the latter in stimulating general economic expansion. The public control of the money supply may of course be defended on other grounds. It is likely that the government's open-market operations will affect general liquidity and therefore general activity much more decisively than will the credit policies of the private banking system. This strongly suggests the possibility that money may become "a creature of the State" earlier than we imagine. Increasing government preoccupation with the problem of economic stability in general and that of depression in particular is indicative of such a possibility.

4

The Theory of Inflation

〰〰〰〰〰〰〰〰〰〰〰〰〰〰〰〰〰〰〰〰〰〰〰

THE TRADITIONAL explanation of inflation runs largely in terms of changes in the money supply, the gold stock, and the cost of money (interest). While doubtless helpful in explaining inflation, these stock concepts are theoretically inconclusive and practically inadequate. Even the concept of "liquid assets" (e.g., accumulated savings out of past incomes) is incomplete, though admittedly important. The quantity-theory type of explanation has been greatly improved by the income-expenditure approach to inflation, such as developed by Keynes during World War II. By functionally relating expected expenditures to disposal income (national income after taxes) in relation to the value of available output at base prices, Keynes originated the concept of the "inflationary gap"—not only to emphasize the strategic significance of the *flow* of money incomes in influencing the general price level but to show the primary importance of fiscal measures (e.g., tax and borrowing) for wiping out the "inflationary gap." [1] This gap concept is our starting point.

[1] For further studies, see Keynes, *How to Pay for the War* (Harcourt, New York, 1940); T. Koopmans, "The Dynamics of Inflation," *Review of Economic Statistics,* XXIV, 1942; A. Smithies, "The Behavior of Money National Income under Inflationary Conditions," *Quarterly Journal of Economics,* LVII, 1942; W. S. Salant, "The Inflationary Gap: Meaning and Significance for

The Concept of the Inflationary Gap

The inflationary gap for the economy as a whole may be defined as *an excess of anticipated expenditures over available output at base prices.* Anticipated expenditures are given by consumption-saving patterns plus the tax structure, while available output is given by conditions of employment plus the technological structure. The problem is one of keeping expenditures down to the level of current output instead of letting those expenditures bid up the value of that output.

How does the inflationary gap start? Let us first take the case of a wartime consumer-goods inflationary gap. The level of wartime national income is determined by government war expenditures plus civilian consumption expenditures. This gives us a certain value of total output at a certain price level, say, $200 billion. Of this output the government claims, say, $90 billion, leaving $110 billion for civilian consumption. This is the amount of consumer goods at preinflation prices against which a proportional amount of money income must be paid out, if price stability is to be maintained. But suppose the economy is paying out money income at the rate of $230 billion by using past income or by creating new purchasing power. Suppose, further, that the government taxes away $50 billion out of the $230-billion national income paid, leaving a total disposable income of $180 billion. This is the amount of money income which may be spent for available output; but we have seen that the total civilian goods amount to $110 billion at the old prices. When, therefore, disposable income of $180 is left free to compete with available output of $110, an inflationary gap becomes inevitable. The process involved in the development of this gap can be seen better in the following model.

Policy Making," *American Economic Review,* June, 1942; L. R. Klein, *The Keynesian Revolution* (Macmillan, New York, 1947), Chap. 6; S. E. Harris, *Inflation and the American Economy* (McGraw–Hill, New York, 1945); "Ten Economists on Inflation," *Review of Economic Statistics,* February, 1948.

National income being paid = $230 billion
Taxes (Federal, State, and local) = $50 billion
Disposable income = $180 billion (230 − 50)
Gross national product at preinflation prices = $200 billion
War expenditures = $90 billion
Available output for civilian consumption = $110 billion
  (200 − 90) at preinflation prices
Therefore: the inflationary gap = $70 billion (180 − 110)

Actually, of course, disposable income of $180 billion is not all spent; a part of it is saved. If people normally save 20 per cent of their income, $144 billion would be left *actually* free to bid up prices in the above example, and the actual inflationary gap would be $34 billion (144 − 110) instead of $70 billion. If people voluntarily saved as much as $70 billion, the inflationary gap would be wiped out. Another "natural" solution would be to let the value of available output rise to the level of disposable income. Why not increase taxes to reduce the amount of disposable income? It is easier said than done, even in wartime. And yet a drastic change in the tax structure is the most effective method of wiping out the inflationary gap, as will be shown later. On the other hand, available output for consumption purposes cannot obviously be increased at the expense of war production. The practical alternatives open to the government authorities in these circumstances are to increase taxes and to induce savings.[2]

In wartime, investment outlays are equal to war expenditures plus government-sanctioned private investment, and as such they are largely independent of the level of current income and amenable to statistical prognosis. In peacetime it is more difficult to estimate beforehand what the level of total investment will be, since the bulk of investment decisions are made by private individuals. In so far as investment outlays can be known beforehand, it will not be difficult to estimate the amount of consumer goods available for public con-

---

[2] For a full discussion of anti-inflation policies, see the next chapter.

sumption and therefore the inflationary gap, given a certain tax structure. The development of an inflationary gap during a postwar boom is illustrated in the following diagram.

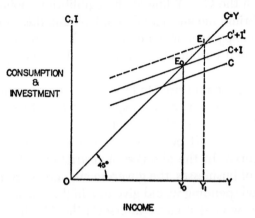

FIG. 1. THE INFLATIONARY GAP

In the above diagram, the vertical axis measures consumption and investment, while the horizontal axis measures income (gross national product). The 45° line measures the quantitative relation of consumption expenditures to various levels of income; any deviation from the line indicates that consumption is larger or smaller than income. The 45° or C = Y line may be regarded as a zero-saving function. The C curve represents a schedule of consumption expenditures which people would make according to their normal habits, and is functionally related to the levels of income postulated.[3] The C + I curve represents the amount people would want to spend for both consumption and investment at all hypothetical levels of income; it lies above the C curve for the simple reason that the amount of consumption *and* investment is larger than that of consumption alone. For simplicity's sake the C + I curve is drawn so as to parallel the C curve,

[3] For a detailed explanation of the consumption function, see Chap. 10.

thus indicating that the amount of investment is the same at all levels of income. Since income is equal to investment plus consumption, it follows that the intersection of the $C + I$ curve with the $C = Y$ line at the equilibrium point E_0 gives us equilibrium income Y_0. We shall assume this Y_0 income to be *full employment* income. Income Y_0 corresponds to the value of total output at a given price level in our previous model.

Now suppose that private businesses, the government, and consumers, together, want to spend for investment and consumption more than before at all levels of income. The result is the upward shift of the $C + I$ curve to the level of the $C' + I'$ curve. In the absence of restrictions, the combined attempts of businesses, the government, and consumers to increase total spending would give us a higher income, Y_1. Note that the new $C' + I'$ curve intersects the $45°$ line at E_1. Yet available output is E_0Y_0, which is obviously smaller than income E_1Y_1 (or OY_1) by the vertical distance between the points E_1 and E_0. This latter difference between what the economy would spend (E_1Y_1) and what it has available (E_0Y_0) is the inflationary gap which must be wiped out if the prices of output E_0Y_0 are to be prevented from rising. For any increase in total spending in conditions of full employment, that is, beyond E_0Y_0, which is just equal to full employment income OY_0, would result in price increases instead of greater output and employment. The problem, therefore, is one of lowering the $C' + I'$ curve to the level of the old $C + I$ curve so that the former will cross the $45°$ line at E_0, or, if possible, of preventing the $C + I$ curve from rising to the level of the $C' + I'$ curve. In terms of policy, this may mean that the government will have to cut down its own expenditures and discourage excessive private capital outlays and consumption expenditures. Regardless of particular policy measures to reduce total spending, the inflationary gap can be wiped out only by the reduction of effective demand if output cannot be increased for lack of unemployed resources. The situation becomes complicated when we consider an "open system" with foreign trade relations, for we shall have to add to aggregate investment another unpredictable variable: namely, a net foreign balance.

Analysis of the inflationary gap in terms of such aggregates as national income, investment outlays, and consumption expenditures clearly reveals what determines public policy with respect to taxes, public expenditures, savings campaigns, credit control, wage adjustments—in short, all the conceivable anti-inflation measures affecting the propensities to consume, to save, and to invest, which together determine the general price level. It is by influencing those propensities, directly or indirectly, that the monetary-fiscal authorities hope to wipe out the inflationary gap and therefore prevent further price increases.

Inflation and Full Employment

Thus far we have said nothing about the possibility of increasing output. If the production of consumer goods could be increased *pari passu* with effective money demand, the inflationary gap would be greatly narrowed. But an increase in available output is exceedingly slight during a war and an immediate postwar period, since the economy in such a period usually operates at full employment. A full-employment economy, however brought about, is highly susceptible to inflation. In the long run there is no problem of inflation, particularly in those dynamic and expanding economies which are capable of increasing output to match with expanding demand.[4] For in longer periods population may increase and swell the labor supply, technological advance may augment

[4] *Cf.* A. H. Hansen, "Can We Meet the Challenge of Inflation?" *New York Times Magazine,* July 7, 1946.

productivity, and new resources may be discovered—so that full employment can be maintained continuously without price inflation.

But in the short run "the stubborn and intractable fact about an economy already operating at peak levels is that output cannot be expanded except by slow degrees." [5] As indicated earlier, inflation is often attributed to increased demand on the tacit assumption of full employment, or what comes to the same thing, of constant output. But full employment should be explicitly stated as a limiting factor on the supply side. At less than full employment both consumer goods and capital goods (or, as in wartime, both "guns" and "butter") can be produced without general price increases. But once full employment is reached, an attempt to increase output of consumer goods involves the bidding up of factor prices, since the factors of production already employed in capital-goods industries must be induced to shift to consumer-goods industries. At full employment, therefore, a further increase in aggregate demand spends itself largely in raising the general price level instead of enlarging aggregate output and employment. That is why inflation is typically a short-run phenomenon peculiar to a stationary, full-employment economy. In order to achieve full employment without at the same time provoking a runaway inflation, we must inquire into the atomistic elements of the economy which make the inflationary tendency perceptible even before the point of full employment is reached.

Keynes showed why "semi-inflation" is likely to develop with increasing money supplies before the point of full employment is reached.[6] His analysis is helpful for an understanding of slow but steady inflationary pressures which characterize a period of recovery or the early and later stages

---

[5] The President's *Economic Report* (Washington, D.C., January, 1948), p. 43.

[6] *Cf. General Theory*, pp. 296–303.

of a war economy. With an expansion of money at less than full employment, prices rise gradually as output and employment increase—for a number of reasons of which Keynes gives an outline of five of the most important.[7] In less technical terminology these reasons are as follows:

1. *The variety of channels into which increased money supplies may flow.* Effective demand (the flow of monetary expenditures) is divided among the rise of prices, the rise of costs, and the rise of output and employment, the amount of each share depending on the community's choice between consumption and saving and between liquid assets and nonliquid assets, prospective rates of profit, interest rates, and other forces in operation. Since not all the increases in money supplies are spent in increasing output or absorbed by the rise of costs, it follows that the effective demand for some goods and services must increase with increased money supplies 'and, together with rise of costs, exert an upward pressure on general prices. If part of the increased effective demand is diverted to speculative channels (e.g., purchase of old securities), the securities market instead of the commodity market will be stimulated. In this case new output will not increase as much as if new securities were being bought, or as if demand were directed toward nonspeculative channels, and the inflationary pressure on general prices will be all the greater. Obviously this type of analysis is much more fruitful for policy than the traditional analysis of the relation between "blanket" M and V.

2. *The nonhomogeneity of resources.* Since labor, for example, is not homogeneous in skills or efficiency, the use of less and less efficient labor will lead to a diminishing return from a fixed quantity of capital equipment in terms of output as output increases and as more labor is applied to that

---

[7] For interesting comments, see J. Lintner, "The Theory of Money and Prices," and A. Smithies, "Effective Demand and Employment," in *The New Economics* (S. E. Harris, ed., Knopf, New York, 1948).

equipment. If skilled labor is scarce relative to demand, the use of less skilled and less experienced labor will involve a higher unit labor cost and therefore the rising supply price of output. Similarly, capital equipment is nonhomogeneous in quality and types. Some part of equipment, therefore, involves an increase in what Keynes calls "prime costs" (factor costs plus opportunity costs) per unit of output and therefore increasing marginal prime costs. This means that the supply price (cost of production) will rise, and the demand price (to be paid by buyers) with it.

3. *The perfectly inelastic supply of particular resources.* Since some unemployed resources are short of supply relative to demand, a series of "bottlenecks" is bound to raise factor prices and therefore commodity prices in some sectors of the economy. If unemployed resources are substitutable, as they would be in the longer period, such "bottlenecks" need not occur to divert demand to other directions via higher prices. But in the short period some particular resources are likely to have a supply elasticity of zero. Accordingly, the supply of particular commodities will become completely inelastic and their prices will have to rise to discourage the demand for those commodities. The supply of durable consumer goods in an immediate postwar period is a case in point.

4. *Increases in wage rates.* As output increases and as business booms along the road to full employment, each group of employed workers will press for higher money wages and get them, though seldom as high as will compensate for the rising cost of living. As long as there are unemployed workers, entrepreneurs will for obvious reasons not give money wage increases to the full extent of the cost of living. However, entrepreneurs are disposed to meet demands for higher wages more than halfway in a period of an increasing effective demand. Wage increases are likely to be discontinuous, since they depend on the unpredictable psychology of the workers as well as on the no less unpredictable policies of manage-

ment and organized labor. Wage increases, however discontinuous, will exert an upward pressure on general prices, in part through their influence on costs and in part through their influence on aggregate consumer demand.

5. *The possibility of increasing marginal cost.* In the short run some variable factors other than labor entering into marginal cost may have different degrees of price elasticity of supply and therefore show varying degrees of price rigidity. If, for example, the supply of particular raw materials is perfectly inelastic (i.e., nonsubstitutable), an increase in the demand for such raw materials will lead to what amounts to "quasi-rent," a factor price which is much higher than if supply were elastic. (If supply were perfectly elastic, increased output and input would be possible with constant marginal cost.) Under these circumstances, the marginal cost curve will move upward via diminishing returns,[8] and its position may also shift upward. In either case increasing marginal cost is associated with higher prices, according to the familiar principle of equating marginal cost to marginal revenue.

Analysis of Inflationary Pressures

Inflationary pressures arise from both the demand side and the supply side. By "demand" is meant the *income* demand or the demand of money income for things, while "supply" here means available output for which money income can be spent.[9]

---

[8] This tendency of diminishing returns and therefore of increasing marginal cost may not be as strong in a monopoly-dominated economy, since "economies of scale" considerably offset the tendency of marginal product to fall. One writer goes as far as to say that under such circumstances it is possible to increase output and employment without lowering real wages (i.e., without inflation). (See A. Smithies. *op. cit.*, p. 566.) But it is debatable whether particular monopolies would in fact react to constant or even rising returns by maintaining or lowering prices.

[9] For a good illustration of concrete factors affecting demand and supply, see the President's *Economic Report, op. cit.*

E

DEMAND SIDE

On the demand side, the major inflationary factors are: (a) the money supply, (b) disposable income, (c) consumer expenditures and business outlays, and (d) foreign demand. In a postwar period, the increased money supply is mainly due to an inordinate increase in demand deposits resulting first from government spending and then from bank expansion of loans and investments. Expansion of bank credit is at once a cause and an effect of inflationary pressures, since it reflects partly an enlarged income stream resulting from the use of bank credit and partly a growing business and personal demand for funds due to higher prices and costs. A postwar increase in the money supply, however brought about, is a presumption in favor of a high rate of spending.

Disposable income (i.e., income payments to factors after personal taxes) is likely to remain at a high level partly because of postwar relaxation of high wartime taxes but largely because of a high level of postwar national income. A part of disposable income is saved, to be sure, but most of it is spent on consumption (e.g., wage receipts and dividends after taxes). Since household consumption (as distinguished from community consumption related to national income) is a function of disposable income, the larger the amount of disposable expenditure the larger the absolute amount of consumption expenditure. Consumer demand is greatly stimulated, moreover, by the reduction of current savings, by the use of accumulated savings, by the possession of liquid assets (other than savings, e.g., readily cashable securities), and by the extension of consumer credit, thus adding to the inflationary pressures. In the absence of mass unemployment and of direct wartime controls wage increases are likely to be pushed by trade union action beyond general productivity, to increase consumer demand as well as business cost.

Capital expansion takes on a speculative character during an inflationary boom. New equipment and plants and excessive inventories are often financed by speculative borrowing, not to mention an increase in replacement demand. And most of business expenditures find their way into the income stream via dividends, wages, and other income payments. When postwar public expenditures for capital development, defense, education, etc., are added to expanding private investment, there is bound to be a terrific upward pressure on total spending, with the result that the inflationary gap increases still further—unless, indeed, consumption expenditures are supposed to decrease.

An additional factor in the increased monetary demand is foreign expenditures for domestic goods and services. This factor is particularly significant if a country maintains an export surplus, as the United States tends to do. The inflationary impact of foreign demand is weakened to the extent that the marginal propensity to import offsets additional expenditures for domestic goods and services out of the increased national income due to that foreign demand. If foreign countries cannot increase their sales of goods and services to the United States, for example, and thus obtain dollar exchange, they will probably liquidate some of their holdings of dollar balances, sell their gold, and spend the proceeds of loans and grants that may be provided by the United States. It is therefore very likely that foreign demand will exert considerable inflationary pressure on domestic areas of shortages which may be "a focal point of spreading inflation."

SUPPLY SIDE

In contrast to a sharp rise in the monetary demand, the supply of goods and services is likely to increase but slightly in a postwar period. The basic limiting factor is of course full employment. Shortages of labor, equipment, and raw materials partly account for the inadequate supply of certain goods, but exports (e.g., American wheat and steel) doubtless aggravate the supply situation. An export surplus in conditions of full employment is doubly inflationary, since it increases domestic income on the one hand and decreases domestic supplies on the other. Moreover, mere concentration of exports of commodities that are subject to especially strong domestic demand is often enough to increase inflationary pressure at home.

The supply situation may be aggravated by yet another factor, namely, a wage-price spiral. Theoretically, wage increases in substandard-wage areas or industries do not necessarily precipitate a race between wages and prices, but in fact demands for wage increases often lead to price increases. A plausible explanation may be found in the general practice of businesses to adjust themselves to cost increases "by increasing prices rather than by absorbing them in whole or in part by reducing profits." [10] The highly inelastic nature of demand in a postwar period encourages businesses to raise prices with increasing payrolls and other costs. Wage-price spirals in particular areas or industries serve to spread inflation throughout the whole economy.

ROLE OF EXPECTATIONS

The process of inflation cannot be fully explained in terms of excessive spending relative to available output; expectations play an important role in the speed of inflation. During inflation the expectation of higher prices usually stimulates general demand for inventories or consumer goods. Relative prices, so important in measuring inflationary pressure on "strategic spots," are greatly affected by expectations concerning wages or incomes. The latter in turn affect the income-elasticity of demand, i.e., consumer reactions to different commodities in response to a rise in income. The brighter the prospect of higher money incomes, the stronger the likelihood that consumers' income-elasticity of demand will be greater than unity. A rise in expected income, therefore, in-

[10] The President's *Economic Report, op. cit.*, p. 40.

duces businesses and consumers to spend more and faster. Mere expectation of wage increases often induces some businesses to increase prices even before upward wage adjustments have actually taken place. In this respect it is useful to refer to the price-elasticity of supply to see how quickly production can be adjusted to changing prices. Anticipated shortages of particular commodities influence the price-elasticity of supply. Furthermore, expectation of continued foreign demand, such as was explicit in the American export surplus and implicit in the American foreign-aid programs during the postwar period, greatly stimulates current general demand at home.

These and many other dynamic influences, coming as they do from both the demand side and the supply side, lead to speculative business and consumer spending and add to the existing inflationary pressures.

The Effects of Inflation

The impact of inflation is felt unevenly by different groups of individuals within the national economy. It is in the light of its specific effects that the social, political, and economic arguments for or against inflation are ordinarily understood. The ultimate test, however, of the desirability or undesirability of inflation lies in the overall effect of inflation on the economic stability of the nation as a whole. Generally speaking, inflation inflicts more harm on low- and fixed-income groups than on high- and flexible-income groups. This generalization needs to be qualified, however. Let us then examine the concrete effects of inflation on various economic groups.

DEBTORS AND CREDITORS

Debtors as a group fare well during inflation, since they are not only in a better position to repay their debts but also allowed to pay them in money whose purchasing power is lower than when they borrowed. In other words, in repaying their debts during inflation debtors forgo less in goods and services than if they had to repay during a period of low prices. The face value of debt obligations remains the same, it is true, but the purchasing power of money may be so low that the debtors are only too glad to get rid of such inflated money (worthless during a hyperinflation). Businessmen, farmers, and consumers who borrowed funds prior to the inflation all stand to gain by inflation in so far as they meet their debt obligations out of inflated currency. Even though debtors are usually more numerous than creditors, it does not necessarily follow that the former should welcome inflation. It is unlikely, though conceivable, that debtors as a group will resist anti-inflation measures in general, since debtors are at the same time members of one or another group which is adversely affected by inflation.[11]

Creditors, on the other hand, stand to lose by inflation, since they receive in effect less in goods and services than if they received the repayments during a period of low prices. Banks and individual lenders and other creditors may not be worse off than some other groups during inflation if, for instance, they are repaid in a foreign currency whose value has not depreciated or in kind (i.e., goods and services). The adverse effect of inflation on some creditors is often more than offset by its favorable effect on other groups to which they may belong simultaneously. For example, an individual who is at once a creditor and an investor in equities may find his dividends more than compensating for the loss of purchasing power in interest income (e.g., from bonds or savings accounts).

THE ENTREPRENEUR

Inflation is a great stimulant to business enterprise, and the entrepreneur, whether he is a manufacturer or a mer-

---

[11] Keynes attributes the historical deterioration in the value of money partly to "the superior political influence of the debtor class" and partly to "the impecuniosity of Governments." (See his *Monetary Reform*, p. 12.)

chant, stands to profit greatly by rising prices. He finds his inventories appreciating in value to the precise extent that the value of money is falling, and therefore can sell them at better prices. Moreover, the time lag between price increases and rising costs serves as an additional source of windfall gains. Until the costs of labor, raw materials, equipment, money capital, etc., catch up with general prices, the entrepreneur may expand production or carry larger inventories even with borrowed funds, as speculators usually do, and thus make fortunes overnight, so to speak. Reference has been made to the fact that businessmen react to higher costs by increasing prices rather than by absorbing them in reduced profit margins. It is not therefore surprising that the consumer should blame businessmen's "exceptional profits" for "the hated rise of prices," although the truth of the matter is that such profits are a consequence rather than the cause of high prices. Yet the fact remains that inflation does convert the entrepreneur into the "profiteer," who is the object of common hatred and who, incidentally, destroys general confidence in the justice of the functional distribution of income.[12]

WAGE–SALARY EARNERS

Although wage earners can chase "galloping" prices, they seldom win the race, with the result that their *real* wages and their standard of living are lower than if general prices and the cost of living in particular did not run away. To the extent that wage earners succeed in getting wage concessions commensurate with the cost of living, they avoid taking the brunt of inflation. Some unions do succeed in obtaining wage

[12] Keynes made the observation that by getting more than the "normal profits" which are a prerequisite to the functioning of business enterprise, businessmen in effect justify an attempt to distribute income beyond what productivity roughly warrants. This may be used as a powerful argument for excess profit taxes during inflation, since such taxes are consistent not only with the general anti-inflation program but also with the perpetuation of capitalism based on "normal profits." (See his *Monetary Reform*, pp. 29–30.)

contracts containing "escalator clauses" to make up for a decrease in real wages which would be caused by further increases in the cost of living.[13] Those who depend exclusively on fixed salaries for a living (including veterans living on pensions and educational allowances, survivors and social security beneficiaries, and those receiving public assistance) are severely affected by inflation, since upward income adjustments take time or are impossible in some cases. Salaried groups are further handicapped by the fact that they are less well organized than wage earners to press for higher pay to compensate for a fall in *real* income. Inflation seems to have taught organized labor everywhere to be more conscious than ever of the significance of real wages and to get away from traditional "money illusions."

INVESTORS

Inflation bestows favors on investors in equities but is rather harsh on investors in fixed-interest-yielding bonds and other similar titles to money. Equity dividends increase as a result of increasing corporate earnings, while bond income remains fixed. To the extent, however, that investors diversify their investments, as institutional investors normally do, they protect themselves against the devastating consequences of the falling value of money. The small middle-class investor has much to lose during inflation, since he usually places his savings in fixed-interest-bearing securities, insurance, and savings accounts. In many countries the small investor has had his savings largely, and sometimes completely, wiped out by the violent depreciation of the purchasing power of money. Such an experience has serious implications for economic progress, in so far as instability in the value of money discourages the common practice of saving and therefore blocks a principal source of investment in a free-market economy. This applies to an undeveloped country with greater force

[13] *Cf.* The President's *Economic Report, op. cit.,* p. 37.

than to an industrially advanced country, since the former country is in need of social progress via further capital formation, while the latter's major economic problem consists in instability due in part to "oversaving." This point will receive further attention.

FARMERS

Farmers in general are a favored group during inflation, not only because prices of farm products increase but because prices and costs paid by them (including interest and taxes) lag behind prices received. This is particularly true of those producing foods and other highly inflation-sensitive products. In many countries governments have found it necessary to cajole farmers into dishoarding the products which they hoarded in anticipation of higher prices. Farmers as debtors can free themselves from the burden of mortgages at the expense of the mortgagees, and pay interest and amortization and other fixed sums of money in depreciated currency, and thus share doubly in the advantage.

Thus we must conclude that inflation redistributes wealth and income in such a way as to hurt consumers, creditors, small investors, and low- and fixed-income groups, and to benefit businessmen, debtors, and farmers. It is interesting to observe, in this connection, that the vigorous anti-inflation proposals of President Truman during 1947–48 "received a hostile reception . . . from many business and industry groups," but "labor and consumer groups in general were in favor of most or all of the provisions." [14] Inflation enables one group to gain at the expense of another for a while, but what is even more disturbing is its dangerous implications for the stability of the economy as a whole. To this subject we shall now turn.

[14] *New York Times*, February 8, 1948.

Inflationary "Boom and Bust"

In this section we shall analyze the deflationary forces which an uncontrolled inflation would set in motion and which, if unchecked, would irresistibly lead to a serious deflation of aggregate demand. While this type of analysis can be more meaningfully made with reference to general business cycle theory, it nevertheless serves to emphasize the danger of *laissez faire* with respect to a persistent inflation. A "bust" need not accompany a "boom," but the phrase "boom and bust" current during an inflationary boom dramatizes the need for anti-inflation policy.[15] It is convenient to analyze the deflationary forces associated with consumption, investment, and foreign demand.

CONSUMPTION

A deflation of consumer demand during inflation may arise principally from (1) a distortion of normal income distribution (e.g., profit-wage relation), and (2) the adverse psychological effect of reduced *real* income on the consumer. If the normal (in the sense of the secular trend) distribution of income is such that two-thirds of a given income goes to wage groups and one-third to nonwage groups, it is plausible that a runaway inflation may change the distribution to give the former three-fifths and the latter two-fifths. The shift of money incomes from low- and fixed-income groups to the "profiteer" tends to reduce the consumer's ability to keep pace with rising prices and thus to accentuate consumer resistance to high-priced goods and services. Thus by reducing the purchasing power of the most important element of the consuming public—wage-salary earners—relative to that of

[15] For example, the President's *Economic Report* states: "But what most fully justifies every effort to halt an inflation is the certainty that, if it runs its course unimpeded, it will spread in its wake the disaster of falling markets, unemployment, and business losses." (*Op. cit.*, pp. 43–44.)

nonwage groups, inflation may well be sowing the seeds of its own destruction, so to speak.

If, furthermore, a gain in money income incident to rising prices is offset by a loss in real income, as is likely during a galloping inflation, the resulting deterioration of the purchasing power of the consumer dollar must have a sobering effect upon the so-called "money illusion" that the consuming public may have. A serious loss of real income induces a cautious psychology which dictates a withholding of consumer demand. As a consequence consumer demand may fall to a level too low to permit absorption of the full output of consumer goods. Postponement of demand for *durable* consumer goods would have as damaging an impact on aggregate demand as a decline in the demand for capital goods in general. This means that in a highly advanced economy the consumption-goods industries are subject to a greater volatility of activity than in an undeveloped economy whose output of durable consumer goods is necessarily small. In these circumstances, the alternatives of "boom and bust" are potentially stronger even with favorable conditions for the private inducement to invest.

INVESTMENT

A period of rapidly rising prices is a period of inordinate inventories and capital expansion. Inflation, however, produces a price structure which is highly sensitive, and vulnerable to fluctuations in business and consumer expectations and in capital and consumer outlays. A reduction in consumer spending, however actuated, increases business uncertainty and diminishes profitable investment opportunities. As a result anticipatory purchases and speculative accumulations of inventories may break down. Serious maladjustments in the profit-wage relation are bound to occur during a runaway inflation, thus causing a distortion of the price-

income structure which foreshadows an "inventory crisis."
If inflation persists, the business world becomes more and more apprehensive about the typical alternatives of "boom" and "bust." A sharp decline in consumer spending, coupled with a price-wage spiral, breeds uncertainty and spreads pessimism. Yet businessmen are as a rule reluctant to reduce prices in response to decreased consumer demand or to accept lower profit margins to absorb higher costs. Such an unwillingness is characteristic of a monopoly-ridden economy. Under these circumstances some markets become glutted and weaken, thus accentuating "bearish" sentiment and spreading a recession of output, employment, and income throughout the whole economy in a widening downward spiral.

Contraction of inventories and capital expenditures, once it has started, will weaken consumer demand, since it involves a further reduction of employment and income in manufacturing industries and particularly in durable-goods industries. Even if an initial decline in consumer demand may not immediately induce a decline in business demand, such a decline may well take place autonomously as a result of the operation of "exogenous" factors outside the price and credit systems. Decreased capital outlays, however induced, lead to decreased expenditures on consumer goods by workers in capital-goods industries as well as by workers in consumer-goods industries. The result is of course a net decrease in aggregate demand, with a depressing effect on aggregate output and employment. In so far as decreased investment merely reduces speculative accumulations of inventories and imprudent capital expansion, it will not necessarily lead to a serious recession of economic activity. But it is open to question whether private investment can be adjusted downward to the right level, since the fear of a "bust" may not serve to restrain capital expansion in a degree conducive to a healthy readjustment of prices. Furthermore, it is difficult to effect a smooth downward readjustment of capital outlays just in those areas or industries needing such a readjustment.

Because private investment in a free-market economy is the resultant of innumerable individual decisions which are influenced by profit expectations, interest rates, the quantity of investible funds, the degree of risk and uncertainty involved, and many other factors, an adequate countercyclical investment program requires much more than "the vision and initiative of business management"; experience suggests that in the absence of government action as "a balancing factor" private investment only reinforces the typical pattern of "boom and bust."

FOREIGN DEMAND

Not only a decline in consumer and business demand but a similar change in foreign demand contributes to a "bust." This latter change has serious repercussions on those countries whose foreign trade represents a large part of total trade or whose exports consist largely of capital goods. A fall in foreign expenditures on exports may arise from (a) too high export prices due to price inflation in exporting countries, (b) a drain on importing countries' gold and foreign exchange reserves due to high export prices elsewhere, (c) deflation or devaluation in importing countries, leading to a lower propensity to import, (d) an abnormally high export surplus in a leading trading country like the United States, leading to adverse balances of payments and therefore to programs of import austerity in importing countries, and (e) too high exchange value of exporting countries' currencies relative to that of importing countries' currencies.

Whatever its specific cause or causes may be, a decline in foreign demand, if not offset by a corresponding increase in domestic demand, will have the effect of reducing output and employment in export industries, with a spreading impact on the whole economy. A decline in foreign demand contributes to a depression of domestic business activity, since that initial decline in foreign demand brings about a multiple contraction of national income via the reverse operation of the foreign-trade multiplier which will be explained later. When capital goods constitute a major part of a country's exports, as in the case of American exports, that country is more susceptible to fluctuations in foreign economic activity. This means that if the foreign demand for American capital goods, for example, declines sharply due to any of the above-mentioned causes or a combination of them, the possibility of an inflationary "bust" is all the greater.

Inflation and Deflation

If the choice is between inflation and deflation, most people will probably prefer inflation. The reason is not far to seek. That is to say, it is generally considered worse to provoke unemployment via deflation than to disappoint the *rentier* via inflation.[16] To be sure, inflation inflicts injustice on the *rentier* class, whose incomes are fixed and unadjustable, but it provides the economy subject to underemployment with maximum output and employment. In other words, inflation is better than deflation as far as aggregate production and employment are concerned, but worse than deflation as far as the distribution of wealth and income is concerned. Needless to say, a hyperinflation must be ruled out in comparing the desirability of inflation and that of deflation. The optimum situation would of course be one in which full employment is maintained side by side with maximum equity in the distribution of wealth and income. Since inflation, however, hurts those who have a low marginal propensity to consume

[16] See Keynes, *Monetary Reform*, pp. 44–45; also P. A. Samuelson, "Everybody Talks about Inflation. But—," *New York Times Magazine*, August 15, 1948.

more than it does those having a high marginal propensity to consume, a redistribution of income from the former to the latter, which inflation induces, may well contribute to stability in the long run, as will be shown later.

But the dichotomy between inflation and deflation is a false one, since both are socially undesirable and economically unsound. The crux of the matter is that the smooth functioning of a free-market economy presupposes and requires stability in the purchasing power of money. Volatile fluctuations in the value of money upset consumption, saving, investment, and employment—all of which are effected or planned by individuals or groups of individuals *in terms of money* and *on the assumption of a stable measuring rod of value*. Both inflation and deflation injure general confidence in the stability of value of this common measuring rod and therefore in the possibility of a continuing stable economy. But the value of money need not and should not be allowed to fluctuate so as to jeopardize the whole money economy.

An economy accustomed to the problem of periodic and chronic underemployment experiences considerable difficulty in adjusting itself to the problem of full employment and of accompanying inflation. For it is politically more expedient to increase aggregate demand than to deflate the money incomes of the economy.[17] While warning against the inflationary danger of a full-employment economy, the public authorities are nevertheless hesitant to apply vigorous anti-inflation measures for fear of precipitating a recession. Deflation is so unpopular that the new word "disinflation" has been coined in some quarters to indicate the kind of anti-inflationary deflation that does not smack of depression.[18]

---

[17] *Cf.* R. A. Musgrave, "Fiscal Policy in Prosperity and Depression," *American Economic Review*, May, 1948.

[18] See *The Economist*, London, January 17, 1948.

5

Anti–Inflation Policies

~~~~~~

ALL ANTI–INFLATION measures ever tried or proposed
have this in common, that they aim mainly at reducing aggregate monetary expenditure, with available output taken as
a given datum. Our theory of inflation indicates three lines of
action to combat inflation; namely, (a) monetary measures,
(b) fiscal measures, and (c) nonmonetary measures. We
shall evaluate the theoretical soundness and practical effectiveness of the principal measures of anti-inflation policy.

Monetary Measures

Anti-inflation measures of a purely monetary nature are
largely a matter of central bank policy. In the United States
the Federal Reserve authorities have the power to raise rediscount rates, increase reserve ratios, sell government securities on the open market, and make selective-control adjustments in order to arrest inflationary credit expansion.
These quantitative anti-inflation monetary measures have
definite limitations, although central bank credit controls are
generally more effective in arresting credit expansion than in
stimulating it.

HIGHER REDISCOUNT RATES

In general, higher rediscount rates [1] increase the cost of borrowing for business and consumer spending, and therefore tend to restrain excess activity based on borrowed funds. The supposed sequence is high rediscount rates, less member bank borrowing to meet the demand for loans, less credit for customers at higher bank rates, and less inflationary pressure. The anti-inflation effect of higher rediscount rates may be illustrated by a simple example. Suppose that a member bank takes commercial paper (e.g., 90-day maturity) at par of $1,000 to the Federal Reserve bank to get additional reserves. If the rediscount rate is 2 per cent, the member bank will get $1,000 minus 2 per cent for one fourth of a year (90 days), or $995. If the rediscount rate is raised to 3 per cent, the member bank will get $992.50 instead of $995 for the same paper. Multiply this example by hundreds of rediscounts and you will have an appreciable decrease in the amount of additional reserves which member banks may get for potential credit expansion.

The presumption is that bank rates (interest rates on loans charged by commercial banks) will rise *pari passu* with higher rediscount rates to discourage business and consumer borrowing for excessive spending. In the final analysis, however, the effectiveness of high rediscount rates as an anti-inflation measure turns on whether commercial banks have easy access to additional reserves. If they have, then high rediscount rates are largely insignificant for credit control during inflation. Let us consider some relevant offsets to the anti-inflation effect of high rediscount policy.

[1] The Federal Reserve authorities raised the rediscount rate from 1 per cent to 1¼ per cent, effective January 12, 1948, and again to 1½ per cent, effective August 13, 1948, as a result of the Treasury's action to raise the rate (yield) on short-term government securities from 1⅛ per cent to 1¼ per cent. (The rediscount rate must be higher than the Treasury's short-term rate, since banks could otherwise adjust their reserves more cheaply by borrowing at, say, 1⅛ per cent than by selling securities yielding, say, 1¼ per cent.)

F

1. *Large amounts of short-term government securities held by commercial banks.* If and when commercial banks are in possession of large amounts of short-term government securities, as in a postwar period, they can increase or replenish their reserves (a) by selling some of those securities to the Federal Reserve banks, or (b) by monetizing maturing securities without replacement. Banks needing additional reserves are usually willing to sacrifice the yield on short-term securities for the sake of liquidity, since the cost of borrowing from the Federal Reserve banks is likely to be higher than that of getting the same amount of reserve funds by selling low-yield securities during inflation. What is more, commercial banks can get additional reserves by selling government securities at their own option; the initiative lies with commercial banks, not with the Federal Reserve banks—as long as the Federal Reserve banks stand ready to purchase all the government securities offered at any time. But this inflationary effect of sales of bank holdings is subject to the constraint that there are no such offsetting forces in operation as a Treasury "budgetary surplus" (excess of revenue over cost) and a large number of nonbank buyers. As will be explained in connection with debt management, the Treasury could use all or part of a budgetary surplus to retire government securities held by the Federal Reserves by drawing down its balances at commercial banks—i.e., the budgetary surplus kept in the form of deposits—and thus reduce bank reserves. But it is unlikely that the actual surplus to be so used will exceed the amounts of securities sold by bank holders or the volume of securities maturing within a short period, say, one year. Thus banks do not have to depend on sales of securities to the Federal Reserves for additional reserves; they merely let them mature without replacement. It is also unlikely that there will be a large number of nonbank buyers of government securities, inasmuch as fixed-income-yielding assets are unattractive during inflation. This

implies that the Federal Reserve banks would buy much more bank-held securities than they could sell to nonbank investors, thus expanding bank reserves unwittingly. Under these circumstances the existence of large bank-held securities is a strong presumption for monetary expansion despite high rediscount rates.

2. *Nonbank holdings of short-term or redeemable government securities.* High rediscount rates might also fail to prevent monetary expansion, if nonbank holders (e.g., insurance companies, dealers, and other institutional and individual investors) of government securities were generally inclined to convert their holdings into cash. And why should they be expected to prefer cash to government securities? The plausible explanation is that fixed-income-yielding assets lose much of their appeal when prices are rising, as mentioned above. Conversion of nonbank holdings into cash would probably have the effect of (a) increasing the velocity of money incident to increased cash balances and of (b) increasing the volume of bank-held government securities due to further sales of issues to the banking system by the government for purposes of "refunding" operations (i.e., further government borrowing to pay off existing debt obligations with the proceeds so obtained). The first consequence means an immediate increase in aggregate effective demand, that is, total expenditure on consumption and investment, while the second means a potential increase in bank reserves and therefore in the total money supply.

It is of course conceivable that nonbank holders convert their holdings into cash merely to hold the proceeds idle. If so, an increase in the money supply due to the above conversion would not increase total spending. But there is no good reason to suppose that nonbank holders would hold the proceeds idle. The contrary is more likely, since there is a strong tendency to get out of money and into goods when prices are rising. Even if the holders in question failed to spend the cash proceeds, there would still remain the inflationary implication of the "refunding" by the sale of additional issues to the *banks*. But it is well to recall that there is no simple mechanical connection between monetary expansion and price increases. The main point here is merely that the very possession of large liquid assets like short-term or redeemable bonds implies potential monetary expansion and, more often than not, greater spending, and therefore it implies a possible offset to high interest rates.

3. *Federal Reserve support policy.* The anti-inflationary effect of higher rediscount rates would be considerably offset by the inflationary effect of increased bank reserves, if the latter effect were sustained by a policy of supporting the government securities market. As a matter of public policy the Federal Reserve System may maintain a policy of keeping up the price of government bonds for two reasons: namely, (a) to keep interest charges on the public debt as low as possible, and (b) to prevent the "demoralization" of the capital market, that is, to protect the financial position of financial institutions holding government bonds. Quite apart from the wisdom of such a policy, it is necessary to understand first why the high selling price of government bonds has the above-mentioned effects. These relations may be illustrated by a simple example.

It is well to recall the role of interest as a go-between relating income and capital. Thus we know that if the interest rate is known, *annual income*—which is the unknown—can be found by multiplying interest rate by capital value (e.g., $0.02 \times \$10,000 = \$200$) and the unknown *capital value* by dividing annual income by interest rate (e.g., $\$200/0.02 = \$10,000$). But the *interest rate* that may be earned on a capital asset, that is, annual *yield* on an "investment," in turn is given by annual income divided by capital value (e.g., $\$200/\$10,000 = 0.02$). All these relations of course logically follow one another.

To return to our original point, it is not difficult to see why the high price of government bonds has the effect of keeping down the interest cost of public debt. In our example the capital value of an "investment" is $10,000, which is the equivalent of the selling price of so many government bonds. If, therefore, the price of government bonds should be allowed to fall from $10,000 to, say, $5,000, the interest rate or the yield on government bonds would double, or rise to 0.04 (4 per cent per annum). Such a doubling of the interest rate on long-term government bonds would have a serious effect on the annual interest charges on the public debt. If the public debt outstanding totaled $250 billion and the interest charges averaged $5 billion at the current market interest rate of 2 per cent, the cost of servicing the public debt would increase to $10 billion with a doubling of the interest rate, that is, at 4 per cent. Since such a rise in the average rate of interest on the public debt implies more taxes or more borrowing, it is not strange that the Federal Reserve authorities should be interested in maintaining the high price of government bonds or, what is the same thing, in keeping the interest low and stable.

Similarly, though less convincing, the Federal Reserve authorities might be interested in not "demoralizing" the capital market. And why should the capital market be disturbed in the absence of the Federal Reserve support policy? The mechanical answer lies in the fact that a rise in the interest rate gives rise to *capital losses*. In our example, a doubling of the interest rate from 2 per cent to 4 per cent leads to a halving of the capital value of government bonds, or from $10,000 to $5,000, and therefore to capital losses amounting to $5,000. With a substantial rise in interest rates, bank and other financial holders of government and private securities would experience serious capital losses. It is therefore partly for the purpose of protecting the "capital position" of the banking and financial institutions that the Federal Reserve authorities may maintain a policy of keeping interest rates low and stable.

The rather inflationary effect of this policy can be seen clearly in the light of what actually happens to bank reserves. In order to implement such a policy the Federal Reserve banks must buy as large amounts of government securities as bank and nonbank holders may elect to sell, that is, at par or better. This means that the banks have ready access to additional reserves, while nonbank holders can convert their holdings without capital loss. In either case bank reserves would increase by the amount by which Federal Reserve holdings of government securities increased. Such an increase in bank reserves would of course offset the anti-inflationary effect of any *ad hoc* rise in rediscount rates. Since a period of rising prices is also a period of a strong demand for credit, the banks will probably be able to expand credit on the basis of such additional reserves as they may get through sales of securities to the Federal Reserve banks.

There may be other impediments to higher interest rates as an anti-inflation factor, but the above-mentioned factors seem to be crucial. The main significance of rising rediscount rates lies in the possibility that they may serve as a barometer for business expectations of "tight" money and a lower rate of profit. For a rise in the rediscount rate from 1 per cent to 2 per cent is equivalent to announcing that credit conditions are firmer and that the current rate of interest might be higher than the *expected* rate of profit (percentage return on a capital outlay), as will be shown in the later discussion of "the marginal efficiency of capital." Experience, however, suggests that higher rediscount rates are by themselves powerless to arrest credit inflation, given the powerful downward pressure on interest rates of *a large and growing public debt* and *a constant tendency to "oversave"* relative to the demand for savings.

HIGHER RESERVE REQUIREMENTS

A rise in reserve requirements is anti-inflationary in that it reduces the amount of demand deposits in the economic system and excess reserves of member banks for potential credit expansion.[2] Higher reserve requirements absorb some of excess reserves and thus prevent them from forming a basis for further credit expansion. Suppose, for example, total member reserves amount to $18 billion, of which $16 billion represents the legal reserves and $2 billion the excess reserves. Now let the reserve ratio rise from 20 per cent to 25 per cent. The total demand deposits remaining equal, the legal minimum will then have to be increased to $20 billion, thus more than wiping out the excess reserves. This impairment of the reserve position of member banks would make them more dependent on borrowing from the Federal Reserve banks and therefore more susceptible to the latter's rediscount policy.

Higher reserve requirements as an anti-inflation measure are subject to the following limitations. First, if member banks happen to have *large excess reserves*, the basic legal requirements may have to be changed. Whether the maximum limit under the law can be raised is a question of political decision (Congressional action). Second, *ready access to reserve funds*, as under the Federal Reserve support policy, frees member banks' lending operations from the restraining influence of high reserve requirements. Third, *a large net inflow of gold*, owing to, say, a persistent export surplus, would increase member banks' reserves to offset the anti-inflation effect of higher reserve requirements. Lastly, *a Treasury policy of keeping interest rates low and stable*, as im-

[2] For example, the Federal Reserve authorities raised reserve requirements of New York and Chicago member banks from 22 per cent to 26 per cent in September, 1948, or 4 percentage points less than the maximum limit under the law. The policy was reversed in 1949 when general activity showed a downward trend, and the requirements were lowered from 26 per cent to 24 per cent for the same areas, effective May 1, 1949.

plicit in the Federal Reserve support policy, would favor large member-bank reserves and thus might discourage too drastic increases in reserve requirements.[3]

In this respect the Eccles proposal deserves mention.[4] Former chairman Eccles of the Board of Governors of the Federal Reserve System proposed that the legal requirements be raised from 20 per cent to 25 per cent against demand deposits and from 6 per cent to 10 per cent against time or savings deposits for member banks (to be carried in cash or short-term government securities). He further proposed that the Federal Reserve banks be authorized to impose "special reserves," in addition to the existing legal requirements, for nonmember as well as member banks (to be carried in short-term government securities, as additional deposits with the Federal Reserve banks, as cash in the banks' own vaults, or on deposits with correspondent banks). The immediate object of the special reserve requirements is to freeze large amounts of government securities in the hands of the banks and thus prevent them from being sold to meet the demand for bank loans. The first of these proposals—to raise basic reserve requirements of all commercial banks—is considered as a possible offset to gold acquisitions and purchases of government securities by the Federal Reserve banks. The second proposal, with respect to "special reserves," is in the nature of an emergency anti-inflation measure.[5] Whatever objections may be raised against the plan,[6] drastic in-

[3] The Secretary of the Treasury was reported to have opposed the Eccles plan mainly on the ground that it is incompatible with public debt management. (See *Monthly Letter*, National City Bank of New York, December, 1947.)

[4] Testimony before a Joint Congressional Committee, November 25, 1947.

[5] Testimony before a Joint Congressional Committee, April 13, 1948.

[6] For example, the Federal Advisory Council, an advisory group of leading bankers from each of the Federal Reserve banks, opposed the Eccles plan on the grounds that it might cause such credit deflation as to check production, that it would be "a step toward socialization of banking," and that the present powers of the Federal Reserve System and the Treasury are adequate, if fully used. (See *Monthly Letter, op. cit.*)

creases (i.e., beyond the present upper limit) in legal reserve requirements are consistent with the general anti-inflation program as well as with the general principle that monetary policy should be determined by reference to its own standards rather than to fiscal considerations.

OPEN–MARKET OPERATIONS

Another conventional device to check credit expansion is open-market policy, that is, *sales* (purchases during recession) of government securities by Federal Reserve banks to the public. The process of reducing member reserves via this method is simple. As the buying public (e.g., bond houses, trust companies, and dealers) purchases and pays for the government securities offered, the public reduces its checking accounts by the amount of the purchases, and the member banks (or nonmember commercial banks) lose their reserve accounts at the Federal Reserve banks by a similar amount. Member banks losing reserves in this way tend to adopt a more cautious credit policy, and general credit conditions are expected to become tight, other things remaining equal. But, just as in the case of rediscount policy or of reserve requirements, other things do not remain equal. Though a powerful regulator of general liquidity, open-market policy is subject to the following offsets.

First, open-market policy is rendered inoperative by a *support policy* of supplying banks with reserves at their volition when they offer government securities to Federal Reserve banks for sale. With the Federal Reserve authorities committed to such a policy, government securities in the hands of member banks are potential *legal reserves*. For banks can always count on liquidating their holdings of government securities in order to improve their reserve position or to get additional reserve for credit expansion. Moreover, if nonbank holders of government securities can sell them to Federal Reserve banks in the absence of other buyers and deposit the proceeds at member banks, the latter's *deposits* as well as reserves will increase. Thus the total money supply is bound to increase under the support policy.

It is quite possible, therefore, that member banks may sell large amounts of short-term government securities to Federal Reserve banks to meet an actual or expected rise in reserve requirements or to counteract the effect of higher rediscount rates. Thus, for example, the anti-inflation effects of higher rediscount rates and higher reserve requirements during the postwar year 1948 were largely neutralized by the inflationary effect of Federal Reserve support purchases of short-term government securities offered by the member banks needing reserve adjustments. Here again we can see something of a conflict between short-run monetary policy and long-run fiscal policy. For while a support policy may be justified by a large public debt and on the ground of effective debt management, such a policy undoubtedly weakens the effectiveness of open-market operations and other measures of anti-inflation monetary policy.

The Federal Reserve authorities are therefore confronted with a serious dilemma, namely, (a) either to modify the support policy in the interest of credit control but at the risk of demoralizing capital markets, or (b) to maintain the support policy at the risk of further inflationary monetary expansion.[7] Solutions to this dilemma are necessarily controversial, but all discussions point to general agreement on the desirability of maintaining low and stable *long-term* rates. Some are of the opinion that a small rise in *short-term* rates should be permitted, on the ground that such a rise would not increase the annual cost of the public debt significantly or demoralize capital markets (especially the long-term government bond market) seriously. The implication of pre-

---

[7] *Cf.* M. S. Szymczak, "Our Federal Reserve Policy Today" (speech before 3rd Annual Federal Reserve Forum, Minneapolis, Minnesota, October 11, 1948).

occupation with stability of the government bond market for open-market policy as an anti-inflation weapon is therefore anything but cheerful.

Moreover, the anti-inflation open-market policy could be somewhat offset by increased member borrowing from, as well as by increased sales of Treasury bills and acceptances to, Federal Reserve banks. Imports of gold would also be another offset here as in other cases. Then there is always the possibility that the government may resort to large-scale deficit financing irrespective of the inflationary consequences, depending on the nature of the national program. Finally, too much reliance on the open-market policy serves to overemphasize the effectiveness of monetary policy based upon the crude quantity theory of money to the neglect of other policies.

CONSUMER CREDIT REGULATION

The selective credit control mechanism known as "Regulation W" is a newcomer in the field of countercyclical monetary policy.[8] Here we are mainly concerned with this mechanism as an anti-inflation weapon. The regulation of consumer credit is based on the observation that the monetary demand for consumers' *durable* goods is extremely unstable and of strategic importance to general price movements and to the levels of aggregate output and employment. The *raison d'être* of consumer credit is graphically expressed in the statement that "the richer a nation is in its stock of durable goods, the more unstable its economy is likely to be."[9] As far as a

[8] For the first time the Federal Reserve authorities were empowered (by Executive Order No. 8843 issued August 8, 1941) to regulate the volume of installment credit buying, in order to minimize the wartime inflationary pressure and to divert resources to war production. "Regulation W" was thus introduced but terminated in November, 1947, in line with the general "decontrol" movement; it was revived in September, 1948, as part of the general anti-inflation policy. The terms of the regulation were somewhat relaxed in March, 1949, owing to a general deflationary trend.

[9] *Cf.* R. M. Evans, "Regulation W—Its Role in Economic Stability," *Federal Reserve Bulletin*, April, 1949, pp. 343–347.

period of full employment is concerned, the regulation of consumer credit is designed (a) to check inflationary credit expenditures on consumers' durable goods, and (b) to minimize the possible danger of undue installment credit expansion to the future stability of the economy.

To see how the mechanism can restrain consumer spending on durables, one must understand the principle involved in its operation. In conditions of full employment "Regulation W" is made to restrict the total volume of installment credit buying (a) by *raising* the minimum *down payments* on specified goods, (b) by *extending* the *coverage* of selective consumers' durable goods, (c) by *lowering* the maximum *maturities* (payment period) on all installment credits subject to regulation, whether to finance the purchase of the specified goods or not, and (d) by *lowering* the maximum *exemption* costs of installment purchases of goods specified. The following model will perhaps help clarify the meaning of these requirements.

Hypothetical Quantitative Adjustments
in the Consumer Credit Regulation

Requirements	Quantitative Adjustments	
	Restrictive	Relaxed
Minimum down payments	20%	15%
Selective coverage of consumers' durables	50 items	40 items
Maximum maturities on installment credits	15 months	20 months
Maximum exemption costs of installment purchases	$50	$100

Brief explanation of the above model is in order. "Minimum down payments" are taken to mean amounts to be paid in cash for purchases of specified goods. Thus, if a television set costs $500, a buyer must put up $100 initially and pay the rest on an installment basis, given a 20 per cent requirement ratio. But if the monetary authority wished to relax this requirement, it could lower the requirement from 20 per cent to 15 per cent, as shown above, and the buyer would then put up $75 instead of $100. The higher the minimum down payment requirement, the more restrictive an installment purchase is likely to be. By "selective coverage" is to be understood the scope of the regulation with respect to particular consumers' durable goods to be included. Thus the authority may include automobiles, furniture and household equipment, washing machines, radio and television sets, etc., the number of items covered depending on the strategic importance of particular goods to aggregate output and employment. If, for instance, housing contributes to national income significantly, furniture and household equipment may be included during inflation and excluded during deflation. The greater the extent of coverage in this respect, the more anti-inflationary is the effect. If a deflationary trend is in sight, the number of items covered should be reduced, as from 50 to 40 in the above model.

"Maximum maturities" refer to the length of payment periods for paying off the debts incurred in installment purchases. Thus, if a down payment of $100 is made on a $500 television set, the buyer may arrange to pay the remaining $400 by giving a first installment payment of $40 and an equal monthly payment of $24 thereafter, given a 15-month maturity requirement. Obviously a 20-month maturity requirement would reduce considerably the amount of the installment payment, to a monthly sum of $18 after an initial installment payment of $40. Merchants would thereby be prevented from extending longer maturities to induce larger volumes of installment purchases during a period of inflation. In reality merchants are more inclined to ease down payment than to extend maturities or reduce prices during such a period. But a combination of the down-payment requirement and the maturity requirement would check inflationary installment sales arrangements which merchants might otherwise make. As for the "exemption" requirement, a $50 exemption requirement would be more restrictive than a $100 exemption, since a larger volume of installment purchases would be subject to regulation when the maximum cost of a purchase exempted is $50 than when it is $100.

Thus it can be seen that appropriate quantitative adjustments in the various requirements of the consumer credit regulation are capable of restraining excessive installment buying or of stimulating it, as the case may be.[10] The technique must be revised from time to time, in accordance with the requirement of concrete circumstances and in the light of actual experience. Although "Regulation W" is not yet a permanent part of Federal Reserve monetary policy at this writing, the increasingly dominant role played by installment buying and the dynamic nature of the demand for consumers' durable goods are a strong presumption in favor of permanent consumer credit control as a countercyclical weapon. This reasoning can more clearly be seen in connection with later discussions of antideflation measures.

MARGIN REQUIREMENTS

Another selective control weapon in the hands of the Federal Reserve authorities is "margin requirement" regulations. Like consumer credit control, this weapon is selective with respect to the field of application and countercyclical in effect (i.e., to combat both inflation and deflation). Here we are primarily concerned with margin requirement regulations as an anti-inflation measure. This weapon is designed to prevent the typical "boom-bust" pattern attributed to such a stock market collapse as occurred toward the end of 1929.

[10] Indicative of the inflationary implication of the *absence* of such regulation is the fact that installment credit jumped from $1.8 billion during World War II to some $7.2 billion upon the removal of "Regulation W" in November, 1947.

The "get-rich-quick" speculative mania of the 1920's would probably have been impossible had there existed margin requirement regulations; it was not until 1934 that the Securities Exchange Act gave the Federal Reserve authorities a mandate to issue margin requirement regulations applicable to all banks, brokers, and dealers.

The mechanism involved is fairly simple. The demand for speculative credit is to be controlled by regulating the amount of credit which one may secure to purchase stocks. The "margin" refers to the amount of cash one must put up in addition to what one may borrow on his stock from a bank, a broker, or a dealer. Thus, if a loan of $9,000 is secured by stock worth $10,000, the *margin* is said to be $1,000, or 10 per cent of the value of the stock. Therefore, with a 10 per cent margin requirement, one can borrow 90 per cent of the value of his collateral security. With a margin ratio of 100 per cent, one can borrow *nothing,* as was actually the case during 1946–47. We may generalize by stating that *the higher the margin required, the more cash one would have to put up or the less credit one could obtain for the purchase of stocks.* To see the effects of margin requirements, we may consider the following three cases, namely, margin ratios of 10 per cent, 75 per cent, and 100 per cent.

With a 10 per cent margin ratio, a speculator with $1,000 could buy 100 shares of stock at $100 each, and make $500 profit on the $9,000 borrowed, given a rise of 5 points ($5 per share). With a 75 per cent ratio, a cash payment of $1,000 could buy about 13 shares at $100 each, and net about $65 profit on the borrowed fund of $325 (25 per cent of $1,300, which is the market value of the shares), given a rise of 5 points. With a 100 per cent ratio, a speculator with $1,000 cash to invest could buy 10 shares at $100 each, and make only $50, given a rise of 5 points. Obviously no credit is involved in this case. Thus the demand for speculative credit could be reduced by raising the margin requirements.

What are some of the implications of margin requirement regulations? First, high margin requirements have the effect of *diverting investible funds from speculative to productive channels.* This is important during a period of rising prices, since the use of credit for the expansion of plant and equipment or for carrying larger inventories would make more goods and services available relative to effective demand and thus help minimize inflationary pressure. It is therefore no accident that the margin ratio was raised to 100 per cent during the postwar boom year 1946–47. And it is well to recall, in this connection, that trading in *existing* securities (as distinguished from new issues) does not lead to *new* production. If, however, credit institutions were well supplied with "idle" funds seeking profitable outlets, they could lend liberally to both speculators (financial investors) and producers (real investors). But there is no good reason to suppose that the supply of "idle" funds is plentiful during a "boom."

Second, high margin requirements have the effect of *checking undue monetary expansion.* With high margin requirements in effect, commercial banks (both member and nonmember) would be prevented from manufacturing so much speculative "bank money" on a fractional reserve basis as to increase the total money supply significantly. Otherwise the money supply would increase relative to real income (output) to increase an upward pressure on general prices. As was explained earlier, in conditions of full employment real income can increase by only a small degree. This means that in the absence of high margin requirements there is likely to be more purchasing power ready to bid up the prices of scarce goods and services than can be offset by available output. Although there is no simple connection between the money supply and expenditure, a period of rising prices is highly conducive to a flight of money into goods. Thus when the purchasing power of money is deteriorating rapidly, there is a strong presumption in favor of the view that an increase in the money supply would increase effective demand or expenditure much more than if the value of money remained stable.

Third, the *income effect* of higher margin requirements must not be overlooked. To see this effect clearly, reverse the assumption and suppose that speculators could make great profits on "borrowed money." Since it is a truism that "easy money" is easy to spend, aggregate spending is bound to increase under those circumstances. The "get-rich-quick" psychology of stock-market speculators might well lead to reckless spending as well as to a mania for "easy money." Such spending would have secondary effects on the incomes and expenditures of other income recipients, thus increasing effective demand relative to effective supply. High margin requirements would *reduce the inflationary effect of speculative profits upon the income-expenditure structure of the economy,* and thus would *contribute to the prevention of a "boom-bust" development.*

Lastly, high margin requirements *go a long way toward eliminating the threat of speculative activity to the stability of the economy.* The risks and uncertainties attending the corporate form of business organization would be greatly minimized, under margin requirement regulations, so that the economy could enjoy the advantage of "venture capital" without the disadvantage of volatile fluctuations in aggregate demand. This is not to say, of course, that margin requirements alone stabilize activity, but it does emphasize the usefulness of the weapon in minimizing cyclical disturbances. Needless to say, margin requirements should be lowered to foster "bullish" sentiment in times of low activity.[11]

[11] In line with a general downward trend, stock-market activity became "bearish" during 1949, and the margin ratio was lowered from 75 per cent to 50 per cent, effective March 30, 1949. In the presence of offsetting non-monetary factors the lower requirement failed to have a sustained stimulating effect on stock-market activity.

G

Fiscal Measures

Fiscal policy with respect to inflation includes all the measures of a monetary nature which the executive branch of the government adopts or intends to adopt in connection with (a) government spending, (b) taxes, and (c) public borrowing. Fiscal policy has come to be recognized as the potentially most powerful instrument of economic stabilization. But fiscal policy, being largely a matter of unpredictable political decision, cannot be relied upon to the exclusion of purely monetary measures for combatting inflation. In this section we shall deal with the major anti-inflation measures stemming largely from fiscal considerations.

GOVERNMENT SPENDING

During inflation the government is supposed to decrease its own spending to counteract an increase in private spending. More concretely, the government must simultaneously reduce expenditures and increase revenues to achieve a cash surplus to be used in an anti-inflation manner. To maintain or even to increase taxes is not too great a problem during an inflationary "boom," but to reduce expenditures is quite another matter, particularly during an immediate postwar period. For example, almost four-fifths of the estimated United States expenditures in 1949 was allocated to national defense, veterans, interest, international affairs, and tax refunds, which President Truman considered as an inevitable reflection of "the costs of war, the effects of war, and our efforts to prevent a future war." [12] The reality of irreducible minima on the one hand and the fear of deflation on the other often deter the drastic downward adjustment of government spending that is required to dampen a principal source of inflation.

Furthermore, the short-run anti-inflation objective of fiscal

[12] *Cf. Monthly Letter* of the National City Bank of New York, February, 1948.

policy may be somewhat upset by the long-run public investment program. For example, the 1949 public investment program of the United States envisaged the financing of such long-range projects [13] as are "much larger than any regular public works program prior to the war." Long-range public outlays, however, can and should be so adjusted in amount and in timing that they will not put a national budget out of control or, more specifically, aggravate the inflationary pressures in shorter periods. The greatest single obstacle to anti-inflation public spending is a warlike international situation which necessitates an expanding national budget. So great a threat to economic stability is the prospect of an expanding armament program that Marriner S. Eccles characterized it as "the certain road . . . to a ruinous inflation." [14]

Barring political or military considerations, public spending is a manageable variable; it is capable of being deliberately increased or decreased according to the overall requirements of the economy as a whole. By reducing its spending the government can partly offset the inflationary pressures arising from unregulated private spending. In other words, aggregate demand relative to the limited supply of goods and services during a period of full-employment inflation is reduced to the extent that the government cuts down its own spending. Yet a reduction of government expenditures is not by itself sufficient to minimize the inflationary pressures; the government must not only reduce its spending but must also tax away or perhaps borrow a substantial portion of spendable money in the hands of the general public.

TAXES

As shown earlier, taxes determine the size of disposable income in the hands of the general public and therefore also the magnitude of the inflationary gap, given the available supply

[13] Including the welfare program, educational aid, housing, health, and public works.
[14] Testimony before a Joint Congressional Committee, April 13, 1948.

of goods and services. Moreover, the maintenance of a balanced national budget or, better yet, of a budgetary cash surplus, depends largely on the amount of tax receipts. It is axiomatic that during inflation the existing tax structure should be retained, that tax cuts should be resisted, and that new taxes should be adopted or tax rates increased, if possible —to reduce the amount of spendable money in the hands of the general public. But care must be taken not to deflate the money incomes of the country via taxation so much as to provoke a recession of economic activity. The degree of flexibility that is required to reverse too effective an anti-inflation tax policy is difficult to achieve, for political and perhaps psychological reasons.[15] It is partly such difficulties involved in tax adjustments that make the monetary-fiscal authorities turn to purely monetary measures to avoid either inflation or deflation.

It is important to investigate which group or groups of taxpayers should be taxed most heavily in order to reduce aggregate demand at "the strategic points" of an inflationary economy. The fiscal authority must take into account shifting, incidence, distributive justice, and many other effects of particular taxes on particular groups of taxpayers. In general, anti-inflation taxation must aim at reducing current incomes which otherwise would be spent in increasing prices. Particular taxes must aim at reducing particular demands rather than aggregate demand. Perhaps the most effective anti-inflation tax is a personal income tax with as high basic and surtax rates as required by the progress of inflation. Such a tax would reduce the consumption function (to be defined later) and so minimize the inflationary pressures. In this respect it was entirely consistent with the general anti-inflation program that President Truman vetoed proposed tax-cut bills during 1947–48.[16]

---

[15] On this point, see R. A. Musgrave, *op. cit.*

[16] Congress finally passed a bill reducing the personal income tax by overriding the President's veto in March, 1948.

There is one exception to the general principle that the existing tax structure should be maintained or taxes increased during inflation: namely, tariffs. Tariffs should be reduced as much and as fast as possible, to increase imports and thus to allow a part of the increased domestic money incomes to "leak out" to other points of an open system. It is expedient to reduce those tariffs which deter imports of necessities and other items in short supply, as Britain and others did during the postwar period of inflation. But changes in the tariff structure involve difficult "structural" adjustments at home (e.g., a shift of resources from affected industries to export industries or to industries which are independent of foreign demand). Therefore it is likely that a reduction of tariffs, however desirable in a short period of inflation, will meet considerable resistance from sectional interests. Nevertheless, the establishment of the International Trade Organization, with its avowed purpose of promoting multilateral trade via tariff cuts, etc., points hopefully to a future possibility that tariffs may be reduced not only to maintain long-run international equilibrium but also to combat domestic inflation in the short run.

SAVINGS

The type of public borrowing which has a deflationary effect on the money supply and effective demand is one that absorbs existing purchasing power, i.e., money otherwise spent on consumption or investment. The most effective anti-inflation public borrowing takes the form of compulsory saving, otherwise known as "deferred pay." [17] According to this plan, the consumer defers a part of his pay by buying savings bonds which are redeemable sometime after war. Besides being anti-inflationary during a period of wartime scarcity, the plan has the added advantage of releasing deferred purchasing power at the first sign of a postwar recession. A variant

[17] For details, see Keynes, *How to Pay for the War.*

of forced savings is a "forced loan," which has been tried by Belgium, Holland, Czechoslovakia, and Norway. The principle involved is the same in all cases, namely "to withdraw a portion of the note issue, to freeze a portion of the bank deposits, and to issue holdings in a government loan in place of the currency withdrawn and the bank deposits frozen." [18] This latter type of forced savings aims at reducing the money supply in the hands of the general public, particularly of speculators, while Keynes' "deferred pay" plan is designed to absorb a portion of money wage income at the source. Compulsory savings of any kind are expedient during wartime, or a postwar hyperinflation, but hardly practicable in peacetime democracies. [19]

Accordingly, an anti-inflation program must in part rely on *voluntary* savings. Statistics on "successful" savings-bond campaigns are rather unreliable, since new savings may have merely replaced other forms of savings under the inducement of higher interest rates instead of reducing current income. A further flaw in excessive reliance on voluntary savings is that the amount of savings depends partly on the level of income taxes. [20] Since payment of high wartime or postwar income taxes involves not only a decrease in consumption but a decrease in savings, the amount of individual savings on a voluntary basis may not be sufficiently deflationary. Keynes further pointed out that the crucial weakness of voluntary savings as an anti-inflation measure lies in the fact that others do not necessarily follow a good example set by an individual who tries to save in order to protect himself against the consequences of inflation. [21] It may be necessary to make savings

[18] *Cf.* R. G. Hawtrey, "Monetary Aspects of the Economic Situation," *American Economic Review*, March, 1948.

[19] Even in wartime Britain, forced savings as proposed by Keynes were practiced to a small extent. President Roosevelt's budget message of January 6, 1943, alluded to a program of "deferred pay" as a possible alternative to additional taxes, but it was never adopted.

[20] On this point, see Keynes, *op. cit.*, pp. 59–60.

[21] *Ibid.*, p. 70.

bonds more attractive to the general public by raising interest rates, but such a policy would come in conflict with the desire of the fiscal authority to keep interest rates low for servicing the public debt and for floating new issues. It is doubtless desirable that savings bonds should be made non-negotiable and less liquid (i.e., with longer maturities) for the duration of an inflationary period.

DEBT MANAGEMENT

Public debt outstanding may be managed in such a way as to reduce the money supply or to prevent further credit expansion. Anti-inflation debt management usually refers to the retirement of *bank*-held debt out of a budgetary surplus. The general reason for concentrating on the effort to retire bank-held debt is that as long as commercial banks are "loaded" with government securities, they can always sell them on the open market or let them mature and thus acquire additional reserves for credit expansion. As long as commercial banks can count on getting additional reserves in these ways, Federal Reserve credit controls are rendered ineffective. This is where fiscal policy comes to the rescue of monetary policy.

Roughly there are two possibilities, namely, (a) retirement of bank-held government securities *out of a budgetary surplus,* and (b) refunding of bank-held public debt *by sale of bank-ineligible bonds to nonbank investors* (e.g., insurance companies, savings banks, endowed institutions, and individuals). Let us consider these possibilities in some detail.

As far as the anti-inflation use of a budgetary surplus is concerned, it is important to analyze separately three distinct cases involved: (1) retirement of public debt held by Federal Reserve banks, (2) retirement of debt held by commercial banks (including nonmember banks), and (3) retirement of debt owned by the nonbank public.

1. Retirement of public debt held by Federal Reserve

banks out of a budgetary surplus is most deflationary in its effect upon the money supply and bank reserves. In the first place, the accumulation of a budgetary surplus involves a reduction of demand deposits in the hands of taxpayers and therefore also of commercial bank reserves—the extinction of a portion of deposit money in the hands of the general public as well as a reduction of commercial bank reserves. This means that commercial banks' ability to make loans or expand investments is reduced. In the second place, the use of a budgetary surplus kept as demand deposits in member banks for retiring debt held by Federal Reserve banks involves a loss of member-bank reserves and a reduction of otherwise spendable deposit money in the hands of the government, that is, effective prevention of inactive money from appearing as active money. This type of operations was actually tried by the Treasury in the postwar year 1947–48.

2. Retirement of bank-held debt (i.e., commercial banks) is neutral in its effect on the money supply, since bank reserves will thereby be increased to create new money to make up for that portion of the money supply which was extinguished by the budgetary surplus. The danger, though, is that commercial banks may have so much more in government securities maturing within one year than any conceivable budgetary surplus as to *increase* the money supply. Such a danger is explicit in any extraordinarily large bank holdings of short-term government securities, as in immediate postwar years, and implicit in a possible failure to achieve a significant budgetary surplus owing not so much to inadequate tax revenue as to increased public expenditure. However desirable or necessary the reduction of bank-held public debt may be on other grounds (e.g., to broaden the ownership of the public debt and to prevent excessive bank earnings), the use of a budgetary surplus for that purpose does nothing to *reduce* the money supply. Therefore, if a positive anti-inflation effect on the money supply is desired, it will be neces-

can be retired without endangering general liquidity. This question brings us to the second method.

Adoption of the second general method, namely, that of retiring bank-held debt by sale of bank-ineligible bonds to nonbank investors, would involve a loss of spendable money in the hands of the public and also of bank reserves. But it is arguable, though inconclusively, that this type of operations would be ineffective if nonbank investors were reluctant to give up spendable money for government bonds, or if the sale of government bonds to the nonbank investors resulted merely in the surrender of idle funds which would not have been spent anyhow.[22] Much depends on nonbank investors' choice between different types of liquidity (cash and government securities, in this instance), prevailing interest rates on alternative investments, and their expectations in general. To the extent that the public purchases new government securities out of idle money, the second method of debt management will be less deflationary in effect. It is important to remember that in this case, as in the first, diversion of Treasury balances, regardless of their source (tax proceeds or loan funds), to the retirement of bank-held public debt prevents an otherwise inevitable increase in the money supply.[23]

"GOLD STERILIZATION"

Whenever gold inflow is deemed too dangerously inflationary in effect, the government may decide to "sterilize" gold in order to keep bank reserves from increasing with gold acquisitions.[24] To see how gold inflow can be prevented from exerting an inflationary influence on the economy, we must

[22] *Cf.* H. R. Bowen, *The Interest Rate, the Debt and Inflation* (Irving Trust Co., New York, 1946), p. 13.

[23] *Cf.* A. Sproul, "Monetary Management and Credit Control," *American Economic Review*, June, 1947.

[24] The Treasury was reportedly studying the possibility of "sterilizing" gold imports during the inflationary year 1947. See *Monthly Letter*, National City Bank of New York, December, 1947.

sary to direct a budgetary surplus toward the retiremen\
public debt held by the Federal Reserve banks and to "free\
the securities owned by commercial banks.

3. In case a budgetary surplus is used to retire a maturin\
portion of debt held by the nonbank public, the result wil\
also be neutral as far as the money supply is concerned. For
the process of accumulating and using a surplus merely results in a shift of ownership of money from taxpayers to
holders of government securities. It is arguable, however, that,
although there is no net change in the money supply, the shift
of ownership of money from taxpayers to holders of government securities involved in this type of operations may have
a deflationary effect on consumer *spending.* For though taxes
are imposed on all groups and deflate their incomes, given the
public expenditure structure, the shift of money in question
benefits chiefly the *rentier* class, which generally spends less
on consumption than those taxpayers who do not own government securities. If, however, the holders reinvest the proceeds of the redemption, the above deflationary effect of the
retirement of nonbank-held debt on aggregate spending is
rather indeterminate—an interesting problem for empirical
research.

The success of these three types of operations presupposes
a large and continuous budgetary surplus out of which to retire maturing public debt. Yet there is the possibility that the
government may have a budgetary *deficit* instead. Such a
possibility becomes the stronger the greater the pressure on
tax proceeds for other purposes grows. Increases in public
expenditures might even wipe out the budgetary surplus
which could otherwise be used to combat inflation. Should
there occur an excess of expenditure over revenue in the
national budget, the public would get more in income than
it lost in taxes. The result would be inflationary, other
things being equal. Barring these possible offsets, the crucial
question is how much and how fast bank-held public debt

first understand the way in which gold inflow inevitably leads to larger bank reserves. Suppose that $10 billion of gold flows into the United States in a given period, owing, say, to a surplus in the American balance of payments. The Treasury then purchases and pays for the gold with checks drawn on Federal Reserve banks, and the public (importers and sellers of gold) gets $10 billion to deposit in member banks. Accordingly, member banks get $10 billion of new reserves in the books of Federal Reserve banks by presenting the checks for collection. The important consequence is that member bank *excess* reserves increase by $10 billion *minus* whatever portion must be deducted to support $10 billion of new demand deposits. If the reserve ratio is 20 per cent, then the member banks will have $8 billion of new *excess* reserves for credit expansion, $2 billion becoming legal reserves to support $10 billion of new demand deposits. This is where a policy of "gold sterilization" comes in.

The government ordinarily replenishes its depleted account at Federal Reserve banks by depositing gold certificates issued against the gold purchased. In our example, the government exchanges $10 billion of gold certificates for $10 billion of Federal Reserve credits. So far the state of affairs is one in which "everybody is happy"—the government has the gold, the Federal Reserve banks have the gold certificates, the member banks have the excess reserves, and the public has the enlarged bank accounts—except the economic system! For, on the one hand, the increased member bank reserves threaten credit inflation, while, on the other, the gold acquisitions have cost the government nothing but have cost the economic system a considerable loss of real income—that is, a sacrifice of otherwise consumable goods and services for the sake of unpalatable gold. A policy of "gold sterilization" is concerned with the inflationary threat of gold inflow, however. How does the government go about "sterilizing" gold? The process involved is simple.

Instead of paying for gold purchases by drawing down and replenishing its account at Federal Reserve banks, the government "sterilizes" gold *by paying for gold purchases out of the proceeds of the sale of government securities deposited at member banks.* In terms of our example this means that the government must sell on the open market government securities equal to $10 billion to reduce both member bank reserves and demand deposits by $10 billion. What happens is a transfer of balances in the books of Federal Reserve banks from member banks to the Treasury. Thus the government in effect pays for gold purchases with government securities, and locks the gold away from the banking system. The United States adopted such a policy between 1936 and 1938, but discontinued the policy in 1938 for two main reasons, namely, (a) the unduly deflationary effect of the "sterilization" policy on bank reserves and on business activity, and (b) the increasing effect of the necessary sale of government securities on the public debt. This historical experience suggests that the Treasury is unlikely to be very quick to adopt such a policy even when a continuous net inflow of gold adds to the prevailing inflationary pressure. A more immediate reason for the Treasury's cautious attitude might be the belief, right or wrong, that the present powers of the Federal Reserve authorities are adequate to cope with the problem of member-bank excess reserves.

A "gold sterilization" policy has special significance for a country like the United States, which, for one reason or another, is in the habit of acquiring gold in large quantities. Past experience tells us that gold imports may pour into the United States in the future as well, whether to settle debts to the United States, to finance purchases in American markets, or simply for safekeeping. All this implies probable increases in member-bank excess reserves. The result would be no different if gold acquisitions arose from the purchase of domestically produced gold. Although the international position of the United States may be such as to warrant a bias toward "gold sterilization," we must nevertheless be prepared to consider the opposite policy, namely, "gold desterilization."

Gold should be "desterilized" when the situation calls for a measure to increase member-bank reserves. This the government could do by releasing or activating a part or all of the previously "sterilized" gold, or by permitting new gold acquisitions to influence member-bank reserves. The government in this instance issues as much in gold certificates as it cares to increase and spend in deposit credits at Federal Reserve banks. The result is that the public gets additional demand deposits as the government spends the proceeds of the gold certificates issued, while member banks accumulate a corresponding supply of reserves at Federal Reserve banks. The new member-bank *excess* reserves are of course equal to the amount of gold "desterilized" minus the legal reserves necessary to support the public's demand deposits. Thus gold can and should be "desterilized" to check credit deflation, as it can and should be "sterilized" to arrest credit inflation, as the case may be.

OVERVALUATION

In order to control domestic inflation a country might maintain the "overvalued" exchange value of its currency, that is, an expensive currency relative to foreign currencies.[25] An "overvalued" currency is anti-inflationary in effect for three reasons, namely, (a) because of its discouraging effect on exports and therefore of its decreasing effect on domestic money incomes, (b) because of its encouraging effect on imports and therefore of its increasing effect on import expenditures, and (c) because of its cheapening effect on the price of those foreign materials which enter into the domestic cost

[25] For detailed analysis of overvaluation and related concepts see Chaps. 17 and 18. Also see H. S. Ellis, "Exchange Control and Discrimination," *American Economic Review*, December, 1947.

of production and therefore of its preventive effect on an upward cost-price spiral. If, however, other countries are experiencing inflation at the same time, the importing country in question may find it necessary to *appreciate* its currency, that is, to make the domestic currency even *more expensive* in terms of foreign currencies. Otherwise the deflationary effects of overvaluation would be offset by the rising cost of imports (an important consideration for countries using many foreign raw materials).

It is unlikely that a country will maintain an overvalued currency or disregard exchange depreciation solely for the purpose of controlling domestic inflation. For the deflationary implication of overvaluation for the balance of payments may well be more serious than a similar implication for domestic price levels.

Nonmonetary Measures

Anti-inflation policies of a nonmonetary nature include, among others, (a) output adjustment, (b) wage policy, and (c) price control and rationing. These measures are much less practicable than monetary-fiscal ones, for psychological, institutional, political, technological, and other noneconomic reasons. Therefore they can be considered only as supplements to more expedient or flexible measures.

OUTPUT ADJUSTMENT

Increased production is admittedly a basic solution to the problem of inflation, since the inflationary gap arises partly from inadequate output. The practical question is: How much and how fast can total output be increased in relatively short periods? There are a number of possibilities as well as limitations. The most obvious limitation is full utilization of resources, yet it is possible to increase the output of *particular* goods and services, or to prevent total output from declining even in conditions of full employment of resources. This can be done by shifting the already employed resources from the production of the less inflation-sensitive to the more sensitive ones. Such a reallocation, if possible at all, must be accomplished without the usual inducement of higher factor prices. Otherwise the resulting higher money incomes to factors would defeat the purpose.[26] The output of particular goods (e.g., food, clothing, housing, and durable consumer goods in general—which are likely to be in short supply) may be increased by systems of priorities, regulated allocation, and perhaps subsidies, as practiced by some countries during World War II and the immediate postwar period. Therefore the practical effort to increase production during a short period of full-employment inflation must be directed primarily at particular goods and services which are found to be in short supply and whose price movements are of strategic importance to the economy as a whole.

Another difficulty lies in the possibility that monopolistic *costs* may inhibit production in many lines. A distortion of the cost-price structure due to the monopolistic control of factors (e.g., raw materials and labor) tends to raise marginal costs more quickly as output increases, thus checking further production. For this reason the measures to increase production usually include the regulation of, or a vigorous campaign against, monopolistic attempts to raise factor costs in the strategic sectors of the economy (e.g., steel and housing). In peacetime it is politically inexpedient and administratively difficult to keep monopolistic factor prices in check. Some *selective* control methods must be devised to prevent monopoly costs from spreading a restraining influence on the production of goods and services in short supply.

It is sometimes suggested that available output be increased

[26] The inducement of higher factor prices for reallocation purposes would not be self-defeating if the proper monetary-fiscal measures were taken to absorb excess cash balances.

by "longer hours of work." [27] Though "longer hours of work" is one way of increasing productivity, it is not a realistic solution in peacetime, and especially in those countries where trade unionism is a going concern. Besides, "overtime pay" would have to be taxed away or otherwise withdrawn from the income stream if the increased production due to "longer hours of work" were to have its anti-inflation effect. A more realistic solution for increased productivity may lie in the direction of encouraging technical innovations, as far as industrially advanced dynamic economies are concerned. Wartime experience showed that technical innovations are possible even in relatively short periods.

Total output can be prevented from falling and the output of particular goods and services increased by keeping industrial strife to a minimum. For strikes and other manifestations of labor unrest are likely to prevail during an inflationary "boom," and thus interfere with the general effort to increase output. Therefore, efficient and satisfactory labor-management relations are a prerequisite to removing "bottlenecks" which impede production. Strikes and other forms of work stoppage for political reasons are generally regarded as taboo during the course of inflation. Lockouts and other "strikes of capital" are similarly detrimental to production. In a democracy the most that the government can do to promote better labor-management relations during inflation is perhaps to strengthen the machinery of collective bargaining. *Ad hoc* measures to deal with specific cases involving serious (e.g., nation-wide) work stoppages, however, may necessitate public policy outside the institution of collective bargaining.

Finally, there is the possibility that imports may somewhat offset domestic shortages and so help to minimize inflationary

[27] M. S. Eccles, for example, in a statement before the Joint Congressional Committee, November 25, 1947, said, among other things: "Nothing could be more effective than increased productivity of labor and longer hours of work by everyone."

pressures at home. As a matter of general policy during inflation, a country should import inflation-sensitive goods, i.e., essentials, in exchange for export of luxuries and other nonessentials, as Britain did in the transition period after World War II. It is not difficult to understand why France and other European nations looked to American grants and credits for partial relief in their domestic shortages of consumer goods during the postwar period when their productive and exporting capacities were too weak to pay for needed imports. In so far as short-term credits are made available by the International Monetary Fund and other channels, adverse balances of payments need not stand in the way of partially overcoming domestic shortages via increased imports. Bilateral trade agreements (e.g., between Britain and the Soviet Union) for barter are one way to get around balance-of-payments difficulties and to import urgently needed products (e.g., Russian wheat for Britain and railway equipment for Russia).

WAGE POLICY

During wartime inflation public control of money wages is expedited by the necessity of keeping down the cost of war production as well as by the patriotic willingness of organized labor to co-operate with the government. But there is no such *raison d'être* for maintaining direct wage controls in peacetime. Yet during inflation wages and other costs cannot be left completely free to chase prices upward. In a country where wage determination is largely a matter of collective bargaining the major responsibility of keeping wages in line with the general cost structure rests with trade unions. What, then, should a trade union wage policy be during inflation?[28] There are certain broad criteria by which trade unions may formulate an appropriate wage policy.

[28] For an interesting discussion of this problem, see A. Braunthal, "Wage Policy and Full Employment," in *Planning and Paying for Full Employment*, pp. 128–146.

H

First, it is considered necessary that trade unions' demands for higher money wages should be made *pari passu* with increases in general productivity, i.e., increased output per worker. If this criterion is observed, higher wages do not generally lead to higher unit cost and therefore to higher unit price. There is, however, no mechanical connection between productivity and money wages, as far as monopolies are concerned, since the monopolists can keep down wages irrespective of productivity by restricting output of goods and input of factors. It is often argued that higher productivity would give rise to either higher money wages or lower prices and therefore to higher real wages, but this argument tacitly assumes perfect competition and long-run equilibrium.[29]

Second, trade union demands for higher money wages would be justified even during inflation where substandard wages exist, since the higher wages would merely reduce abnormal profits made possible in part by paying wages below the competitive level. Even in this case there is no assurance that the higher money wages, if granted, would not lead to price increases. For businessmen are generally reluctant to absorb wage increases by reducing their profit margins even when productivity clearly warrants it. Such a reluctance would be the greater the more prevalent was labor immobility.

Third, it is considered advisable for trade unions to refrain from pressing for wage increases on the grounds of the cost of living, except when the general anti-inflation program fails to prevent the prices of essentials from rising.[30] This criterion imposes on the government the responsibility of keeping down consumer prices and on trade unions the responsibility of preventing their higher wage demands from causing consumer prices to rise. If the government cannot assume such a responsibility, then it would be better to let trade unions

[29] See, for example, F. D. Graham, "Wage Fallacies," (letter to the editor) in *New York Times*, January 5, 1947. Compare it with my "Present Wage Structure," also in *New York Times*, August 9, 1947.

[30] *Cf.* Keynes, *How to Pay for the War*, p. 57.

get higher wages on the grounds of the cost of living and then tax away or borrow a part of the increased wage incomes.

It is not at all certain that trade unions will support the government's anti-inflation program by observing the above criteria; much depends on the mutual attitudes of the government and organized labor. Blanket suspension of wage increases [31] is obviously difficult to achieve in peacetime, especially where and when trade unionism is a powerful political force. The whole question of wage policy during inflation is further complicated by the fact that wages are income as well as cost, and therefore by the basic fear that a deflationary wage policy may precipitate a train of uncontrollable deflationary movements.

PRICE CONTROL AND RATIONING

Many countries adopted price control and rationing during World War II and some retained them during the immediate postwar period. The United States continued price control and rationing until June, 1946, and President Truman asked for their partial restoration in his anti-inflation message to Congress of November 17, 1947, though in vain.

The function of price control is to establish the legal upper limits beyond which the prices of particular goods may not rise. Price control has the political advantage of being popular during a period of rampant "profiteering" and runaway inflation. But there are some flaws in price-fixing as an anti-inflation measure.

Though conceding some measure of price control as "a valuable adjunct" to his main proposal (i.e., "deferred pay"), Keynes, for example, objected to price control on the ground that it fails to bring about equilibrium, namely, the needed balance between purchasing power and available output.[32] For price control increases the pressure of consumption and

---

[31] See, for example, Mr. Eccles' testimony before the Joint Congressional Committee, November 25, 1947.

[32] Keynes, *op. cit.*, p. 57.

merely leads to "shop shortages" and "queues" and therefore to "great injustices of distribution." He considered price control as a poor alternative to "old-fashioned inflation," that is, the conventional method of restriction via higher prices. Keynes therefore would have us reduce the volume of purchasing power via taxation and forced savings and then allow the consumer to exercise a free choice in allocating his purchasing power among different consumer goods. Thus price control, if unaccompanied by any restriction on the amount of purchasing power, is not only unfruitful as anti-inflation policy but detrimental to consumer freedom and welfare. Moreover, when administrative difficulties in enforcing price-fixing and legal restrictions against black marketing are considered, price control pales by the side of monetary-fiscal policy.

The main function of rationing is to divert consumption from those articles of consumption whose supply needs to be restricted for some special reasons. In the absence of rationing the tendency is for the wealthy few to bid up the prices of scarce consumer goods so high that the majority of the consuming public cannot afford to buy any. When the supply of necessities is short, as during a war or a postwar period, it is obviously objectionable to let the price system do the trick, that is, to perform the function of rationing. Rationing has the effect of limiting the variety and amount of goods available for consumption in a way conducive both to consumer price stability and to distributive justice.

Rationing, however, has been criticized on the ground that it involves "a great deal of waste, both of resources and of enjoyment." [33] A waste of "enjoyment" is a dubious objection to rationing during a period of general scarcity, but it is true that the wide variety of consumer need, taste, and habit renders rationing somewhat ludicrous. Moreover, the prac-

[33] Keynes, *op. cit.*, pp. 51–54.

tical difficulty of covering a sufficient number of consumer goods by a rationing coupon would leave the pressure of purchasing power free to divert production in the direction of the unrationed articles. Thus a sensible program of rationing should aim at diverting consumption from particular articles whose supply is below normal rather than at controlling aggregate consumption.

PART II

Interest, Income, and Employment

6

The Liquidity-Preference Theory

THE LIQUIDITY-PREFERENCE theory is an integral part
of the general theory of effective demand; it explains the nature of the demand for liquid assets and its relation to the
interest rate, prices of nonliquid assets, expected rates of
profit, investment, and employment.

Liquidity-Preference—the "Propensity to Hoard"

HOARDING AND SAVING

It is useful to begin with a comparison of the concept of
hoarding with that of saving. *Saving* may be defined as *the
excess of income over consumption outlays.* Saving always
means the failure, willful or otherwise, to spend on consumption out of a given income; it is in fact the complement of
consumption outlays. That is to say, consumption outlays
and savings equal a given income.[1] The above definition
applies to both individual saving and community saving.

If an individual earns $100 a month and spends $80 on
consumption, then his savings in that period are $20. Similarly,
if the gross national product in a given year amounts to $100
billion and consumption outlays to $70 billion, the commu-
nity's total savings must be $30 billion. For some purposes dis-

[1] For further details, see Chap. 10 (on the consumption function).

posable income (national income after taxes) may be used to determine the amount of total savings. As far as the concept of saving is concerned, it is immaterial how the $30 billion so saved is used, provided that it is not spent on consumer goods; savings may be kept as savings accounts in the bank, put "in the mattress," or used to purchase securities, new capital equipment, or additional inventories. Thus savings are related to income and to consumption outlays.

Hoarding, on the other hand, is related to the supply of money and to the interest rate. Hoarding may be defined as *people's desire to hold wealth in the form of money.* To hoard is in effect not to spend money on nonliquid assets. Consumption expenditure is the logical alternative to saving; a desire to lend or invest is the logical alternative to hoarding. If saving involves the sacrifice of consumption, hoarding involves the sacrifice of an interest income which is forgone by not lending or investing. The choice between money and nonliquid assets presupposes the choice between spending (on consumption) and saving.

This concept of hoarding differs from the concept of saving in that it is essentially *psychological.* What is stressed in this concept of hoarding is *a psychological tendency* to hold wealth in the form of money, not *the amount of hoards.*[2] Hoarding, as such, may be translated into a schedule of various amounts of money which people may wish to hold at various rates of interest. Thus conceived, hoarding is merely another expression for *the demand for money* or, to use Keynesian terminology, a schedule of "liquidity-preference." It is this

[2] Keynes introduced the concept of "liquidity-preference" to distinguish what he meant by "hoarding" from what others meant by it. He considered the "propensity to hoard" as substantially the same as his own concept of liquidity-preference, but warned against interpreting the "propensity to hoard" to mean "an actual increase in cash-holding." (See *General Theory,* p. 174.) For the actual amount of money held by the community is equal to the total money supply and is independent of the *demand* for money. What the concept of "liquidity-preference" is designed to convey is the *demand* for money, not an increase in the money supply or a decrease in the velocity of money.

demand for money or liquidity which, together with the supply of money, influences fluctuations in the interest rate and therefore the volume of investment.

FORMS OF HOARDING

Before going any further we must clarify the relation between the hoarding and the velocity of money. The traditional treatment of hoarding runs in terms of an explanation of the decreasing effect of hoarding on the velocity of money and therefore on general prices. Thus hoarding in the traditional formulation is synonymous with a decrease in the velocity of money. Whether hoarding decreases the velocity of money and therefore depresses production and trade depends largely on particular forms in which people want to hoard a part of their income. If one hoards by putting "money in the mattress," one is obviously withdrawing spendable money from circulation. It is such an act of hoarding that is popularly blamed for depression. Even this type of hoarding may not be so harmful to production and trade if its psychological effects are taken into account. A large amount of "money in the mattress" certainly depresses the economy during the period in which it is accumulated at the expense of spending, but it may well generate such a sense of security as to induce people to spend more out of current income or to hoard less out of future income.

If, on the other hand, an act of hoarding takes the form of putting money in the bank to hold it idle (e.g., savings accounts and inactive checking accounts), the result may not be harmful at all. For the presumption is that this type of hoarding "provides the offsetting facilities for some other party," as Keynes has pointed out.[3] It is arguable, however, that even though the banks would rather utilize your money in the bank to earn interest income than leave it idle, they may not always succeed in finding willing borrowers who

[3] His speech in the House of Lords, May 18, 1943.

will use it. One could go a step further and argue that even if borrowers were found, they might not spend the proceeds in such a way as to stimulate production and trade. Barring these adverse possibilities, an act of hoarding in the form of keeping bank deposits can be said to have no detrimental effect on the economy. Furthermore, if one considers the well-known favorable psychological effect of large public holdings of idle money in the form of savings accounts, etc., one can hardly deny that people's desire to spend more out of current income may increase as a result of past hoarding.

It is clear that hoarding cannot be deplored without reference to what forms it takes or how it affects the general public psychologically through a dynamic series of income periods. It is to Keynes' credit that he revised the concept of hoarding in such wise as to relate it directly to the monetary theory of interest and the general theory of employment. In his view, if hoarding has any effect on the general price level, it is primarily through its influence on the interest rate. It is a change in people's disposition to hold money rather than a change in the velocity of money that is involved in the Keynesian concept of hoarding. In other words, Keynes emphasizes not the amount of hoards, but people's psychological propensity to hoard and its influence on the interest rate and therefore on the volume of investment. The subsequent sections will show how the "propensity to hoard" is related to the interest rate, the money supply, the volume of investment, and employment.

THE LIQUIDITY FUNCTION

Having made an initial choice between spending and saving, people have yet another choice to make between holding the accumulated savings in the form of cash balances and holding them in the form of nonliquid assets. This latter choice gives us a schedule of liquidity-preference, or a schedule of amounts of money to be held at various interest rates. In making this choice people compare the marginal utility of holding money and the marginal disutility of forgoing interest income. Given the level of income, the demand for money varies with the interest rate. In other words, *liquidity-preference is a function of the interest rate, increasing as the interest rate falls and decreasing as the interest rate rises.* The reason for this inverse correlation between liquidity-preference and the interest rate is that at a lower rate of interest less is lost by not lending money out or investing it, that is, by holding on to money; while at a higher rate holders of cash balances would lose more by not lending or investing.

Figure 2 illustrates the relation of liquidity-preference to the interest rate. The L curve represents the liquidity function or the demand for money, which slopes downward to the right, indicating that at a lower interest rate more would be held. The M curve represents the total amount of money, which is assumed to be fixed and inelastic with respect to interest. That is to say, the monetary authority leaves the money supply unchanged regardless of changes in the interest rate. At the r_1 rate of interest, the amount of money people wish to hold and the amount of money in existence coincide. In other words, the demand for money to hold and the supply of money are in equilibrium at E, and r_1 (or Q_1E) is the equilibrium rate of interest. This means that people have no inducement to increase or decrease the stock of money by lending or investing. At a higher rate of interest, r_2, however, people would want to hold OQ_2 of cash balances and lend or invest the rest, or Q_2Q_1. Thus at a higher rate of interest, people's liquidity-preference is low, since they can gain more by lending money out or investing it (e.g., purchase of securities to earn a return of Or_2).

Contrariwise, people's liquidity-preference would increase, that is, by OQ_3, if the interest rate fell to r_3. For they would lose more by lending money out or investing it. But they cannot hold more than OQ_1 of money, since that is all there is to hold. The tendency, therefore, is for the holders of non-liquid assets to sell some of their holdings to get liquid. Consequently, the supply of nonliquid assets increases, whereas the demand for them is decreasing *pari passu* with the increasing demand for liquidity, so that the value of nonliquid assets must fall. When the value of nonliquid assets falls the interest rate must rise, since they are inversely correlated with

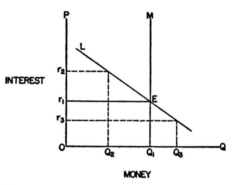

FIG. 2. THE LIQUIDITY FUNCTION

each other via capitalization (i.e., capitalized value = annual income/interest rate; e.g., $1,000/0.05 = $20,000). The interest rate would increase to r_1, so that the demand for money to hold and the supply of money would be once again in equilibrium and the tendency to hold more or less money would disappear.

If the demand for money is stable and inelastic, as the traditional theory assumes it to be (due to preoccupation with the transaction motive and with a frictionless world of certainties), an attempt to reduce the interest rate via increased money supplies will be so successful as to raise output and employment to the full. But the liquidity function may be *unstable* and *elastic* with respect to the interest rate, as Keynes emphasized, *if our knowledge of the future is incalculable and our propensity to hoard to satisfy the speculative motive is predominant and volatile.*

If the liquidity function is as elastic (at the lowest practical rate of interest) and volatile as Keynes supposed it to be, then an attempt to reduce the interest rate by monetary expansion may prove disappointing. For an expansion of money leads, in these circumstances, to a less than proportional fall in the interest rate, given a highly interest-elastic

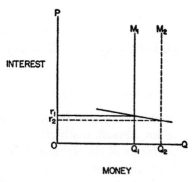

FIG. 3. AN INTEREST–ELASTIC
LIQUIDITY FUNCTION

liquidity function, as shown in Figure 3. An increase in the money supply from M_1 to M_2 leads to an insignificant fall in the interest rate, from r_1 to r_2. If the liquidity function were horizontal straight (i.e., perfectly elastic), no increase in the money supply would affect the interest rate. Such a function is conceivable when the speculative motive for liquidity (to hold money in anticipation of higher interest or lower security prices; or to postpone current purchase of securities) is the preponderant factor in the demand for money to hold. (The liquidity function would be the more inelastic the more dominant the transaction and the precautionary motives.)

If the interest rate fails to fall sufficiently, owing to the interest-elastic liquidity function, real investment and employment will be discouraged. For the high interest rate both as *cost* and as *income* makes *real* investment less attractive than *financial* investment. The sequence is the elastic demand for liquidity, the high interest rate, the smaller scale of real investment, and the lower level of employment. The conclusion is inevitable that the more elastic the demand for money, the more ineffective central bank credit controls and the more unreliable interest policy for full employment. As will be shown later, an interest-elastic liquidity function is one of the reasons for persistent tendencies toward underemployment equilibrium. Experience seems to support the Keynesian view of the elasticity and instability of the liquidity function.[4]

The Liquidity–Preference Theory of Interest

In a world of uncertainties the desire to hold money as a store of wealth is an almost instinctive mechanism. This desire is not only an index of the degree of our feeling of uncertainty about the future but is capable of changing our present economic calculations and behavior. The desire to hold liquidity to satisfy the transaction and precautionary motives is rather stable. In other words, the demand for cash balances to satisfy these motives is relatively interest-inelastic. But the demand for cash balances to satisfy the speculative motive is highly interest-elastic. The interest-elasticity of demand for liquidity, the supply of money remaining equal, makes a significant difference to interest policy and therefore to the inducement to invest.

THE DEMAND FOR MONEY AND THE INTEREST RATE

In general, people desire to hold cash balances, first because it is convenient to have liquid assets around, secondly because future cash needs are uncertain, and thirdly be-

[4] *Cf.* L. R. Klein, *op. cit.*, p. 72.

cause spending appears less attractive than holding cash. To put it differently, people tend to hold cash balances for the purpose of (a) conducting ordinary transactions, (b) meeting emergencies, and (c) gaining speculative profits through future changes in prices. While the traditional theory stresses the first two, the Keynesian liquidity-preference theory places major emphasis on the last motive. Since the need for cash balances for transaction purposes is fairly constant except during a hyperinflation, and since fairly constant amounts of cash balances must be set aside to meet emergencies (business or personal), it follows that the preference for liquidity to satisfy the *speculative motive* is the most flexible factor influencing the aggregate demand for money.

The demand for liquidity, together with the supply of money, determines the interest rate. An increased preference for liquidity will raise the interest rate, since more must be offered to induce people to part with liquidity or not to hoard. Conversely, a decreased preference for liquidity will lower the interest rate, since less has to be offered to "bribe" people to give up cash holdings in favor of nonliquid assets. The relation between liquidity-preference and the interest rate is shown in Figure 4 (A). Given the supply of money, M, an increase in people's liquidity-preference from L_1 to L_2 leads to an increase in the interest rate from r_1 to r_2. The reason for this tendency is that when the desire to hold money is stronger and when the monetary authority does not increase the money supply to satisfy that increased desire to hold money, a higher premium must be paid to induce the marginal hoarder to part with liquidity so as to release more money for nonliquid assets. At the r_1 rate of interest, the new demand for money exceeds the supply of money by Q_1Q_2. Obviously, this interest rate fails to bring demand and supply into balance. Only at the higher rate of interest, r_2, is the new demand for money in equilibrium with the supply of money, that is at E_2. Hence r_2 (or Q_1E_2) is the equilibrium rate of interest.

I

Conversely, a decrease in liquidity-preference from L_2 to L_1 would bring down the interest rate from r_2 to r_1.

Figure 4 (B) shows a change in the interest implicit in the changing value of nonliquid assets (i.e., securities). Suppose the demand for securities decreases from D_1 to D_2 owing to an increased preference for liquidity, indicating that people consider it more advantageous to hold their wealth in the form of cash. Consequently, people will try to dispose of securities in the market from S_1 to S_2 (i.e., an increase in sup-

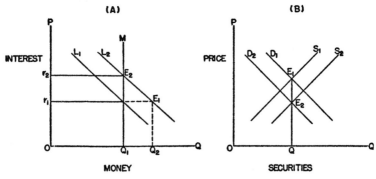

FIG. 4. LIQUIDITY–PREFERENCE AND INTEREST

ply). The upshot of the decrease in the demand for securities and the increase in their supply is the lower value of securities, QE_2. This fall in the value of securities means a rise in the interest rate, since a higher reward (i.e., an interest income) must be offered to induce people to hold their wealth in the form of securities rather than in cash. Thus the influence on the interest rate of a change in people's liquidity-preference can be shown indirectly via its influence on the value of nonliquid assets.

LIQUIDITY–PREFERENCE AND THE MONEY SUPPLY

Theoretically the Federal Reserve banks can influence the interest rate by influencing the volume of bank credit. For example, the Federal Reserve banks can buy government securities on the open market and thus provide member banks with additional reserves for credit expansion. But whether open-market purchases of government securities by the Federal Reserve banks will lead to a fall in the interest rate depends partly on people's liquidity-preference. If people prefer government securities to cash, they will be reluctant to sell their holdings of such securities, so that the Federal Reserve banks may not be able to purchase enough of them to increase member banks' reserves and so decrease the interest rate.

Conversely, if people's demand for cash is stronger than their demand for government securities, they will be more willing to part with their government securities and thus enable Reserve banks to purchase enough of them to increase member reserves. Although short-term government securities are almost as liquid as cash, people still can choose between those interest-yielding securities and noninterest-bearing but convenient cash. This choice between two kinds of liquidity is all the more important when one considers the potential power of open-market operations and a secular tendency among investors to desire stable interest income.

Given central bank credit policy, the money supply can vary with banks' liquidity-preference. It is banks' liquidity-preference, together with individual savers' liquidity-preference, that concerns the so-called "loanable-fund" approach to the interest rate. In contrast to Keynes' emphasis on *people's* liquidity-preference and therefore on the *demand* side of liquidity-preference, the loanable-fund theorist treats liquidity-preference, if at all, as a *supply* factor. While savers' and banks' liquidity-preference affects the interest rate via its influence on the supply of "loanable funds," the interest rate in question is of smaller significance than the interest rate which is determined by people's demand for money to hold and by an autonomous supply of money. For the interest rate in the case of the loanable-fund theory refers to bank rates on loans, while Keynes' liquidity-preference theory has to do with *the entire interest structure,* including rates on bank loans, savings deposits, and bonds. That is why Keynes speaks of *the* interest rate rather than interest rates. But in so far as bank rates influence other interest rates, it is useful to investigate the effect of banks' liquidity-preference on the supply of loanable funds.

Suppose a bank anticipates great difficulty in getting cash, owing, say, to a firmer central bank credit policy. The bank in question will try to improve its liquidity position by raising its loan rates to discourage further loans. Multiply this example by the thousand, and you will have a significant reduction of bank credit. The demand for loanable funds remaining unchanged, a decrease in the supply of loanable funds incident to the banks' increased liquidity-preference will lead to higher interest rates. The same applies to a case where member banks are greatly indebted to the Reserve banks. Whatever may impair or endanger the liquidity and reserve positions of member banks, the result is an increased preference for liquidity at the expense of loanable funds. The effect of banks' liquidity-preference on the supply of loanable funds and therefore on interest is shown in Figure 5.

The D curve represents the schedule of customers' demand for loanable funds. The demand is assumed to have an ordinary elasticity and to remain constant. The S_1 curve is the original schedule of supply of loanable funds, and it intersects the demand curve at E_1 to establish the equilibrium rate of interest, r_1 (or Q_1E_1). Now the banks' increased preference for liquidity decreases the supply of loanable funds to S_2, which intersects the demand curve at E_2 to establish a higher equilibrium rate of interest, i.e., r_2 (or Q_2E_2). The amount of loanable funds that would be demanded or supplied is OQ_1 at the r_1 rate of interest and OQ_2 at r_2 respectively. By how much the banks will actually be able to raise their rates depends, however, on the elasticity of demand as well as on the possibility of a change in demand (i.e., the steepness of the curve and a shift in the position of the curve).

The Interest Rate and Investment

The significance of the monetary theory of interest reduces itself to the fact that a change in the interest rate, together with the anticipated rate of profit, determines the rate of investment and therefore the level of employment, given the propensity to consume. We shall assume (a) that the banking

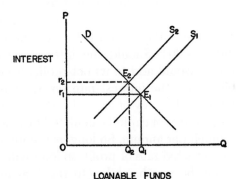

FIG. 5. BANKS' LIQUIDITY–PREFERENCE
AND INTEREST RATES

system is in a position to manipulate the interest rate, (b) that the investing firms follow the principle of maximizing profits, and (c) that all the investment outlays are made by private firms. With these assumptions in mind, we shall proceed to examine the relation between the interest rate and investment and its effect on aggregate employment.

THE INTEREST RATE AND THE MARGINAL EFFICIENCY OF CAPITAL

The decision to invest, that is, to produce or purchase capital goods, is influenced principally by (a) the current rate of interest, and (b) the expected rate of profit. The current rate of interest refers to the prevailing rate which is paid to overcome people's liquidity-preference, and the expected rate of profit (what Keynes calls "the marginal efficiency of capital") is a percentage return on a capital outlay over the original costs (excluding the interest cost). These two are independent variables, but the former influences the latter significantly.

If, for example, a capital outlay of $10,000 is expected to yield an annual net return of $800 after allowing for all costs except interest charges, then the marginal efficiency of capital is 8 per cent. Now suppose the outlay was financed by borrowing at an interest rate of 5 per cent. Then the firm planning to make that capital outlay would get a net annual profit of $300 (= $800 — $500). Should the interest rate fall to 3 per cent, the firm would add to its net profits $500 annually ($800 — $300). Thus the interest rate serves as the mechanism by which the efficiency of capital is discounted, that is, the value of the services of capital calculated in terms of a percentage of so much per annum. So long as the interest rate is lower than the expected rate of profit, so long will the investment in question be worth while (to the firm making it). Otherwise there is no sense in borrowing to finance the investment. Therefore, from the standpoint of individual firms which must use borrowed funds for capital expansion, the lower the interest rate on loans, the greater the inducement to invest.

The above relation between the interest rate and the marginal efficiency of capital is not at all vitiated—though it may be obscured—by the fact that in modern conditions many firms make capital outlays out of their own reserves (e.g., depreciation allowances and undistributed profits) rather than out of borrowed funds. In this case, however, the interest rate enters into investment decisions as an income rather than as a cost consideration. A firm with accumulated reserves has a choice between investing and lending, depending on the comparative advantage of those alternatives. If the interest rate is higher than the expected rate of profit, the firm will *lend* its reserves for an interest income (e.g., purchase interest-yielding bonds). Conversely, if the interest rate is lower than the expected rate of profit, the firm will *invest* by expanding plant and equipment or by increasing inventories.

The sum of all the marginal efficiencies of capital of different types is the marginal efficiency of capital for the whole

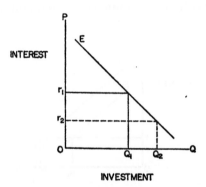

FIG. 6. THE INTEREST RATE AND INVESTMENT,
WITH A GIVEN MARGINAL EFFICIENCY
OF CAPITAL

economy. We cannot here enter into a discussion of the determinants of the marginal efficiency of capital, and it may suffice for the moment to indicate the interrelationships among the interest rate, the marginal efficiency of capital, and the volume of investment. From the foregoing discussion follows our first proposition: *the lower the interest rate, the larger the volume of investment, given the marginal efficiency of capital.* Figure 6 shows that with the marginal efficiency of capital remaining equal, more investment is made at a lower rate of interest. The E curve stands for the efficiency of capital at a given level of consumption, and constitutes a *de-*

mand curve (for capital) to the entrepreneurs planning investment commitments. In reality the demand curve is likely to be highly interest-inelastic, as will be explained later.

The second proposition is that *the higher the marginal efficiency of capital, the larger the volume of investment, given the interest rate.* Figure 7 illustrates this proposition. The marginal efficiency of capital curve shifts upward to the right, that is, from E_1 to E_2, thereby increasing the demand for capital. The result is that the volume of investment increases from

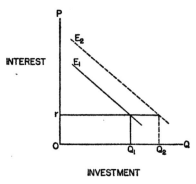

INVESTMENT

Fig. 7. The Marginal Efficiency of Capital
and Investment, with a Given Rate
of Interest

OQ_1 to OQ_2, the interest rate remaining equal. These propositions suggest that either the interest rate should be lowered to the level of the marginal efficiency of capital or the marginal efficiency of capital raised to the level of the interest, whichever is the more expedient. In the short run, in which technological improvements and general economic development are usually precluded, the marginal efficiency of capital cannot be raised significantly, and the lowering of the interest rate may be, therefore, a more realistic alternative.

In Figure 6 the marginal efficiency of capital is shown to be rather interest-elastic, so that a slight fall in the interest rate leads to a more than proportional increase in the volume of investment. Under such circumstances, the interest rate is significant for income and employment. In other words, *if the general demand for capital is highly elastic, low interest policy leads to fruitful results. If the general demand for capital is inelastic, no downward change in the interest rate will stimulate the inducement to invest.* If we make the favorable assumption that the demand for capital is interest-elastic,[5] a decrease in the marginal efficiency of capital can

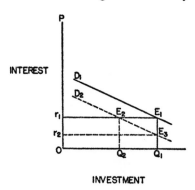

FIG. 8. THE LOW INTEREST RATE AND THE
ELASTIC DEMAND FOR CAPITAL

be offset by the lowering of the interest rate to maintain the desired level of employment. Such a situation is illustrated in Figure 8.

A fall in the general demand for capital (i.e., a temporary collapse of the marginal efficiency of capital) from D_1 to D_2 leads to a decrease in the volume of investment, i.e., from Q_1 to Q_2, given the r_1 rate of interest. Suppose that OQ_1 is the volume of investment which is compatible with full employment. In order to maintain this full-employment investment in the face of the collapse of the marginal efficiency

[5] The demand curve would be horizontal straight if investment opportunities were unlimited, as classical economists supposed them to be.

of capital we must lower the interest rate from r_1 to r_2, which is equal to the lower marginal efficiency of capital at E_3. Otherwise the volume of investment would fall to OQ_2, and the level of employment with it. Thus the volume of investment compatible with full employment can be maintained even if the marginal efficiency of capital falls, provided that the interest rate is lowered as much as the marginal efficiency of capital and the demand for capital is interest-elastic.

7

Interest Policy and Full
Employment

IT WAS shown earlier that high interest rates are helpful in combating inflation even though there may be somewhat off-setting forces in operation. In this chapter we shall consider whether a cheap-money policy is an effective or desirable means for promoting full employment. The usefulness of purely monetary policy for economic stabilization depends partly on the answer to this question.

Rationale of the Low Interest Rate

There are a number of reasons why the low interest rate may be regarded as a desideratum from the standpoint of achieving and maintaining full employment.

1. *The low and stable interest rate has a healthy effect on the capital market and therefore on investment.* An intimate relation exists between *financial* investment (e.g., old securities traded on the stock exchange) and *real* investment (i.e., production of new capital assets) in the business world. The interest rate is the mechanism whereby this relationship is established in the capital market. The low and stable in-

terest rate has a stabilizing effect on the capital market, since it minimizes or eliminates possible capital losses due to a rise in the interest rate, or—what amounts to the same thing —falling security prices. This may be illustrated by a simple example. Suppose one bought a bond for $1,000 bearing 4 per cent interest to earn an annual income of $40 (annual income = interest rate × capital value). Now suppose that the interest rate for this type of bond rises to 5 per cent. At 5 per cent interest, one can get an annual income of $40 by investing $800, that is, by paying the price of $800 for a bond bearing 5 per cent interest (capitalized value = annual income/interest rate). Therefore a capital loss of $200 is involved in the rise of the interest rate from 4 per cent to 5 per cent. Such capital losses not only demoralize the capital market but also discourage *real* investment.

The demoralization of the capital market due to rising interest disturbs real investment via its effect on the new investment market and the marginal efficiency of capital. If prices of old securities traded on the stock exchange are falling because of rising interest, new ones cannot be floated in the new investment market except at falling prices also, thus inducing prospective investors to postpone security purchases to avoid capital losses. Hence there will be less "venture capital" available to new enterprise and investment. Moreover, if the community prefers liquidity to securities for fear of capital losses, the interest rate will rise still further and security prices will fall likewise, to demoralize the capital market even more. If the quotations for existing securities are low owing to rising interest rates, the prospective returns on new *real* investment (the marginal efficiency of capital) will be low relative to the interest rate and the inducement to new investment all the smaller. For in this case it is clearly less profitable to build new capital assets than to buy claims to existing assets. Thus, the low and stable interest rate, if it is maintained, would make the marginal efficiency of capital seem not too low relative to the interest rate, and so stimulate new investment.

2. *The low interest rate is conducive to long-term capital formation.* Although the low interest rate is generally regarded as an insignificant factor in investment decisions on the ground that interest is a minor element of cost for most businesses,[1] it is an important consideration for *some* forms of investment. Construction and public utilities fall under this category. Because of the great durability of the capital assets involved, construction and public utilities are especially sensitive to changes in capital costs. When it is realized that these industries play a substantial role in the formation of capital in all advanced economies, it is not difficult to see why low long-term rates are a significant factor in economic stability. The lowering of mortgage interest rates, together with other favorable conditions, would doubtless promote stability in the private-construction industry. Similarly, total gross investment would be increased considerably if public utilities and other similar industries could obtain loan-capital at lower long-term rates. Moreover, in so far as a considerable portion of the total sales of durable goods is effected on credit (e.g., household equipment and automobiles in the United States), low interest rates, coupled with other liberal terms of lending, would no doubt help minimize the usual volatility that is associated with durable-goods industries and at the same time sustain high consumption expenditure.

3. *The low interest rate facilitates loan-financed public investment.* Perhaps the most important single reason that the interest rate should be kept low and stable is the increasing importance of loan-financed public investment. This follows from the fact that private investment in a free-market economy is inherently unstable. If public investment must

---

[1] *Cf.*, e.g., J. R. Ebersole, "The Influence of Interest Rates upon Entrepreneurial Decisions in Business," *Harvard Business Review*, XVII, 1938; also F. A. Lutz, "The Interest Rate and Investment in a Dynamic Economy," *American Economic Review*, December, 1945.

be increased to supplement cyclically or chronically deficient private investment in order to sustain full employment, there is a strong presumption in favor of a low and stable interest structure to facilitate such public investment. For the low interest rate lends itself to large-scale deficit financing and so minimizes the interest on the public debt. The low interest rate means a rise in the price of government securities, which in turn expedites the flotation of new issues.[2] The rise in the government securities market increases public confidence in the general securities market and therefore in future activity. Thus, in an economy subject to unstable private investment loan-financed public investment is considered by some as the *raison d'être* of the low interest rate [3] and a zero rate of interest considered by others as desirable and necessary.

4. *The low interest rate is instrumental in minimizing the secular tendency of savings to outrun investment in advanced capitalistic economies.* Income-elasticity of saving in those economies is such that even at a zero rate of interest people tend to save.[4] If there is no longer any justification for a high interest rate on the grounds of saving,[5] it follows that the interest rate should be kept as low as practically possible *to stimulate investment to offset large savings out of high income,* which take place anyway in wealthy economies. Available evidence suggests that there is no significant correlation between the interest rate and savings, as far as wealthy capitalistic economies are concerned. It is therefore increasingly felt that people should not be paid a reward in the shape of interest for saving more than the economy can invest, and that "a reduction in the rate of interest towards

---

[2] A stable government bond market also protects the *rentier* class against capital losses, and thus contributes to high marginal efficiencies of many types of *private* capital.

[3] See, e.g., Lord Beveridge, *Full Employment in a Free Society* (London: George Allen & Unwin Ltd., 1945), pp. 336–341.

[4] *Cf.* J. H. Riddle, *Interest Rates and Federal Reserve Policy* (Bankers Trust Co., New York, 1946), pp. 4–5.

[5] Keynes, *General Theory,* p. 375.

[the] vanishing point" to stimulate new enterprise and investment is a sensible, though immediately impracticable, proposal.[6]

5. *The low interest rate is more expedient than wage reduction for solving the problem of mass unemployment.* The manipulation of the interest rate is more feasible than the deflation of money wages, since trade unionism is here to stay. More important, a decrease in aggregate demand due to wage reduction is obviously self-defeating. Thus flexible interest policy is considered preferable to flexible wage policy, at any rate in the short run. Keynes gave the benefit of the doubt to the idea that the interest rate my be reduced by wage reduction, but was quick to add that the release of cash due to a reduction in the total wage bill might well be offset by a rise in people's liquidity-preference due to the popular unrest accompanying the wage reduction.[7] In such a case the low interest made possible by the release of cash cannot be maintained. It is now generally agreed that low interest rates can and should be achieved by methods other than wage reduction, such as low rediscount rates, open-market purchases, low reserve requirements, low taxes, public-debt monetization, and similar *monetary-fiscal measures to increase general liquidity* and to reduce "liquidity premiums."

Some Deterrents to Low–Interest Policy

Desirable as the low interest rate may be from the standpoint of full employment, there are a host of institutional and psychological deterrents to a cheap-money policy. These difficulties are reflected in various arguments against low interest rates.[8] We shall consider some of these arguments in the following order.

---

[6] Keynes, "National Self–Sufficiency," *Yale Review*, May, 1933; also R. F. Harrod, *Towards a Dynamic Economics* (Macmillan, London, 1948), pp. 129–159.

[7] Keynes, *General Theory*, pp. 263–264.

[8] *Cf.* H. R. Bowen, *op. cit.*

1. Low-interest policy is criticized at times on the ground that low interest rates, together with high taxes, discourage a man from building up a fortune to pass along to his heirs and therefore reduce an incentive to business development and leadership. It is counterargued that the development of an idle *rentier* class, which high interest rates promote, is not needed for an efficient business leadership. Keynes, for example, considered it desirable and inevitable that "the functionless investor" now receiving a "bonus" in the form of interest for "no genuine sacrifice" should gradually disappear to make room for genuine risk takers.[9] At any rate, the resistance of the *rentier* class to a cheap-money policy in general and to low long-term rates in particular is an institutional factor that cannot be overlooked.

2. Low interest rates are said to discourage thrift and to increase economic insecurity for the aged and dependents. It has been argued, on the other hand, that high interest rates may have the effect of reducing thrift, since high-interest income renders saving less necessary. As for economic insecurity, one answer is that progressive income taxes and extensive social-security programs rather than high interest rates should provide security. This is tantamount to reducing people's liquidity-preference to satisfy the precautionary motive, and therefore the interest rate which must otherwise be paid to overcome such a preference for liquidity. A further counterargument is that security should be provided by principal rather than by interest income. It is doubtful that people who save for "the rainy day" are very much influenced by changes in the interest rate. Nevertheless, the thrift-security argument will more often than not stand in the way of a cheap-money policy.

3. Low interest rates are further criticized on the ground that they reduce the income of banks and educational and charitable institutions. As far as the latter two are concerned,

[9] *General Theory*, p. 376.

their tax advantages are likely to offset their reduced interest income. If interest income is inadequate, some would have these institutions supported out of taxes. But reduction of the income of banks is more serious.

It is feared that a reduction in interest income would force commercial banks to increase service charges to such an extent as to "price themselves out of the market." Whereupon the government would subsidize the private banking system and eventually take it over. Apart from such an eventuality, the loss of interest income creates a grave problem for commercial banks, in spite of the growing importance of *interest-yielding* government securities in their investment portfolios. If the government is committed to a policy of maintaining a low and stable long-term rate of interest, commercial banks will probably have to seek additional sources of interest income even in less reliable, and often risky, loans and investments. Yet commercial banks cannot very well depend on increased investments in low-grade private bonds, let alone equities, for the simple reason that such investments would subject them to the danger of serious losses due to changing market values. The downward trend of interest on bank loans along with the average yield on long-term government bonds (2.63 per cent average for 1929–47) [10] suggests that the net returns on loans will not bear as favorable a relation to the net returns on investments as in the past. To the extent, however, that a cheap-money policy, together with other measures, promotes full employment, commercial banks will be able to increase their earnings by expanding loans and investments as well as by increasing service charges.

4. A cheap-money policy is considered fundamentally objectionable on the ground that it may undermine the accepted "concept of a return to ownership" and strip the capitalistic system of "a basic element of its most characteristic institu-

[10] See the President's *Economic Report*, January, 1948, p. 130. Interest on bank loans for the period 1929–47 averaged 3.17 per cent.

tions." [11] Keynes and others, on the other hand, consider a falling rate of interest irresistible in such wealthy capitalistic economies as the American, not only because the drive for continuous full employment is bound to call forth at least partial "interest-free financing," but because large savings out of full-employment income will be forthcoming even at a zero rate of interest.[12] Moreover, they regard a falling rate of interest, and "the euthanasia of the *rentier*" with it, as a prerequisite to a system of "private enterprise" which is compatible with "that degree of material wellbeing to which our technical advancement entitles us." [13] Apart from these arguments for and against a falling rate of interest, the actual opposition of those who favor the perpetuation of "a return to ownership"—even at the expense of a reward for genuine risk and enterprise—looms large in the background.

Thus a cheap-money policy may be acceptable in principle, but not necessarily in fact. These institutional and psychological obstacles to a falling rate of interest are the practical reasons for not relying upon the manipulation of interest rates for full employment, and also for the increasing emphasis placed on fiscal policy as the main instrument of full-employment policy.

[11] *Cf.* H. C. Wallich, "The Changing Significance of the Interest Rate," *American Economic Review*, December, 1946.
[12] Keynes, *General Theory*, p. 376, and "National Self–Sufficiency"; also R. F. Harrod, *op. cit.*
[13] Keynes, "National Self–Sufficiency."

8

Non–Keynesian Theories of Saving and Investment

THE MODERN theory of employment as well as of economic fluctuations runs in terms of an analysis of the savings-investment process. Consumption and investment are the two most important strategic variables in the determination of aggregate income and employment. An appraisal of non-Keynesian theories of savings and investment will serve as a background against which the Keynesian theory of the savings-investment plan may be better understood. For this reason it is useful to examine the classical savings-investment theory and the underconsumption theory and to indicate wherein these theories differ significantly from the modern theory of saving and investment.

Classical Savings–Investment Theory

With classical economists,[1] the savings-investment analysis is an analytical device to explain the determination of the interest rate, not that of the levels of output and employ-

---

[1] For interesting discussions of the classical position, see A. P. Lerner, "General Theory," in *The New Economics*, and "Alternative Formulations of the Theory of Interest," *ibid.*; also L. R. Klein, *op. cit.*, pp. 79–90.

ment. Just as the price is determined by the demand and supply of a commodity, so is the interest rate determined by the demand and supply of savings. It follows from this that any change in the going rate of interest creates a disparity between savings and investment, just as a deviation from the equilibrium market price means that demand and supply are not in balance. What is unique about this classical view of savings and investment is that the interest rate serves as the mechanism whereby savings are brought into equilibrium with investment regardless of the level of income.

A variant of the classical view of the savings-investment equilibrium is based on Say's law. Translated into modern terms, Say's market law that supply creates its own demand means that savings are automatically the same as investment without the benefit of any mechanism to bring savings into equilibrium with investment. This version assumes that investment opportunities are unlimited at the going rate of interest (an infinitely interest-elastic investment function) and that savings are highly responsive to changes in the interest rate (a relatively interest-elastic savings function). Thus whatever the interest rate may be, there is a corresponding horizontal straight investment curve to intersect the nonhorizontal savings curve at some point. Savings are, in this view, an increasing function of the interest rate, and automatically flow into a proportional amount of investment. What is implied here is that there can be no such thing as oversaving or underinvestment; the theory simply does not admit of the possibility of an excess of savings over investment.

If, on the other hand, savings are a function of income, the savings function may not be elastic with respect to interest. Similarly, if investment opportunities are found to be definitely limited at the going rate of interest, the investment function may be quite interest-inelastic. Once it is recognized that savings and investment are functionally related to the level of income rather than to the interest rate, it is not difficult to see why there should be the theoretical possibility of an excess of savings over investment. For it is possible that savings and investment may change with the level of income in such a way that the savings and investment curves will not intersect each other. Such a possibility is strong in a wealthy capitalistic economy that tends to save more than it can invest, so that the interest rate, however low, fails to bring savings into equilibrium with investment. Thus, when the unrealistic assumptions of perfectly interest-elastic investment and relatively interest-elastic savings (in the schedule sense) are dropped, there is no automatic savings-investment equilibrium regardless of the level of income.

In the first version of the classical savings-investment analysis the choice of interest as an equilibrating mechanism seems to be the main difficulty. This difficulty is the direct result of the classical habit of assuming income to be a constant. When this assumption is dropped, the savings-investment equilibrium is found to depend on a change in the level of income. Income rather than interest is now considered to be the proper equilibrating mechanism. In the second version the failure to recognize the semiautonomous nature of the demand for capital (i.e., an investment function related partly to interest and income but largely to noneconomic variables) is held responsible for the unrealistic assumption of unlimited investment opportunities. This assumption has led to the denial of the possibility of underinvestment, as well as to the conclusion that overconsumption (or its inverse, undersaving) is the principal cause of depression. This last statement concerning "undersaving" leads us to a consideration of a sophisticated neoclassical variant of the savings-investment theory associated with K. Wicksell, L. Mises, F. Hayek, L. Robbins, and others. A consideration of this variant is important because it throws much light on the rather naïve yet popular notion that depression is caused by unbalanced

budgets, insufficient savings, inadequate "venture capital"—
in short, by spendthrifts who disregard the classical virtue of
saving.

The starting point of this "undersaving" theory is a theory
of the relation between "the natural rate" and "the market rate"
of interest. The natural rate is the equilibrium rate of interest
which equates savings and investment to give a stable price
level, while the market rate is taken to mean the going rate
of interest determined by the conditions of money markets.
The concept of "the natural rate" is more difficult to define,
since it differs from writer to writer. As a first approximation
the natural rate of interest might be thought of in terms of
the rate of profit determined by the productivity of capital.
As such, the natural rate of interest is somewhat related to
Keynes' concept of "the marginal efficiency of capital," particularly in the form in which G. Myrdal and other Swedish
writers developed and adopted the concept. As the adjective
"natural" suggests, the market rate, it is argued, should not
deviate from the "natural" rate, if the general price level is
to remain stable—or, what is the same, if savings and investment are to be balanced. Otherwise an unnatural state of
affairs would develop in which general prices would be abnormally high or low. Let us pursue the argument further
to see where it will lead us.

When the market rate falls below the natural rate, it becomes profitable to expand production, since the cost of borrowing is lower than the rate of return on capital, and prosperity will continue indefinitely. This implies that if the prosperity ever came to an end, it would be because of a mistaken
banking policy of letting the market rate rise and because of
people's failure to keep on saving at the expense of consumption. This is where the notion of "undersaving" as the chief
instigator of depression comes in. In other words, it is implied
that prosperity is assured only if people will sacrifice present
consumption in order to make more "venture capital" avail-

able to producers through the banking system or through capital markets. Spendthrift consumers, not ever-willing investors, are therefore blamed for depression, for it is taken for granted that investment opportunities are inexhaustible at the low market rate of interest. This of course is the opposite of the Keynesian theory of savings and investment, as shown in later discussions. It apparently never occurs to "undersaving" theorists to ask whether the natural rate may be so low in fact that no practical low market rate will be low enough to stimulate investment. Suppose, for example, that the natural rate under existing technological conditions is 3 per cent. In order for new investment to be worth while the market rate of interest should be much lower than 3 per cent. But suppose that the existing psychological-institutional complex is such as to bring about an irreducible minimum market rate of 2½ per cent. Is there much scope for expanding new investment in these circumstances? The answer is probably no.

Unless, therefore, the forces that determine "the natural rate" are made clear instead of being merely assumed, the explanation of monetary disequilibrium in terms of a discrepancy between the natural rate and the market rate is unrealistic. For no matter how much people are willing to save for the sake of capital formation, thus tending to lower the market rate, the natural rate may not be high enough for investors to make use of these savings even at a low market rate. It is to Keynes' credit, in this respect, that he showed what forces were behind his concept of "the marginal efficiency of capital." Once those forces influencing the anticipated returns over cost on new investment have been made clear, it will not be difficult to see the possibilities and limitations of raising "the natural rate" above the market rate to stimulate investment or of lowering the market rate below the natural rate for the same purpose, as can be seen later.

The Underconsumption Theory

The underconsumption or oversaving theory is the link between the classical and Keynesian theories of savings and investment. The most articulate and most consistent underconsumption theory is associated with the name of J. A. Hobson.[2] Like Malthus, Sismondi, and Marx before him, Hobson traced a tendency to oversave to the unequal distribution of wealth and income inherent in capitalist society. He reasoned that "an undue exercise of the habit of saving" leads to "an accumulation of capital" in excess of what is required to maintain the level of consumption, which is necessarily kept down by the maldistribution of income. With him the sequence is the unequal distribution of wealth and income, excessive savings, overinvestment, general overproduction, and mass unemployment.

Hobson's contribution to the modern theory of savings and investment consists in (a) the notion that the prosperity of a nation lies in spending, (b) the explicit statement of the fact that capital formation owes its origin and existence not so much to saving as to the actual or expected demand for consumption, and (c) the suggestion that income redistribution is fundamental to any serious program of stabilization. There is much in all this that is penetrating, but it is strategically incomplete. It is useful to indicate the major flaws involved in Hobson's underconsumption theory.

The crucial flaw in Hobson's theory lies in the tacit assumption that what is saved is actually invested, that is, in a tendency to identify "oversaving" and "overinvestment." Hobson apparently supposed, as did classical economists of whom he was critical, that the interest rate always equilibrates sav-

---

[2] *Cf.* J. A. Hobson, *Economics of Unemployment* (London, George Allen & Unwin Ltd., 1923). For sympathetic discussions of Hobson see Keynes, *General Theory*, pp. 366–370; also L. R. Klein, *op. cit.*, pp. 135–138. For a recent variant of the underconsumption theory see H. G. Hayes, *Spending, Saving, and Employment* (Knopf, New York, 1947).

ings and investment so that saving and investing appeared to him to be one and the same process. What worried Hobson was not excessive savings *per se* but excessive investment, that is, a glut of capital goods which may lead to general overproduction. A glut in the capital-goods market is supposed to spread to the consumption-goods market by creating unemployment not only in the capital-goods industries but also in the consumption-goods industries. This is certainly plausible. What is not so plausible is the assumption that excessive savings automatically pass into investment. For it is much more likely in modern conditions that excessive savings out of full-employment income will not be so easily offset by investment. There is, for this reason, a growing feeling that the real problem of modern capitalism is *how to make excessive savings pass into investment*. This problem, however, will be mitigated to the extent that measures are taken to prevent excessive savings. This seems to be Hobson's point, for it follows that reform measures to redistribute wealth and income toward equality are quite explicit in his stress upon underconsumption.

It is interesting to observe that those, including Hobson, who emphasize oversavings do not take for granted the existing system of income distribution but would rather change it in such a way as to increase consumption and at the same time promote "distributive justice." Therefore, apart from the formal error of mistaking oversavings for overinvestment, the underconsumptionist emphasis on the need for a more equitable distribution of wealth and income makes a powerful appeal to all those who espouse the "egalitarian" principle of one sort or another. There are, on the other hand, those like Keynes who sympathize with the underconsumptionist quest for a greater equality in the distribution of wealth and income but who nevertheless take the existing property relations as given in the short run and concentrate on the effort to promote investment. This latter group seems disposed to think that it is more realistic for purposes of countercyclical stabilization to relate oversaving to "the motives to production," as Malthus did, or "the inducement to invest," as Keynes put it, than to relate it to the need for income redistribution. In other words, while income redistribution has an intrinsic value regardless of the problem of economic stabilization, the short-run emphasis must, it is felt, be placed primarily upon the adverse implications of underconsumption or oversaving for the expected rate of a return on new investment. For this reason it is considered unrealistic to expect excessive savings to materialize in proportional investment and then to worry about the consequences of "overproduction," whereas the first and foremost concern of a wealthy capitalistic economy is to find profitable investment opportunities to offset what it is capable of saving within the framework of its established habits and institutions.

Keynes, however, considered the underconsumptionists' preoccupation justified if and when investment is left "unplanned and uncontrolled," since in conditions of *laissez faire* with respect to investment there is no way of increasing employment except by increasing consumption.[3] That is to say, if investment opportunities for private investment are inadequate, the rate of investment must, in Keynes' view, be "socially controlled" or else effort must be concentrated on increasing consumption expenditure. In view of the practical difficulty of controlling private investment Keynes considered it "wisest" in longer periods to support simultaneously all kinds of measures for increasing both consumption and investment.[4] But he differed from the underconsumptionists in thinking that it is not only necessary but possible to regulate the investment side of aggregate demand in such a way as to achieve the desired level of employment. Furthermore, Keynes argued that there is much social advantage in

[3] *General Theory*, p. 325.
[4] Keynes, *op. cit.*

increasing investment, since the community can thereby raise the standard of living without reducing physical productivity. This he considered to be the practical answer to the under-consumption theory. This argument may be accepted as cogently applicable to those undeveloped countries where the standard of living is kept down by the sheer lack of capital for effective industrialization, but it is debatable whether the argument can be applied with equal force to advanced economies. For in the latter the standard of living could be raised by a combination of a somewhat slower rate of capital formation and a much faster rate of consumption. But all this is a long-run consideration. In the short run the Keynesian emphasis on investment may be considered plausible for the following reasons.

1. The demand for investment goods (i.e., capital equipment as well as inventories) is typically elastic with respect to price, and therefore volatile fluctuations occur first and above all in the activity of capital-goods industries. Moreover, private investment decisions are subject to all kinds of unpredictable influences, economic and noneconomic. Hence the stabilization of investment comes first of all if aggregate demand is to be kept stable.

2. At less than full employment, expenditure on capital goods immediately leads to expanded expenditure on consumer goods by workers in capital-goods industries as well as by those in consumer-goods industries; whereas the initial expenditure on consumption does not immediately stimulate activity in the capital-goods industries, since no new equipment has to be produced until all the unemployed equipment has been put to use. Hence a recovery program calls forth, first and above all, expansion of capital outlays.

9

Aggregate Demand and National Income

THE KEYNESIAN savings-investment theory, alternatively called the theory of effective demand, is the heart of modern monetary analysis. Here we see a complete break with the classical tradition. Traditional preoccupation with individual prices and quantities on the tacit assumption of stability of aggregate demand has given way to a new theory of output and employment as a whole based on the more realistic assumptions of unstable aggregate demand and underemployment savings-investment equilibrium. Investment is no longer seen to be unlimited at low rates of interest, but is seen to depend on the level of income, the marginal efficiency of capital, the propensity to consume, and other factors largely outside the price system. Keynes formulated a simple but powerful analytical tool, namely, the income-expenditure analysis expressed in the fundamental equation $Y = C + I$ (the economics counterpart of Einstein's equation $E = mc^2$ that has led to the development of atomic science). The next few chapters will be devoted to the explanation and qualifications of the variables of this equation. The subsequent analysis will show why Y has been chosen as the central variable.

Aggregate Demand and Employment

In contrast to classical emphasis on the supply side, Keynes placed major emphasis on the demand side. He traced fluctuations in the levels of output and employment ultimately to changes in demand. The theory of effective demand is an attempt to explain the relevant factors which cause changes in the aggregate demand for the products of the whole economy and the effects of such changes on the levels of aggregate output and employment. More specifically, the theory is concerned with analysis of how and why it is that aggregate demand is periodically and often chronically deficient and unstable in the capitalist economy; it is also interested in indicating alternative means of stabilizing unstable aggregate demand.

Aggregate demand in the statistical sense is made up of (a) private consumption expenditure, (b) private investment outlays, (c) public investment outlays, and (d) foreign expenditures on domestic goods and services over and above domestic expenditures on foreign goods and services. As such, aggregate demand is a flow of monetary expenditures on final output in a given period. The following table illustrates the composition of aggregate demand in the statistical sense.

Table I tells us an interesting story. In the bottom depression year 1933, consumer outlays amounted to about 82 per cent of aggregate spending, and investment outlays 18 per cent. What is most striking is the fact that *private* investment was far smaller than public investment, indicating that capital went "on strike." Yet public investment was none too large—a reflection of the then prevailing attitude toward public finance.[1] The small net foreign expenditure clearly

---

[1] In an open letter in the *New York Times* (December 31, 1933) Keynes appealed to President Roosevelt for a bold program of compensatory spending, but in vain. When Keynes visited President Roosevelt in 1934, he found, much to his disappointment, that the President was still unimpressed with

TABLE I. COMPOSITION OF AGGREGATE DEMAND IN
THE UNITED STATES

(In billions of dollars)

Year	Aggregate Demand	Consump- tion	Investment		
			Private	Public	Foreign
1933	55.8	46.3	1.3	8.0	.2
1939	90.5	67.5	9.0	13.1	.9
1944	210.6	110.4	5.7	96.6	−2.1
1948	231.8	164.5	30.5	28.0	8.8

Source: The President's *Economic Report,* January, 1948, p. 109. The years
are arbitrarily selected from the series in order to sharpen the issue.
Detail will not necessarily add to totals because of rounding.

indicates the world-wide scope of the Great Depression. A
total expenditure of $55.8 billion was the lowest between 1929
and 1947, and was reflected in an all-time high record of unemployment numbering some 15 million, or about 28 per cent
of the total labor force in 1933.[2] By 1939, the beginning of
World War II, aggregate demand had improved, reflecting
in part increased consumption and in part increased investment. Unemployment was reduced to less than 10 million.
By that time "compensatory spending" (i.e., public investment outlays to supplement deficient private investment) had
become an integral part of American public finance, thus
making fiscal policy a definite countercyclical weapon. The
increased public outlays, however, were not due entirely to
this change of attitude; they partly reflected the beginning
of defense financing against the background of the European
war.

the merits of large-scale public investment. Miss Frances Perkins, then the
Secretary of Labor, informs us that the President might have been persuaded
to adopt bold deficit spending for recovery had Keynes explained the "multiplier principle" to him in nontechnical language. (See her *The Roosevelt I
Knew,* Viking Press, New York, 1946, pp. 225–226.)

[2] The labor force in America is estimated to be increasing at an annual
average rate of 500,000. It is necessary to allow for a change in the labor
force in order to compare meaningfully the levels of unemployment in widely
separated periods.

Radical changes in the composition of aggregate demand during the war year 1944 are indicative of the enormous possibilities of "autonomous" investment (i.e., capital outlays independent of the level of income). Private investment was drastically reduced, thus indicating that government purchases of war goods dominated the investment scene. Public investment reached a record high of $96.6 billion, or about 87 per cent of the total investment. Despite price control and rationing, consumer outlays also increased, owing largely to payroll increases. Net foreign demand, however, was negative in the sense that foreign purchases of American goods and services were less than American purchases from abroad, the main reason being that Germany, Italy, Japan, and their overrun countries completely stopped trading with the United States and its allies during the war. As might be expected, unemployment was reduced to a monthly average of 2,142,-000, or about 3 per cent of the total labor force—"full employment" in the technical sense (from 2 to 3 million are usually excluded as "frictionally" unemployed at any moment).

In the postwar "boom" year 1947, public investment was cut down with the reduced defense expenditure, and private investment once again dominated the investment front. Net foreign expenditure increased phenomenally, thus indicating the acute postwar needs of the war-devastated countries as well as the gradually improved foreign trade relations between the United States and the rest of the world. Consumption expenditure increased absolutely but remained about 70 per cent of total demand, that is, about the same proportion as during the war. Unemployment, however, was reduced to what was considered to be an irreducible minimum, or 1,643,000.

Some generalizations emerge from the above analysis of historical changes in aggregate demand in the United States.

1. There is a direct correlation between aggregate demand

and employment (or an inverse correlation between aggregate demand and unemployment).

2. The proportion of consumption expenditure to the total flow of expenditures remains rather stable irrespective of changes in the absolute amount of consumer outlays.

3. The absolute volume of private investment fluctuates drastically, increasing sharply during prosperity and decreasing likewise during depression.

4. Autonomous public investment, regardless of motive, is capable of increasing total expenditure significantly by supplementing inadequate private investment and private consumption.

5. The greater the amount of net foreign expenditure, the smaller the burden on domestic investment, private and public, to fill the gap between total expenditure and domestic consumption expenditure.

There is still another sense in which the concept of aggregate demand has a significant bearing upon employment analysis, namely, *in the schedule sense.* Aggregate demand in this sense is a schedule of what the economy as a whole is disposed to spend on the total output at its various hypothetical levels. Obviously this concept of aggregate demand is a tool of equilibrium analysis, for aggregate demand, as such, determines the equilibrium level of income, given an aggregate supply schedule (a schedule of what the economy must receive to cover the cost of production at various levels of output). It was in this sense that aggregate demand was seen earlier as producing an inflationary gap. The following diagram illustrates how a change in aggregate demand may produce an overemployment or an underemployment level of income.

The vertical axis measures aggregate demand made up of consumption expenditure and investment outlays, while the horizontal axis measures national income (or output). The 45° line represents the supply schedule, and is identical with income. Schedule $C + I$ intersects the 45° line at E_0 to give full-employment income Y_0, indicating that aggregate demand and aggregate supply are in equilibrium; what the economy wishes to spend is identical with the value of available output at a given price level. If aggregate demand increases, as shown by schedule $C' + I'$, we get overemployment income Y_1 and the inflationary gap measured by the vertical distance between E_0 and E_1. Schedule $C'' + I''$, on the other hand, gives us underemployment income Y_2 and

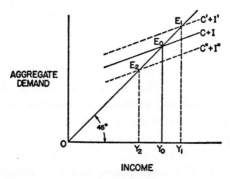

FIG. 9. AGGREGATE DEMAND AND
EMPLOYMENT

the deflationary gap measured by the vertical distance between E_0 and E_2. Detailed explanations of the shape or position of the aggregate demand curve must be postponed, but the present model may be adequate to show how useful the schedule concept of aggregate demand is for employment analysis.

Concept of Gross National Product

We have seen that the total amount of consumer, business, government, and foreign expenditures constitutes aggregate demand in the statistical sense or in the schedule sense, depending on whether the expenditures in question are realized or expected. Aggregate demand in the statistical sense is nothing but the expenditure side of realized *gross national product*. This identity of aggregate demand and gross national product arises from the dual nature of a monetary transaction, that is, from the fact that *income* and *expenditure* are merely two aspects of one and the same transaction. An income is to a seller what an expenditure is to a buyer; the same dollar which a buyer spends is also an income to some seller. Therefore, gross national product may be defined as *the value of final output produced in a given period* or as *the sum of all the monetary expenditures on current final output*. If, for example, the value of aggregate final output in a given year amounts to $200 billion, it indicates that all the buyers of the economy together spent $200 billion on its output. This is merely stating the obvious statistical truth that the economy receives no more and no less than what the buyers spend on its output.

If we break down the components of gross national product, we obtain the equation $Y = C + I$, where Y represents gross national product, C consumption, and I investment. This is Keynes' simplest formulation of the static relations among three variables Y, C, and I. Variable I may or may not include government and foreign investment.

The qualification "final" in the above definition means that the expenditures (or incomes received in producing) on such intermediate products as raw materials used up in the manufacturing process are excluded to avoid double counting. The term "gross" signifies inclusion of the expenditures involved in making good capital consumption, that is, the depreciated and obsolete capital equipment.[3] It follows that we must subtract the amount spent on replacements to arrive at *net* national product. Now, net national product is identical with

[3] *Cf.* Keynes, "The Concept of National Income," *Economic Journal*, March, 1940; also S. Kuznets, *National Income and Capital Formation* (New York, 1937).

national income provided that sales taxes and other business taxes are excluded from prices at which output is sold, since the value of current output at market prices which exclude indirect taxes is equal to the sum of factor costs (e.g., wages, interest, dividends, rents, and undistributed profits). The concept of national income is useful in measuring the relative importance of productive factors if it is in terms of payment classification. Expressed as a net flow of goods and services, the concept of national income is a measure of the productivity of the economy, i.e., the dollar value of the net product.

The concept of net national product is useful in long-run analysis, since it measures economic growth, that is, the rate at which the stock of capital goods may increase. Since the standard of consumption is a function of a change in the stock of capital equipment, net national product is significant for measuring long-run welfare.

But *gross* national product is the most significant concept for *short-period employment analysis*. If our major concern is to determine the level of employment in the short period, we need to be interested only in the flow of aggregate output, regardless of what portion of that output ought to represent replacements in the long view.[4] The short period in question is an analytical concept (i.e., operational rather than clock-time) which indicates the possibility of adjusting the *rate* of operation within the limits of *fixed* plant and equipment. This is also Keynes' concept of the short run. The short period

[4]This is apart from the statistical difficulty of distinguishing the new from replacement units of a given capital good. In connection with the concept of gross national product, M. Gilbert and G. Jaszi have argued that resources could be increased in the short run without adding to the stock of capital or making replacements. (See "National Product and Income Statistics as an Aid to Economic Problems," in *Readings in the Theory of Income Distribution* [London, George Allen & Unwin Ltd., 1950], p. 48.) This argument presupposes the presence of excess capacity or, at full employment of equipment, the possibility of making significant improvements in the physical productivity of existing equipment and labor. Wartime experience suggests that such a pre-supposition may be realistic.

is conceived to be short enough to preclude any significant change in the stock of capital goods—a period in which the ratio between the output of new capital goods and the existing stock of capital goods is very small. Such a view of the short period is probably realistic, since the structure of durability (of capital goods) is nearly constant in the short period. Taking this view, we do not need to subtract from gross national product any depreciation allowances to determine the rate of capital consumption or of net capital formation. That is, we can neglect that part of total output which must otherwise be deducted as merely making good the depreciated and obsolete equipment. Therefore, unless specified to the contrary, we shall mean gross national product whenever we use the term "national income" or simply "income."

Whichever concept of national income may be used for a particular purpose, the fact remains that national income estimates are the most comprehensive measures of the aggregate economic activity and the aggregate yield of the whole economy, and perhaps the most important single guide to both short-term and long-range economic planning everywhere. Largely as a result of Keynes' analytical contributions we now have national income analysis which consists in (a) analysis of income formation and propagation, (b) analysis of the relevant factors affecting the behavior of the components of national income, and (c) analysis of the effects of the change in any particular element of national income on general activity and particularly on the level of employment. It is useful to summarize Keynes' contributions to the national income analysis as follows:

(1) The variables of the Keynesian income equation $Y = C + I$ are all in *monetary* terms, thereby facilitating *dynamic* income-expenditure analysis as well as public monetary-fiscal policy for economic stabilization.

(2) Those variables are all "measurable," "observable,"

and "operational," [5] thus facilitating the determination and verification of the quantitative relations among such macrounits as income, consumption, savings, and investment.

(3) The complex and diverse elements of the spending stream have been reduced to a manageable number of simple yet strategically relevant variables, thus rendering the elimination process "understandable" and "transparent." [6]

(4) Traditional preoccupation with the *allocation* of national product based on analysis of "composition of national product" and on the tacit assumption of full employment (i.e., constant aggregate output) has been largely superseded by new emphasis on the determination of the *level* of aggregate output and employment.

(5) The focusing of attention on national income or aggregate demand has opened a new vista, among others, for the fruitful study of the hitherto neglected problem of income distribution, thus linking the problem of inadequate output with the problem of inequitable distribution—two fundamental evils of our society, to borrow D. H. Robertson's phrase.

(6) National income data resulting from research inspired by the income-expenditure approach are now an accepted basis for public policy with respect to both inflation and deflation. The helpful concepts of the inflationary gap, the deflationary gap, and the savings gap stem directly from the national income analysis. Similarly, the all-important concept

[5] The adjectives are due to J. Lintner, "The Theory of Money and Prices," in *The New Economics*, p. 526.

[6] *Cf.* J. Tinbergen, "The Significance of Keynes' Theories from the Econometric Point of View," in *The New Economics*, p. 231. Some economists are inclined to add to Keynes' simple models such variables as relative price changes, time lags, the stock of existing capital, accumulated liquid assets, the standard of living, population growth, etc. These additional variables must indeed be taken into account to make the income approach meaningful in a changing world, but some are rightly worried lest the simple Keynesian models should be made too complicated to be of practical use. (See, for example, S. E. Harris, "Keynes' Influence on Public Policy," in *The New Economics*, pp. 21–22.)

of the consumption function is related to the Keynesian concept of gross national income.

Much of this summary is ahead of our understanding, but it is intended to serve as an introduction to the theories of the consumption function, the savings-investment equilibrium, and affinitive macroeconomic relations as well as to their policy implications.

10

The Consumption Function

IN 1929 the gross national income in the United States was
$103.8 billion and consumption expenditure $78.8 billion. In
the depression year 1933, when the income went down to
$55.8 billion, consumption also decreased to $46.3 billion.
When in 1934 the income increased to $64.9 billion, con-
sumption increased to $51.9 billion. But note that consump-
tion increased by only $5.6 billion between 1933 and 1934,
whereas the income during the period increased by $9.1 bil-
lion. Again, when the income increased by $28.1 billion be-
tween 1946 and 1947, consumption increased by only $20.8
billion. It is easy to see why consumption and income should
move in the same direction, but why did an increment of income lead to a smaller increment of consumption both during the depression year 1933–34 and during the "boom" year
1946–47? The answer lies in the nature and characteristics
of the consumption function in the United States. This
chapter will be devoted to the explanation of the consumption function as a determinant of national income.

The Concepts of the Propensities to Consume and to Save

THE PROPENSITY TO CONSUME

The propensity to consume, otherwise known as the consumption function, indicates the relation between C and Y

in the income equation $Y = C + I$, that is, $C(Y)$—a functional relationship between two aggregates, i.e., total consumption and gross national income. The consumption function may be better understood in terms of the income demand for consumer goods. Thus viewed, consumption C represents the *amount* of consumer expenditures made at *a* given level of income, whereas the propensity to consume $C(Y)$ is a *schedule* of consumer expenditures at *various* income levels. Figure 10 illustrates the functional relation between consumption and income.

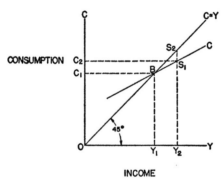

FIG. 10. THE PROPENSITY TO CONSUME

In the diagram, the C axis measures consumption expenditures and the Y axis gross national income. The linear function of 45° is the unity line that indicates the relation of consumption to income for each income level at which consumption and income are equal—a line along which the horizontal co-ordinate is identical with the vertical co-ordinate. The C curve represents the consumption function or the propensity to consume, which is conceptually similar to an ordinary market-demand curve.[1] The C curve moves upward to the

---

[1] This income-demand schedule and an ordinary Marshallian demand schedule differ in that the independent variable is *income* in the one case and *price* in the other, and that there is a *direct* correlation between income and consumption but an *inverse* correlation between price and consumption.

right, indicating that consumption increases as income rises. But note that the C curve rises less steeply than the unity curve after the intersection ("break-even") point B, indicating that the increase in consumption is smaller than the increase in income. At income Y_1, consumption and income are shown to be equal ($OY_1 = OC_1$). As the income rises to Y_2, consumption also increases to C_2, but the amount of consumption expenditures (OC_2) is smaller than the income (OY_2). What happens to the portion of income not consumed? It is *saved*, as indicated by the vertical distance between S_1 and S_2 at income Y_2. The amount saved is positive and increases as income rises after the intersection point, but it is negative below the intersection point. Thus the consumption function measures not only the amount spent on consumption but also the amount saved. This is so because the propensity to save is merely the propensity not to consume. The 45° line may therefore be regarded as a zero-saving line, and the shape and position of the C curve indicate the division of income between consumption and savings.

As long as we know that savings are the complement of consumption, we need not have a separate savings schedule. To make the relation between consumption and savings clearer, however, we might draw such a schedule. Figure 11 is an attempt to show in one diagram, for comparison, both the propensity to consume and the propensity to save.

In Figure 11 the vertical axis measures both consumption and savings and the horizontal axis measures income. The curves C and S are consumption and savings schedules respectively. At each level of consumption there is a corresponding level of savings. Thus when consumption is 100 per cent at income Y_1, savings is zero where the S curve intersects the income axis. At income Y_2, consumption is OC (or s_2S_2, since consumption is income minus savings) and savings are OS (or s_1s_2, since savings are income minus consumption, that is, $s_1S_2 - s_2S_2$). The vertical length s_1S_1 is necessarily equal to the vertical length s_2S_2, since they are merely two ways of measuring the same thing. The important point to note is that the vertical distance between s_1 and s_2, representing the amount of savings at income Y_2, is the same as that between S_1 and S_2. Thus we can derive a savings function from a consumption function. In the diagram the C and S curves are both straight, but if the C curve were convex, the S curve would necessarily have to be concave. We do not

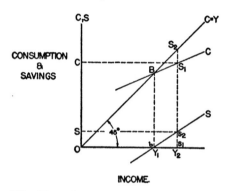

FIG. 11. THE PROPENSITIES TO CONSUME
AND TO SAVE

have to be bothered with the shape of these curves at this juncture, however. The important point is merely that the propensity to save is, to repeat, the complement of the propensity to consume, and can therefore be subsumed in the latter function.

Given the propensity to consume, national income will be divided in some proportion between consumption and savings. Now the next question is: in what *proportion* will income be so divided? The answer requires the explanation of the characteristics of the propensity to consume, that is, the *average* and *marginal* propensities to consume.

THE AVERAGE PROPENSITY TO CONSUME

The propensity to consume is the function that relates consumption and income. In terms of our diagram it is the entire C curve with a definite position and slope. By contrast, the concept of the *average* propensity to consume is the *ratio* of consumption to income, or C/Y. If, for example, the gross national income is $200 billion and consumption expenditure $160 billion, the average propensity to consume is 0.8, or 80 per cent. Thus the value of the average propensity to consume for any income level may be found by dividing consumption by income. Expressed as a per cent of income, the average propensity to consume in the United States in ordinary times is estimated at 88 per cent.[2] This means that the public ordinarily spends about 88 per cent of total income on consumption and saves the rest, or 12 per cent.

In terms of our diagram this means that the average propensity to consume is a single point on the C curve which indicates the *proportion* of income consumed or saved. The C curve is made up of a series of such points. The average propensity to consume (C/Y) may decline as it moves along the C curve to the right, as can be shown by a flattening C curve measuring the decreasing proportion of consumption to income at any point on the curve.

Experience shows that the average propensity to consume under normal circumstances is a fraction less than 1. But it is not too important whether a higher or lower *proportion* of income is consumed or saved; *what really matters is the absolute amount of additional consumption or savings as income increases from one level to another*. This point will be elaborated further in our discussion of the *marginal* propensity to consume.

[2] *Cf.* A. H. Hansen, *Fiscal Policy and Business Cycles* (London, George Allen & Unwin Ltd., 1941), p. 237.

THE MARGINAL PROPENSITY TO CONSUME

The concept of the *marginal* propensity to consume is exceedingly important, since it tells us, to borrow Keynes' phrase, how the next *increment* of income will have to be divided between consumption and savings. The marginal propensity to consume may be defined as *the ratio of the change in consumption to the change in income* or as *the rate of change in the average propensity to consume as income changes*. It can be found by dividing an increase (or decrease) in consumption by an increase (or decrease) in income, that is, by the formula dC/dY, where d (delta) indicates the change in consumption or income. If, for example, income increases by $10 billion and consumption by $6 billion, the marginal propensity to consume is 0.6. From the marginal propensity to consume we can derive the marginal propensity to save, that is, by the formula 1 — dC/dY. If the marginal propensity to consume is 0.6, the marginal propensity to save, according to this formula, must be 0.4. The marginal propensity to consume plus the marginal propensity to save equal 1 as a matter of course.

Diagrammatically expressed, the marginal propensity to consume is the *slope* or gradient of the C curve. Figure 12 illustrates the marginal propensities to consume and to save. To ascertain the slope of the C curve we draw a horizontal line of unit length through B (the "break-even" point), and then measure vertically to the first tangent C. We shall find that the ratio of the vertical length AC to the horizontal length BA is 0.6. In other words, the marginal propensity to consume is merely a mathematical concept depicting the slope of the consumption function; but it is a concept which has great social significance, as will be shown later. As for the marginal propensity to save, we extend the vertical line AC at income Y_2 to the second tangent D and then measure the distance between C and D, which is necessarily 0.4, since AD is equal to BA and CD equal to AD minus AC. It follows that the marginal propensity to consume plus the marginal propensity to save equal unity.

Sometimes the C curve flattens out with rising income to show that the marginal propensity to consume declines as income rises. The actual propensity to consume, however, is such as to justify a linear function and therefore $dC/dY = \triangle C/\triangle Y$ (slope at a point = slope over a small range). The marginal propensity to consume, calculated from the data on family budget studies and on the consumption-income time series in

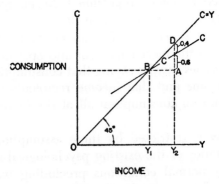

FIG. 12. THE MARGINAL PROPENSITY TO
CONSUME

the United States, is considered approximately constant, i.e., between 0.6 and 0.8 in most cases.[3] It is on such data that the linear consumption line with slope of less than unity is based. The consumption function which moves upward to the right less steeply than the 45° line is an abstract of the observed fact that people are in the habit of spending between 60 per cent and 80 per cent of an increment of income on consumption, and saving the rest. The actual marginal propensity to consume depends on concrete circumstances, but *the essential theoretical requirement* is that the marginal propensity to consume be *between zero and unity*. Otherwise *stable* equi-

[3] *Cf.* L. R. Klein, *op. cit.*, p. 60.

librium analysis would be impossible. This point will be clarified in our later discussion of the multiplier principle.

KEYNES' PSYCHOLOGICAL LAW OF CONSUMPTION

We are now in a position to understand Keynes' psychological law of consumption. This law consists of three related propositions: namely, (a) that *when aggregate income increases, consumption expenditure will also increase but by a somewhat smaller amount;* (b) that *an increment of income will be divided in some proportion between spending and saving;* and (c) that *an increment of income is unlikely to lead either to less spending or less saving than before.* Of the three, the first is the most important and epitomic. We may paraphrase Keynes' law by saying that consumption depends mainly on income and that income recipients always tend to fail to spend on consumption all of the increment of income.

Keynes' law is restricted by three assumptions, namely, (a) the constancy of the existing psychological-institutional complex, (b) normal conditions precluding wars, revolutions, hyperinflations, and other "extraordinary" circumstances, and (c) a wealthy capitalistic economy with a minimum of government intervention in private initiative and enterprise.

The first assumption suggests the short run in which the psychological-institutional complex remains relatively constant. This assumption makes consumption depend on income alone, since it precludes the possibility that the propensity to consume itself may change. To say that consumption depends on income alone is to say that the psychological-institutional complex does not change significantly to alter either the position or shape of the consumption function. This assumption does not logically admit of the consumption function that may shift in response to changes in variables other than income (e.g., income distribution, price movements, population growth, etc.). In the short period it is not perhaps unrealistic to make consumption depend on income alone.[4] Yet it is well to bear in mind the possibility that the psychological-institutional complex may change under the impact of some dynamic influences even in relatively short periods, and the consumption function with it.

As for the second assumption, much depends on what is to be included in "extraordinary" circumstances. A war, a revolution, or a hyperinflation is a clear-cut case, but there may be less obvious cases. Even barring wars and other "extraordinary" circumstances, the cyclical behavior of the consumption function may not be as stable as it might be under *rigid* institutional assumptions. It is widely believed that the consumption function has been shifting upward with increasing general productivity.[5] The behavior of the consumption function within each cyclical period, however, is more controversial.[6]

The third assumption refers to the general atmosphere of *laissez faire* with respect to people's choice between spending and saving. This assumption precludes the extremes of a very indigent community, for which the freedom of choice between spending and saving has no practical significance, and an opulent but rigidly controlled economy in which spending and saving are subject to drastic regulations. This assumption, therefore, can be more meaningfully applied to relatively free "mixed economies" in normal peacetime.

[4] J. Tinbergen, for example, considers it analytically justifiable to make consumption depend on national income alone (in the short run, at any rate, as Keynes does) on the plausible grounds that the distribution of individual incomes is a function of the absolute level of national income; that the marginal propensity to consume is the same over a wide range of income; and that national income is the chief factor affecting aggregate demand and therefore general prices. (See his "The Significance of Keynes' Theories from the Econometric Point of View," in *The New Economics*, p. 223.)

[5] *Cf.* P. A. Samuelson, "Full Employment after the War," in *Postwar Economic Problems* (S. E. Harris, ed., McGraw–Hill, New York, 1943).

[6] See, e.g., "Five Views on the Consumption Functions," *Review of Economic Statistics*, November, 1946.

These assumptions will have to be relaxed or dropped to make concrete analysis fit changing reality. Keynes' law based on these assumptions may be regarded as a rough approximation to the actual macrobehavior of free consumers in the normal short period. What is vitally stressed in Keynes' law is, to repeat, the tendency of people to *fail to spend* on consumption the *full* amount of an *increment* of income. A persistent failure to spend all the increment of income leads to a "low-consumption and high-saving economy," such as the American economy is described to be. The above tendency is so deeply rooted in people's habits, customs, traditions, and the existing institutional setup that only fundamental structural changes are believed to change it significantly.[7] Obviously such fundamental changes are less likely in shorter than in longer periods.

Technically speaking, it is not just the propensity to consume but the marginal propensity to consume that is supposed to be stable under the above psychological and institutional assumptions. In other words, the position and shape of the consumption function are such that the amount of consumption depends on income alone and the amount of income saved increases as income increases. This suggests that in the short run, in which the propensity to consume is likely to remain constant, the only way to increase the amount of consumption out of a given income is to increase income itself. With an upward shifting consumption function, on the other hand, the amount of consumption could be increased without any increase in income.

Some Relevant Implications of Keynes' Law

On the assumption that consumption depends mainly on income, or what is the same, with the stable consumption function as given, some theoretical and policy implications may be developed here briefly.

---

[7] *Cf.* A. H. Hansen, *Fiscal Policy and Business Cycles*, (London, George Allen & Unwin Ltd., 1941) pp. 254–258.

CRUCIAL IMPORTANCE OF INVESTMENT

If people tend to spend less than the increment of income when output and employment increase, the increased output and employment will be unprofitable, unless *investment* (i.e., monetary outlays on capital goods, excluding such claims as securities) increases to fill the gap between income and consumption. For such a gap means that sales fall short of costs necessary to produce current output. If investment should fail to increase, output and employment would inevitably fall, unless indeed the consumption function rises to wipe out the gap between income and consumption. With the consumption function remaining stable, however, income-employment fluctuations must be sought in the instability of investment. Thus Keynes' stress on investment as the crucial and initiating determinant of the levels of income and employment presupposes the difficulty of raising the consumption function in the short period, or a failure of the consumption function to rise automatically under *laissez faire*.

To make it clear, suppose that the consumption function is rising even in the short period and under *laissez faire*. In this case the gap between income and consumption will be wiped out even with zero investment. If we could count on the consumption function to come to the rescue in this way, we should be spared any serious concern over inadequate or unstable private investment. For the higher the consumption function, the smaller the gap between income and consumption to be wiped out by investment, and the less need for finding profitable investment opportunities. With the consumption function remaining stable, however, the main effort will have to be concentrated on increasing investment. This does not of course preclude the possibility of raising the consumption function in the longer period, along with measures to promote investment, or the desirability of increasing consumption in the short period by changing the income variable without shifting the consumption function upward.

M

This may appear to be a curious way of establishing the strategic importance of investment in the stabilization of income and employment, but it is the most *direct* way to do so. One might attempt to do it in an *indirect* way, that is, by stressing the stability of the savings function in the short run. But since the stability of the savings function is merely the *passive* reflection of the stability of the consumption function, it is more effective to hold the *active* factor—the consumption function—responsible for proving the decisive importance of investment, in the short period at any rate. Moreover, this direct method is consistent with the simple assumption that aggregate output consists of consumer goods and capital goods, and that aggregate employment is made up of the workers producing consumer goods and those producing capital goods. But in emphasizing the crucial importance of investment on the assumption of the short-period stability of the consumption function, we must not overlook the growing importance of the role played by *durable consumer goods,* which are subject to just as *unstable* and *volatile* a demand as capital goods are. To the extent, therefore, that durable consumer goods account for a larger and larger portion of aggregate output and employment, the consumption function will become unstable even in the short period, and the stabilization of activity in the consumption-goods industries will become that much more urgent.

POSSIBILITY OF GENERAL OVERPRODUCTION

Another relevant implication of Keynes' law is that there can be general overproduction and mass unemployment. If the marginal propensity to consume is less than unity, not *all* that is produced (income) is taken off the market (spent) as income increases. In other words, producers fail to get back in sales receipts an equivalent of the amount that must be had to justify current output. Thus supply, far from creating its own demand, exceeds demand only to create a glut of goods and services and therefore general overproduction and mass unemployment.

The plausible hypothesis of the marginal propensity to consume of less than unity helps to invalidate Say's law, which denies the possibility of general overproduction. If Say's law is defended in terms of long-run equilibrium, it is criticized in terms of short-run equilibrium. There is, it is argued, in the long run a tendency for demand to be sufficient to buy all that the economy is capable of supplying. This long-run equilibrium adjustment is supposed to be brought about automatically by market forces alone. On the other hand, it is argued that such adjustment is difficult in the short run, and that therefore general overproduction may set in at least temporarily. If Say's law is defended on the assumption of perfect competition, more realistic assumptions of monopoly and oligopoly (or monopsony and oligopsony) are counterposited. Prices and costs are supposed to be readily adjusted downward to absorb a temporary glut in the market. If prices are lowered, additional purchasing power is thereby released for other goods and services, the amount of extra purchasing power depending on the elasticity of demand with respect to price (usually unit elasticity assumed). Introduction of monopolistic price-cost rigidities, of course, weakens such an argument. If Say's law is explained in terms of the instantaneous adjustment of spending to income, it is criticized in terms of time lags. Thus against the assumption that an act of producing is simultaneously an act of creating proportional effective demand, is set the argument that, though output creates income to the full extent of its value, the income so created is separated from spending both in time and in space.[8]

These are conventional objections to Say's law in varying degrees of sophistication, but none of them is as simple and yet effective as the hypothesis of the marginal propensity to

---

[8] For this last objection see P. Sweezy, *The Theory of Capitalist Development* (Oxford Univ. Press, New York, 1942), p. 137.

consume of less than unity in vitiating the validity of that classical law of markets. Apart from the merits or demerits of alternative methods of dealing with Say's law, the recognition of a possibility of general overproduction has a far-reaching effect upon policy. For the acceptance, however inadvertent, of Say's law leads straight to a policy of *laissez faire*, whereas its rejection implies the necessity of conscious public control for averting general overproduction and mass unemployment.

DECLINING TENDENCY OF THE MARGINAL EFFICIENCY OF CAPITAL

The expected rate of profit may collapse temporarily largely because the consumption function fails to rise to sustain consumption expenditure at a high level. Once the demand for capital goods has started to decline for one reason or another, there is little hope of raising the marginal efficiency of capital, with the propensity to consume remaining unchanged. If the consumption function fails to rise, offsets to the decline in the marginal efficiency of capital must be sought elsewhere; for example, in the cost structure. But even lower costs, if practicable at all, might fail to stimulate the demand for capital during a period of low activity. And yet the only real and ultimate help—a rise in the propensity to consume—may not be forthcoming. Failure of the consumption function to rise would not lead to the collapse of the marginal efficiency of capital, if consumption could be increased by increasing income. But there is no reason to suppose that income increases at a time when investment is declining—unless indeed the government can be supposed to be pouring new purchasing power into the income stream via public works programs or some other channels. Under *laissez faire*, therefore, it is difficult to arrest the declining tendency of the marginal efficiency of capital once the process has started, unless an automatic rise in the propensity to consume is to reverse that process. In longer periods, however, the marginal efficiency of capital is affected by "autonomous" factors, that is, factors independent of the level of income, of which consumption outlays constitute the single most important element.

The other side of the picture is that the stable propensity to save stands in the way of reducing savings to the level of existing investment opportunities. If the propensity to save cannot be expected to decrease automatically, then the economy may find itself trying to save more than it can profitably invest, and thus bring down the marginal efficiency of capital. Thus the marginal efficiency of capital tends to decline when the demand for capital goods is discouraged by the failure of the propensity to save to fall, or, what comes to the same thing, by the failure of the propensity to consume to rise. If the demand for capital goods can be supposed to be infinitely elastic at the going rate of interest, as some seem to suppose, then the stable consumption function will be no problem at all. But there is no reason to suppose, on available evidence, that investment opportunities are unlimited even at the lowest practicable rate of interest. Therefore the stable savings function may properly be regarded as one of the factors tending to lower the marginal efficiency of capital and the level of investment in the short run.

TURNING POINTS OF THE BUSINESS CYCLE

Keynes' law also helps to explain the turning points of the business cycle.[9] The traditional theory based on Say's law had to explain the turning points of the business cycle by postulating the inflexibility of credit policy or the presence or absence of production "bottlenecks," such as equipment short-

[9] Even before Keynes, J. M. Clark conceived of the possibility that the turning points of the business cycle might be explained in terms of the limiting effects of the marginal propensity to consume of less than unity on consumption expenditures, though not in Keynesian terminology. (See his "Capital Production and Consumer Taking: a Further Word," *Journal of Political Economy*, October, 1932.) But the present discussion is due largely to L. A. Metzler, "Business Cycles and the Modern Theory of Employment," *American Economic Review*, June, 1946.

ages and cost rigidities. If it were not for these "rigidities," a given change in output would presumably create a corresponding change in the demand for this output and thus give rise to a "self-perpetuating" cumulative movement upward or downward. Keynes' law leads to the opposite view, that a cumulative process of expansion may end in a recession and a cumulative process of contraction in a recovery without the limiting influences of credit policy and cost changes.

The upper turning point of the business cycle, or a *downturn* from prosperity, is now explained by the ultimate limit set by the marginal propensity to consume of less than unity, that is, by the plausible hypothesis that people fail to spend on consumption as much as the increment of income. Conversely, the lower turning point, or an *upturn* from depression, is explainable in terms of the failure of people to cut down their consumption expenditures to the full extent of the decrement of income. Let us consider the matter further.

The process of expansion during prosperity may come to a stop short of full employment, if an increase in consumption outlays is smaller than the increment of income. To put it in another way, prosperity may turn into a recession before full employment for the simple reason that producers fail to recover in sales receipts an equivalent of what they must have in order to justify current output. Keynes did not explain the downturn of the business cycle in this way; he explained it in terms of the sudden collapse of the marginal efficiency of capital.[10] This is only another way of putting the same idea, since a decrease in the expected rate of profit is nothing else than a disappointment in entrepreneurial expectations due to a decrease in consumption sales. Whether we explain the downturn of the business cycle in terms of producers' disappointment or in terms of consumers' unwillingness to spend the full amount of an increment of income, the result is exactly

[10] *Cf. General Theory*, p. 316.

the same. For to say that producers' anticipated rate of profit is not large enough to cover the cost of production is to say that consumers are not willing to spend as much on final output as the increment of income warrants.

Conversely, if people do not immediately cut down their consumption expenditures by as much as the decrement of income, producers can reduce output and employment to minimize losses without the fear of reducing aggregate demand to the same extent. This is plausible, because it is difficult to give up the accustomed standard of consumption even if a drastic decline of income may require it. Durable consumer goods will be the first to be affected, since the demand for them is typically elastic and their purchase typically postponable. Thus expenditures on clothing, household equipment, and other consumer durables will decrease as income decreases. But it is unlikely that the demand for nondurable consumer goods will decline quite as much as income decreases. For the demand for most of these goods is typically inelastic with respect to both price and income. Thus the marginal propensity to consume of less than unity sets a limit beyond which consumption may not decrease more than income decreases. This fact accounts for the possibility of recovery.

Diagrams may help clarify the matter. Figure 13 shows how and why the downturn and the upturn occur. In Figure 13 (A), an increase in income is shown to result in a smaller increase in consumption expenditure. Beginning with the equilibrium level of income, Y_1, at which what people would want to spend equals what producers would have to get to cover the cost of producing current output, the increase in income from Y_1 to Y_2 leads to the *smaller* increase in consumption expenditure from c_1 to c_2.

The resulting loss, as measured by an excess of cost OY_2 over revenue Oc_2, would have the effect of inhibiting further production and employment and of preventing income from reaching full-employment income Y_0. From then on prosperity takes a downturn, and output and employment will decline until equilibrium income Y_1 is reached. All this is due to the fact that the consumption function is rising upward but less steeply than the 45° line, i.e., the marginal propensity to consume of less than unity. Thus the marginal propensity to consume of less than unity sets a definite limit to the process of expansion. Figure 13 (B) shows the converse of (A), namely, the upturn of the cycle due to the fortunate fact that people tend to decrease consumption by *less* than the decrement of income. Recovery gets under way before income reaches zero.

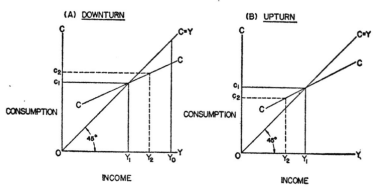

FIG. 13. TURNING POINTS OF THE CYCLE

DANGER OF PERMANENT "OVERSAVING GAP"

If the consumption function is not readily adjustable upward, there may be a continuous "oversaving gap" between the amount people wish to save out of *full-employment* income and the volume of *private* investment businesses find profitable to maintain. If, for example, people wish to save at the rate of $60 billion out of a full-employment income of $200 billion, and businesses find the existing opportunities such as to justify investment at the rate of $40 billion, there will be an "oversaving gap" to the tune of $20 billion annually. The propensity to consume of less than unity at full employment creates a thorny problem of offsetting a large amount of savings to maintain that full employment. The problem is thorny because the possibilities for further investment may be completely "autonomous" with regard to the level of income or the rate of interest. Because the maintenance of a level of investment compatible with continuous full employment depends on such "autonomous" factors as economic development, technological progress, population growth, and political changes—factors outside of the credit and price systems—it is by no means easy to fill an "oversaving gap" at high levels of income.[11]

And yet it is not safe to assume that the "autonomous" factors will operate to expand investment opportunities in just that degree which is necessary to fill the gap. Nor can it be assumed that public investment will increase to just such an extent as to bridge the gap which private investment fails to fill. A real solution may lie in the direction of *raising* the consumption function (or lowering the savings function). An upward shift of the consumption function is, under *laissez faire*, too much to hope for, unless conditions of full employment can be supposed to reduce people's propensity to save drastically.

UNIQUE NATURE OF INCOME PROPAGATION

The marginal propensity to consume of less than unity also accounts for the peculiar way in which an initial injection of purchasing power into the income stream leads to an ultimate expansion of total income. Such an injection leads to smaller successive increments of income in the course of the respending of the original purchasing power. This phenomenon owes its explanation to the fact that income recipients ordinarily spend less than the full increment of income. The

[11] *Cf.* M. Kalecki, "The Maintenance of Full Employment after the Transition Period. A Comparison of the Problem in the United States and the United Kingdom," *International Labour Review*, November, 1945.

"multiplier" by which the initial outlay magnifies total income is directly derived from the marginal propensity to consume. The extent of the magnifying effect of an initial increase in income on the total income at the end of a given period is determined by the way income recipients elect to divide that increment of income between consumption and saving. Given, therefore, the stable consumption function, it will not be difficult to tell in advance what effect an injection of new purchasing power will have on national income and therefore on aggregate employment. This, in combination with the knowledge of the "acceleration" effect of the rate of consumption on investment, will give us a fair measure of dynamic changes in aggregate demand. Both the "multiplier" and "acceleration" principles will be explained in another chapter.

There may be many other implications of the stable consumption function in general and the marginal propensity to consume of less than unity in particular. The above implications do not all rest on the hypothesis that the position of the consumption function remains unchanged; they presuppose the essential requirement that the slope of the consumption function be positive but less than unity.

Factors Affecting the Consumption Function

We have thus far discussed various problems on the assumption that consumption depends on income alone, but there are in fact many "other variables" which may affect the actual consumption function in varying degrees. We shall discuss some of these "other variables" in the following order.

DISTRIBUTION OF INCOME

The way in which national income is divided among various income groups partly determines what the actual consumption function is at any given time. If we simplify our analysis by dividing the national income pie into just two cuts, one for "consuming brackets" and the other for "saving brackets," it is easy to see what kind of consumption function we shall get. If the proportion of the pie going to the "consuming brackets" is very much larger than that going to the "saving brackets," we should expect the consumption function to be *high*. If, on the other hand, the share of the "saving brackets" is relatively large, the consumption function is likely to be *low*. As a first approximation it is useful to consider wage groups as belonging to the "consuming brackets" and non-wage groups as belonging to the "saving brackets." Thus viewed, the wage-profit relation is the most significant variable in the distribution of income.

An economy in which the proportion of national income going to wage groups is relatively large is prima facie a "high-consumption economy." Conversely, a "high-saving economy" is likely where the proportion going to non-wage groups is relatively large. Thus it is possible to identify a "high-consumption economy" with a "high-wage, low-profit economy." [12] It should be added that a "high-wage, low-profit economy" has to do with the way the national income is divided between wage groups and nonwage groups, not with the question of changes in wage *rates*. Should, for example, a "labor government" be in power for a long time, the consumption function would probably become higher as a result of various measures to increase the share of labor groups relatively to that of property groups.

Another way to put the matter is to say that consumption is typically the function of the poor and saving is typically the function of the rich. There seems to be little doubt about the fact that great inequality in the distribution of income keeps the consumption function low and the savings function high. It is a matter of common knowledge that the consumption function is low wherever there are large disparities

[12] See A. H. Hansen, *Economic Policy and Full Employment* (Whittlesey, New York, 1947), p. 48.

between the rich and the poor. If in the future inequalities of incomes and wealth are reduced for one reason or another, the consumption function will doubtless be higher than at present. Quite apart from the normative question of whether inequalities of incomes and wealth ought or ought not to exist, it is patent that the degree of equality in the distribution of income affects the levels of the propensities to consume and to save.

ATTITUDES TOWARD THRIFT

Thrift has long been praised as at once a private and a social virtue. It is regarded as a private virtue because it is an acceptable way of increasing one's private wealth as well as of providing reserves against insecurity. It is considered to be a social virtue on the ground that it facilitates the growth of capital and therefore makes for social progress. Apart from the merits or demerits of this conventional view of saving, there is little doubt about the fact that the actual consumption function is affected by people's attitudes toward thrift. A presumption in favor of thrift, however harmful at less than full employment, may be reinforced by such institutional arrangements as life insurance, corporate savings, and real-estate amortization quotas,[13] to keep the consumption function low.

Only in the field of public spending has the traditional notion of "sound finance" been drastically modified. But then we are concerned with the individual's attitude toward thrift. This attitude toward thrift is governed by a schedule of time preferences. Given the freedom to choose between present consumption and future consumption, the individual will develop a certain attitude toward the relative importance of spending and saving. It may be that people will be so "educated" as to value present consumption more than future consumption. It is also possible that the existing institutional

[13]For a detailed discussion of these institutional factors see A. H. Hansen, *Fiscal Policy and Business Cycles* (London, George Allen & Unwin Ltd., 1941) pp. 238–242.

setup will change in such a way as to minimize the need for saving or to remove the incentives to save. People may in time wake up to the danger of "oversaving" long stressed by economists from Malthus down to Keynes. If people become fully aware of the "paradox of thrift" at less than full employment, the propensity to consume will probably become higher and the propensity to save lower than if they continue to regard thrift as an unmitigated virtue.

HOLDINGS OF LIQUID ASSETS

Another factor affecting the consumption function is the volume of accumulated savings in the hands of individuals. The larger the amount of such holdings, the more likely people are to spend out of current income. For holdings of savings in liquid forms (e.g., savings accounts, government savings bonds, and cash) have the effect of increasing a sense of security on the one hand and of decreasing the urge to save out of current income. A change in the real value of such accumulated savings due to general price changes might also affect the propensity to consume. For instance, a decrease in the real value of such holdings due to price inflation is likely to reduce the propensity to consume, since such a decline in the real value of liquid assets weakens the liquidity positions of the owners and therefore increases pessimism. When people are pessimistic, they do not generally spend much out of current income.

The wartime accumulations of savings and postwar ownings of public debt by individuals are believed to have caused the consumption function to shift somewhat higher. This tendency for the consumption function to shift upward is especially perceptible in a country like Britain, where a rather stringent program of "austerity" caused holdings of liquid assets to increase in addition to the wartime savings.[14]

It is important to know, however, in whose hands the liquid

---

[14]*Cf.* J. E. Meade, *Planning and the Price Mechanism* (London, George Allen & Unwin Ltd., 1948), p. 19.

assets are held, and also how these liquid assets came into existence.[15] If it is the consumers who hold them, then the consumption function may be expected to rise. More exactly, it is the liquid assets held by low-income groups which are most likely to have an upward pressure on the consumption function. If an absolute increase in liquid assets comes about through the monetization of assets held by investors and wealthy individuals (e.g., conversion of bonds into cash through central-bank purchases or on the open market), it is unlikely to raise the consumption function appreciably. If, on the other hand, liquid assets come into the possession of low-income groups via loan-financed public investment, the consumption function is more likely to rise. The volume of liquid assets is not considered to be at par with the level of income as an independent variable in the determination of the consumption-income relation.

TAX STRUCTURE

A change in the tax structure, that is, in the nature and rates of taxes, may influence the actual consumption function significantly. A tax structure which depends mainly on progressive taxes is generally conducive to an upward shift of the consumption function. Conversely, a tax structure based largely on regressive taxes (e.g., sales and excise taxes) is a presumption against a rise in the propensity to consume. For a progressive tax system falls more heavily on the portion of income that is saved than on the portion that is spent. It follows that tax policies aimed at reducing the inequalities of incomes will reduce the propensity to save more than the propensity to consume.

The American tax structure during the 1930's probably had rates progressive enough to prevent an appreciable increase in inequality and therefore a further decline in the pro-

---

[15] On this point see Hansen, "The General Theory," in *The New Economics,* pp. 140–141.

pensity to consume. But it is doubtful that the tax structure during that period was progressive enough to effect such a positive redistribution of income toward equality as to raise the consumption function.[16] It is generally believed that the progressive elements of the United States tax structure in the Federal field are considerably offset by the regressive elements in the State and local field, so that the net effect of the progression on the propensity to consume is negligible.

If a tax cut in, say, a personal income tax should take place because of nonfiscal considerations, it is likely to be of such a nature as to strengthen individual and corporate savings more than the propensity to consume. Needless to say, the tax reductions designed to support consumer demands may well be offset by other tax reductions designed to encourage individual and business savings. Thus a mere decrease in tax rates is no guarantee that the propensity to consume will rise. In combination with spending programs, however, a change in the tax structure is capable of changing the consumption function significantly.

There are many other factors affecting the consumption function. The state of expectations and interest rates are among the most frequently debated factors, but these factors are so indeterminate in their influence on various income groups that we may safely neglect them at this juncture. Perhaps further empirical research will show whether there is a significant correlation between the propensity to consume and the elasticity of expectations or interest rates. As for the influence of general price changes, it is not necessary to consider it separately here, since the principal demand factor determining the general price level is national income.

All these other variables are capable of affecting the consumption function in one direction or the other, even though

[16] See G. Colm and F. Lehmann, *Economic Consequences of Recent American Tax Policy* (Graduate Faculty of New School for Social Research, New York, 1938).

aggregate income is "the ultimate independent" variable influencing the propensity to consume. The reason that these other variables are considered secondary in importance to the income variable is that the effect of any one factor (other than income) on the consumption function is likely to be weakened, if not completely nullified, by the offsetting influence of other factors in operation. Nevertheless, these other variables suggest that the actual consumption function is what it is because of a multiplicity of forces in operation, and throw much light on what must be done to raise the consumption function or to lower it.

11

Savings and Investment

◆◆

THE SAVINGS-INVESTMENT relation has been mentioned off and on without an explicit explanation. We are at last in a position to examine it with a view to understanding its place in the theoretical structure of effective demand and its practical significance for policy. This chapter will deal with (a) savings-investment equilibrium, (b) underemployment equilibrium, and (c) determinants of investment.

Savings–Investment Equilibrium

SCHEDULE CONCEPT OF INVESTMENT

For purposes of equilibrium analysis, investment will be conceived in terms of a schedule measuring various amounts of investment associated with various possible levels of income (or various rates of interest in some cases). This gives us the concept of *the propensity to invest* or *the investment function*. Investment in this schedule sense is a *dynamic* concept of *entrepreneurial behavior*. It tells us how producers as a whole would respond *over time* to changes in income or in the interest rate. Together with the propensity to consume (or its inverse, the propensity to save), the propensity to invest determines the *equilibrium* level of income. Diagrammatically speaking, the equilibrium level of national income

N

is given by the intersection of the investment function and the savings function.

Conceptually, therefore, we can compare investment in the schedule sense to a demand curve measuring the functional relation between various amounts of capital outlays and various levels of income or rates of interest. We can also speak of the income-elasticity or interest-elasticity of the investment function, depending on how responsive the demand for capital goods is assumed to be to the slightest change in income or rates of interest. If we make investment depend on income, we may have either "induced" or "autonomous" investment, the former being an income-elastic investment function and the latter an income-inelastic investment function. For purposes of short-period analysis it is perhaps realistic to consider the propensity to invest to be sensitive to income changes, and therefore to draw an upward-sloping investment curve rising from the horizontal income axis. For national income, it will be recalled, is the chief demand factor affecting the general price level and therefore sales possibilities. In the short period, therefore, investment is "induced" by income changes which measure profit possibilities parametrically.

"Autonomous" investment, on the other hand, is insensitive to income changes, and is usually represented by a horizontal straight line running from left to right parallel to the horizontal income axis. "Autonomous" investment is characteristic of a war economy or of a planned economy in which investment decisions are made on the basis of considerations other than profits and losses. But even peacetime private investment becomes "autonomous" of the level of income to the extent that investment opportunities depend on "exogenous" factors largely outside the economic system, as in the longer period. The distinction between "induced" and "autonomous" investment is shown in the following diagram.

In Figure 14 (A), the I curve represents the schedule of

"induced" investment at various levels of income, and the amount of investment at the Y level of income is YN. A larger amount will be invested as income increases, and a smaller amount as income decreases, given the upward rising investment schedule. At a very low level of income, "induced" investment might become negative, and the I curve would cut through the income axis from above. The steeper the I curve is sloped, the greater will be a percentage increase (or decrease) in the amount invested in response to a percentage increase (or decrease) in income. A change in the entire

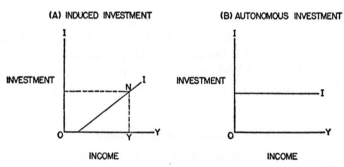

Fig. 14. Investment Schedules

relation of investment to income can be indicated by a shift of the I curve. Thus an upward shift of the curve to the left would mean that amounts of "induced" investment were larger at all levels of income. Conversely, a downward shift of the curve to the right would signify a lower propensity to invest.

The I curve in Figure 14 (B) represents the schedule of "autonomous" investment, the amount of investment being identical at all levels of income. In other words, investment opportunities are such that the amount of investment remains constant, e.g., $30 billion at the zero level of income as well as at a national income of $200 billion. The upward shift of the I curve parallel to the original curve would indicate that opportunities had expanded to call for an increased steady flow of investment, e.g., at the constant rate of $40 billion at all levels of income.

In both cases investment measured by the vertical axis refers to *real* investment, not *financial* investment. For while financial investment involves merely transfers of existing assets (e.g., securities) and therefore no net change in aggregate expenditure, real investment, involving as it does the production and purchase of new capital goods, gives rise to a net increase in total expenditure. Included in capital goods are (a) plant and equipment, (b) inventories, (c) residential construction, (d) public works, and (e) "net foreign investment" (an excess of exports and other credit items over imports and other debit items). It is these outlays that are significant for income and employment analysis, since business cycles are associated mainly with fluctuations in these outlays.

LOGICAL IDENTITY OF SAVINGS AND INVESTMENT

Investment in the statistical sense is always identically equal to savings in the same sense. This identity of savings and investment holds valid at any level of income, and regardless of the obvious fact that decisions to save and decisions to invest are made by different people for different reasons. This identity of savings and investment is implicit in the truism that total income and total expenditure are but two names for the same thing. Since investment is the name given to monetary outlays on things other than consumption, it is nothing but income minus consumption, or $I = Y - C$. But then this quantity is exactly what we understand savings to be, or $S = Y - C$. If both savings and investment are equal to income minus consumption, we get the identity of savings and investment ($S = I$) as a matter of logical necessity. This is one sense in which Keynes talks about the savings-

investment relation, the other being the schedule sense.[1]
The truism may be written:

$$Y = C + I \qquad \text{or} \qquad 100 = 80 + 20$$
$$S = Y - C \qquad\qquad\qquad 20 = 100 - 80$$
$$\text{Hence } S = I \qquad\qquad\qquad \text{Hence } 20 = 20$$

If Y is 100, C 80, and I 20, the value of S is necessarily 20,
which is also the value of I. Since savings are an excess of
income over consumption $(Y - C)$ and investment is income minus consumption $(Y - C)$, these two quantities
must be the same. Thus savings and investment in the statistical sense are always equal *by definition*—in precisely the
same sense that the quantity of money times its velocity equals
the volume of trade times the average price, or $MV = PT$.
Thus we are merely saying that since the sum of all expenditures (Y) consists of the sum spent on consumption (C)
plus the sum spent on things other than consumption (I),
that part of aggregate spending which is not due to consumption necessarily represents the value of savings (S) or
investment (I).

To dispel any possible misunderstanding or confusion, a
further explanation of the identity equation $S = I$ is in order.
The equation is true by virtue of definition only. Income, consumption, savings, and investment are all so defined as to
make savings and investment equal.[2] As such, the equation
is merely a logical relation, with nothing but a set of definitions to account for its existence and justification.

Moreover, the logical identity of savings and investment
refers to *aggregate* savings and investment. The identity holds
valid regardless of the seemingly paradoxical fact that an
individual can save more than he invests. Obviously there

---

[1] *General Theory*, p. 63.

[2] A variant of the definitional, nonschedule savings-investment relation is
found in D. H. Robertson's treatment. See his "Savings and Hoarding," *Economic Journal*, September, 1933.

is no reason why an individual's savings should equal his investment. Yet *all* the individuals of the economy cannot save more than they invest. This is true because an increase in an individual's savings is exactly offset by a decrease in others' savings, so that there is no net change in aggregate savings. Taking investment as a constant, let us see what happens simultaneously when an individual attempts to save more than he is investing. Suppose he attempts to increase his savings by 10 so that his savings are greater than his investment by 10. But at the same time his consumption expenditures decrease by 10, since he cannot save except at the expense of consumption. As his consumption expenditures go down, income of others depending on consumption sales goes down by a similar amount. As others' income decreases by 10, *aggregate income* must decrease by 10. But *aggregate savings* remain unchanged, since an increase in the first individual's savings is exactly offset by a corresponding decrease in others' savings due to a similar decline in the latters' income—their consumption being constant.[3] It follows that the unchanged savings and the unchanged investment are identically equal. It should be remembered, however, that aggregate income has declined.

Thus the identity equation reveals an error of composition. The classical notion that aggregate savings increase with individual savings is vitiated by the reasoning that an individual's attempt to save has a zero effect on aggregate savings because of its decreasing effect on others' incomes and therefore on others' savings. This is in itself a considerable service, but, more important, it is a step nearer to the disturbing conclusion that what is considered to be a private as well as social virtue, i.e., savings, is after all socially harmful when there is less than full employment. For, as will be

[3] An individual's act of saving cannot be assumed to have any such involuntary effect on others' decisions to consume as on the latter's income and savings.

shown later, an increase in people's desire to save at less than full employment actually leads to a decrease in aggregate income and therefore in aggregate savings.

The identity equation is designed to indicate the adverse implications of an attempt to save more than is being invested for aggregate consumption, income, and employment. By relating savings and investment to the "bilateral" relation $(Y - C)$ we can equate a failure to spend to a failure to earn an income and to get a job. For to say that some people's savings increase is to say that their consumption expenditures decrease and that others depending on consumption sales for incomes receive less income. But for this practical significance the identity equation might be considered inconsequential, as some writers are disposed to do.[4] Others defend it in varying degrees of enthusiasm.[5]

The analytical usefulness of the identity equation is severely limited by the absence of an adjusting mechanism. Since the equation is as true as the proposition that two plus two equals four, no mechanism of adjustment is involved. If savings is another name for investment, obviously no time lags are involved to necessitate "sequence analysis." Because it is not a description of an actual process of adjustment, the identity equation is a tool for *static* analysis. A failure to describe an actual *dynamic* process of adjustment between conflicting decisions to save and to invest is the main analytical handi-

[4] *Cf.* G. Haberler, *Prosperity and Depression* (London, George Allen & Unwin Ltd., 1941), Chap. 8; J. R. Hicks, "Mr. Keynes' Theory of Employment," *Economic Journal*, XXVI, 1936; F. A. Lutz, "The Outcome of the Saving–Investment Discussion," *Quarterly Journal of Economics*, Vol. 52, 1938; B. Ohlin, "Some Notes on the Stockholm Theory of Savings and Investment," *Economic Journal*, XLVII, 1937; J. W. Angell, *Investment and Business Cycles* (McGraw–Hill, New York, 1941), pp. 204–210; G. H. Halm, *Monetary Theory* (Blakiston, Philadelphia, 1946), pp. 340–543; W. Fellner, *Monetary Policies and Full Employment* (Univ. of Calif. Press), pp. 7–15; etc.

[5] *Cf.* A. P. Lerner, "Saving Equals Investment," *Quarterly Journal of Economics*, Vol. 52, 1938, and "Saving and Investment: Definitions, Assumptions, Objectives," *ibid.*, Vol. 53, 1938–39; A. H. Hansen, "A Note on Savings and Investment," *Review of Economics and Statistics*, Vol. 30, 1938; L. R. Klein, *The Keynesian Revolution*, pp. 100–103, 110–117; etc.

cap of the identity equation, and also the main reason for the need of a dynamic approach. Keynes suggested the possibility of "dynamizing" the static identity equation by comparing the process of the savings-investment relation to that of the supply-demand relation and by making the equality of savings and investment depend on income changes.[6] We shall discuss this determinate equality of savings and investment subsequently.

DETERMINATE EQUALITY OF SAVINGS AND INVESTMENT

Although savings and investment in the statistical sense are identically equal at all times and at any level of income, savings and investment in the schedule sense are equal *only in equilibrium,* that is, at the equilibrium level of income. To facilitate the exposition let us compare the equilibrium of savings and investment with that of supply and demand. Just as supply and demand can be unequal except in equilibrium, so can savings and investment be unequal except in equilibrium. Just as supply and demand are brought into equilibrium by the equilibrating mechanism of price, so are savings and investment in the schedule sense equilibrated by the income mechanism. Though different with respect to the equilibrating mechanism, the process of equilibrium adjustment is the same in both cases. Supply and demand are equal only at the equilibrium price, namely, that price at which the quantity demanded is exactly the same as the quantity offered. An excess of demand over supply causes the price to rise to the equilibrium level, and an excess of supply over demand causes the price to fall to that equilibrium level. Until and unless they reach the equilibrium price supply and demand are unequal. This process of the supply-demand equilibrium is shown in Figure 15.

In Figure 15 the vertical axis measures price and the hori-

[6] *Cf.* Keynes, "Alternative Theories of the Rate of Interest," *Economic Journal,* Vol. XLVII, 1937, and also *General Theory,* p. 184.

zontal axis measures the quantity of some commodity that would be offered for sale and purchased. The SS and DD lines are the supply and demand schedules. Suppose we begin with price OP_1, at which demand exceeds supply by S_1D_1. This excess of demand over supply raises the price to OP_2 in the next period. But at price OP_2 demand still exceeds supply by S_2D_2, and consequently the price goes up to P, at which supply equals demand. Thus the equilibrium of supply and demand has come about through price changes in sequential periods.

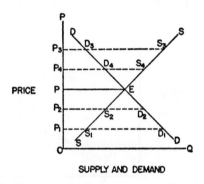

SUPPLY AND DEMAND

Fig. 15. Dynamic Process of Equilibrium
Adjustment of Supply and Demand

If, on the other hand, we begin with price OP_3, at which supply exceeds demand by D_3S_3, the price will fall to OP_4 in the next period and so on until it reaches OP, the equilibrium price at which supply and demand are in balance. This is the familiar dynamic process of market equilibrium. The dynamic process of monetary equilibrium is the same as that of price equilibrium except for the equilibrating variable, which is income in the one case and price in the other.

Let us construct a dynamical model for the equilibrium of savings and investment similar to the above. The three variables involved in this model are independent variable Y and dependent variables S and I. The rate of change of income is functionally related to savings and investment in such wise that income must rise when investment is greater than savings and fall when savings is greater than investment. Savings and investment are equal only at the equilibrium level of income, an income which is neither rising nor falling. Thus the equality of savings and investment is seen as being brought about through the mechanism of equilibrating income. In this model the equality of savings and investment is an equilibrium "solution" of a continuous dynamical system. The equilibrium process of savings-investment adjustment is illustrated in Figure 16.

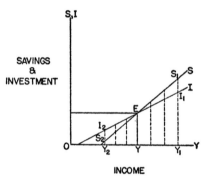

FIG. 16. SAVINGS–INVESTMENT EQUILIBRIUM

In Figure 16 the vertical axis measures both saving and investment and the horizontal axis measures income. The investment function, I, is the same as in Figure 15. The savings function, S, cuts the investment function from below, indicating that stable equilibrium is under consideration.[7] If

[7] There will be *unstable* equilibrium if the I curve cuts the S curve from below, since income would move *away* from the equilibrium level. The I curve may rise so steeply upward to the left as to cut the S curve from below, if the demand for capital goods is highly elastic with respect to income. Such a situation is conceivable (a) when there is an unusual backlog of demand for new capital goods, (b) when the rate of consumption greatly increases as a result of large holdings of liquid assets (e.g., past savings), and (c) when the demand for consumer goods gives rise to a greatly "accelerated" derived demand for capital goods. The probable result would be "explosive" inflation.

we begin with income Y_2, investment exceeds savings by I_2S_2. This excess of investment over savings means business profits, since the smaller the amount of income saved, the larger the amount of income spent and therefore the amount of sales. Consequently, income rises to the next higher level until eventually it reaches the equilibrium level of income, at which savings and investment are in balance. Note that the gap between savings and investment narrows with the

---

Fortunately, the propensity to invest is seldom so sensitive to income changes as to cut the S curve from below, for there are usually offsetting influences in operation.

Consider the following diagram showing unstable equilibrium for a given market and for the economy as a whole.

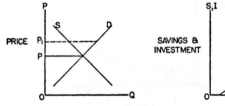

(A) UNSTABLE MARKET EQUILIBRIUM   (B) UNSTABLE S-I EQUILIBRIUM

The market will be unstable if the demand curve cuts the supply curve from below, as in (A). For at P_1 the amount demanded exceeds the amount offered so much that price will rise in the next period and keep on rising, instead of falling to the equilibrium price P. Such a demand curve implies the outright violation of the law of diminishing marginal utility, according to which a demand curve is expected to slope downward to the right. Similarly, the supply curve shown is the reverse of the ordinary one based on the law of diminishing marginal productivity. These demand and supply functions are conceivable, since we know that there are exceptions to the above-mentioned economic laws. The point to remember is that given such demand and supply functions, the slightest price change merely widens the gap between demand and supply so that the price mechanism fails to prevent a tendency of price to move away from the equilibrium level.

The same analysis applies to the whole economy. Here again, there can be no stable equilibrium with so income-elastic an investment function and with not so income-elastic a savings function. For any slight income change will widen rather than narrow the gap between savings and investment, with the result that income tends to move away from the equilibrium level. At Y_1, for instance, investment far exceeds savings, only to push the income up and keep on pushing it up. Thus with an investment curve that cuts a savings curve that is less steep than the zero-saving 45° line, the economy is exposed to inflation and deflation at the slightest income provocation.

rising income and is completely wiped out at the equilibrium level of income. If, on the other hand, we begin with income Y_1, there is an excess of savings over investment to decrease income, over time, to the equilibrium level. Thus, whenever there is a discrepancy between the propensity to save and the propensity to invest, income rises or falls until the equilibrium level is reached.

There is still a better way to show the dynamic process of savings-investment equilibrium adjustment. Figure 17 is such an attempt.

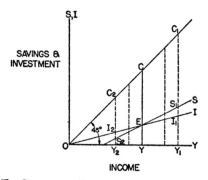

Fig. 17. Savings–Investment Equilibrium
(Alternative form of presentation)

The familiar 45° line has been added to measure consumption relative to savings and investment. At income Y_2, investment exceeds savings by I_2S_2. This means that businesses would receive profits (measured by the distance from the investment schedule to the savings schedule), since the total income received by businesses (the vertical length Y_2I_2 plus the vertical length S_2C_2, or the investment distance plus the consumption distance) is larger than the total payments (the vertical length Y_2C_2), that is, by the amount of I_2S_2. As a result production would be increased and income would rise eventually to the equilibrium level of Y. At this equilibrium level of income the savings and investment curves are seen to intersect at E (the vertical length YE is equal to itself). If, on the other hand, we begin with income Y_1, the amount businesses would be willing to invest is smaller than the amount people would be willing to save, with the result that there is loss by the amount of S_1I_1. The total received by business (S_1C_1 plus Y_1I_1) is smaller than the total paid out by it (Y_1C_1) by the difference between savings and investment, i.e., I_1S_1. This excess of savings over investment would have the effect of decreasing output and therefore of causing income to decline eventually to the equilibrium level of Y.

Thus savings and investment in the *schedule* sense are brought into balance, *over time,* by the equilibrating mechanism of *income.* This way of looking at savings and investment is consistent with the common-sense view that, though decisions to save and decisions to invest are made by different people and often from conflicting motives, these decisions are somehow reconciled in the course of time. Only in this case "the invisible hand" happens to be *income.* Moreover, there is nothing mysterious about this "invisible hand," since income changes are shown to be clearly connected with down-to-earth profits and losses due to disparities of consuming, saving, and investing activities. This implies that income, while influencing savings and investment, may itself be influenced by them. Let us now make consumption and investment independent variables and income a dependent variable in order to see how income is determined by the interaction of the consumption function and the investment function.

By means of another diagram we can now show the initiating role of the propensity to invest in the determination of income in the short period. Let us take the propensity to consume as a constant, according to Keynes' law. For simplicity we may make the further assumption that the investment function is inelastic with respect to income, that is, "autonomous." In Figure 18 the vertical axis measures consumption, investment, and savings, and the horizontal axis measures income. C is the familiar consumption function. The C + I curve above the C curve is the consumption plus investment schedule, obtained by adding vertically to each point of the consumption schedule, a particular level of investment associated with each level of income. In other words, it is the investment function superimposed on the consumption function. The distance between the C curve and the C + I curve measures the amount of investment at a given level of income.[8]

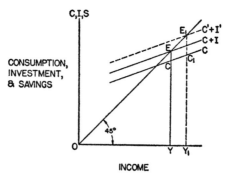

FIG. 18. INITIATING ROLE OF INVESTMENT IN SHORT–PERIOD INCOME DETERMINATION

In Figure 18 the amount of investment is autonomously given so that the C + I curve runs parallel to the C curve, indicating that the amount of investment is the same at all levels of income. The C + I curve intersects the 45° line to give the equilibrium level of income, Y. In other words, what people would wish to consume and what businesses would wish to invest, together, determines the equilibrium level of income at which the amount of that income spent on con-

[8] The distance between the C curve and the C + I curve at any point of income depends on the particular assumption made regarding the level of profitable investment within the framework of the existing investment opportunities.

sumption equals the amount spent on things other than consumption (the vertical length YE is equal to itself). It should be noted that at the equilibrium level of income, Y, savings CE equal investment CE. Thus it can be said that the equilibrium level of income is the unique level of income at which consumption plus investment (the vertical length YC plus the vertical length CE) equal income (the vertical length YE). Similarly, it can be said that Y is the only level at which savings and investment are in balance.

Now suppose that the $C + I$ curve shifts upward for some "autonomous" reasons. The new $C' + I'$ curve intersects the 45° line to give the new equilibrium level of income, Y_1, at which consumption plus investment equal income and savings equal investment. E and E_1 are single positions of shifting equilibrium corresponding to levels of income Y and Y_1— positions in which savings and investment are equal. Thus it is possible (and probably preferable for pedagogic reasons) to show the dynamic process of income determination *directly* by use of the consumption and investment schedules. Yet neither this diagram nor any other so far presented tells us whether the equilibrium level of income is also a *full-employment* level of income. The equality of savings and investment does not tell us whether the economy is at full employment or at less than full employment. The mere absence of any discrepancy between savings and investment is no guarantee that available resources (manpower and materials) are fully utilized in the production of consumption goods and investment goods. To this problem we shall now turn.

Underemployment Equilibrium

The classical notion of monetary equilibrium is one in which savings flow automatically into an equal amount of investment via interest changes to give a full-employment level of income. In modern conditions, however, it is more likely that the equilibrium of savings and investment is reached considerably below the full-employment level. The explanation for the likelihood of "underemployment equilibrium" is to be found in the plausible assumptions regarding the shapes of the strategic functions, namely, (a) the interest-inelastic investment function, (b) the interest-inelastic savings function, and (c) the interest-elastic liquidity function. If the shapes of these functions are what they are believed to be, savings do not automatically flow into proportional investment to give a full-employment equilibrium solution, no

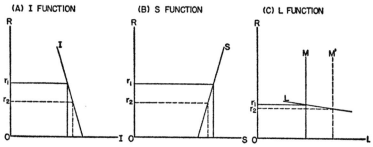

Fig. 19. Shapes of the Investment,
Savings, and Liquidity Functions

matter how flexible the cost-price structure may be. Figure 19 shows the probable shapes of the above functions which account for the possibility of "underemployment equilibrium."

In Figure 19 the vertical axis measures the interest rate in all cases, and the horizontal axis measures investment in (A), savings in (B), and liquid assets in (C). The I curve in (A) is the investment schedule, which is highly inelastic with respect to interest. This we know to be a good first approximation, since there is in most cases no significant correlation between the interest rate and the volume of investment. The interest-inelasticity of the investment function implies that the propensity to invest cannot be expected to rise to intersect the propensity to save to give a full-employment equilibrium level of income when the economy is in equilibrium at less than full employment. In other words, there can be no automatic flow of savings into investment via a cheap-money policy to establish the savings-investment equilibrium at full employment, as the traditional theory assumes.

In Figure 19 (B) the S curve is the savings schedule, which is highly inelastic with respect to interest. As was shown earlier, this too is a realistic assumption, as far as the wealthy capitalistic economies are concerned. If people do not readily respond to interest changes, they may want to keep on saving even when investment opportunities are zero. Thus the interest inelasticity of the savings function implies that the propensity to save cannot be expected to fall if and when the investment function cannot be raised. The result is that the S curve and the I curve intersect to give the equilibrium level of income short of full employment. It might be thought that the savings function could be made more responsive to interest changes by the drastic raising or lowering of the interest rate, but then the liquidity function seems to be in the way.

In Figure 19 (C) the L curve is the liquidity function, which is highly elastic with respect to interest at a low rate. This is due to the fact that the demand for liquid assets to satisfy the speculative motive becomes hypersensitive to interest changes at a very low rate. In other words, people are strongly inclined to demand an almost infinite amount of liquid assets when they expect to gain very little by lending or investing their money, i.e., when the expected interest earnings on nonliquid assets are extremely low. If the L function is perfectly elastic, that is, horizontal straight,[9] it spells more

[9] If the demand for money to satisfy the "transaction" and "precautionary" motives is stronger than that for "speculative" reasons, the L function need not be so interest-elastic. But it is realistic to consider the demand for money to satisfy the "speculative" motive (i.e., to postpone current purchases of non-liquid assets in anticipation of lower prices) as strategically more significant in the actual world of risks and uncertainties.

o

trouble for the economy. The interest-elastic liquidity function has two disturbing implications for investment. First, the inducement to invest is discouraged by the depressing effect on the marginal efficiency of capital of the high rate of interest which must be paid to overcome a strong preference for liquidity. Second, the monetary authority cannot reduce the interest rate significantly by increasing the money supply to stimulate investment. Thus the investment function may not rise to intersect the savings function at a break-even point high enough to give the full-employment equilibrium level of income.

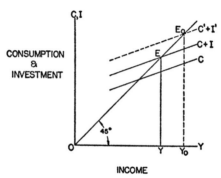

FIG. 20. UNDEREMPLOYMENT EQUILIBRIUM

The shapes of these functions indicate a strong likelihood that the investment function cannot be "induced" by interest changes even if full-employment equilibrium requires it. Figure 20 shows an "underemployment equilibrium" solution.

In Figure 20 the consumption plus investment schedule, $C + I$, intersects the 45° line at the break-even point of E, to give equilibrium income Y and also the equality of savings and investment (the vertical distance between the 45° line and the C curve at the Y level of income). But the equilibrium income Y so given is by hypothesis short of full employment income Y_o. In order that the dynamic process of adjustment may find an equilibrium solution at this full-employment level of income, the consumption-plus-invest-ment schedule must shift upward to intersect the 45° line at E_o, as shown by the dotted $C' + I'$ schedule. Yet there is no likelihood that the investment function will *automatically* shift that way, the shapes of the investment, savings, and liquidity functions being what they are. Accordingly, the economy may find itself in equilibrium at underemployment income Y instead of at full-employment income Y_o.

It must be emphasized that this underemployment equi-librium refers to *private* investment only. If the investment function is a matter of "autonomous" public policy, it can be "planned" upward, and in just that degree which is neces-sary to insure the equilibrium of savings and investment at full-employment income Y_o. Although full employment was not the objective, it so happened that the wartime public investment was increased "autonomously" (i.e., by Congres-sional action regardless of the level of income) at a rate which was compatible with full employment. In other words, the consumption plus government investment (the $C + G$ curve) schedule was raised so high that its intersection with the 45° line gave not only the equality of savings and in-vestment but the full-employment equilibrium level of in-come as a matter of course. This does not mean that "au-tonomous" public investment is the only solution; on the contrary, our primary interest lies in the possibility of "in-ducing" private investment to increase to the desired level. Only when private investment cannot be "induced" to in-crease sufficiently to offset savings, must public investment be relied upon to supplement the private inducement to invest. Otherwise the economy is likely to find an equilib-rium solution short of full employment.

Thus, with the plausible assumptions regarding the shapes of the basic functions of the Keynesian system, it is not dif-ficult to show that "underemployment equilibrium" may be the rule rather than the exception. If the investment function, the savings function, and the liquidity function behave toward interest changes as they are believed to behave in modern conditions, underemployment equilibrium is difficult to avoid, no matter how flexible the price-cost structure may be or how perfect market competition may be in the classical sense.[10] The essential point of this discussion is that full employment is *not automatically assured* as the traditional theory assumes.

Determinants of Investment

We have seen that the levels of income and employment depend on the interaction of the propensity to invest and the propensity to save, or, more directly, on the movement of the consumption-plus-investment schedule. We have also seen that the propensity to consume is subject to various influences. Now it is necessary to investigate the underlying factors affecting the propensity to invest. The propensity to invest, we have seen, is nothing else than the demand for capital goods or capital assets. In our discussion of the interest rate we saw that the demand for capital, otherwise known as "the marginal efficiency of capital," together with the given rate of interest, determines the volume of investment. Therefore, as a first approximation, it is proper to investigate the factors that influence the marginal efficiency of capital in order to understand why the propensity to invest is what it is. In this section we shall consider the major factors, other than the interest rate, that influence the marginal efficiency of capital.

STATE OF BUSINESS CONFIDENCE

"Business confidence" is the general expression for businessmen's subjective evaluation of the profitability of future in-

---

[10] A failure to recognize the shapes of these functions leads to the error of dismissing the savings-investment relation as incapable of producing cyclical disturbances. J. Schumpeter. e.g., argues that saving itself reduces the interest rate and so creates investment opportunities. (See his *Business Cycles,* McGraw–Hill, New York, 1939, Vol. I, p. 188.)

vestment opportunities. Broadly, it epitomizes "hopes of profit" and "fears of loss." More narrowly, the expression refers to businessmen's estimates of the marginal efficiencies of various types of capital assets. As such, business confidence is an important factor influencing the propensity to invest and therefore the levels of output and employment. An understanding of businessmen's *expectations* is essential to a better grasp of the *instability* of the actual investment function in a free-market economy.[11]

We may distinguish between *short-term* and *long-term* expectations. The former are the projections of recent experiences into the near future, while the latter concern "hopes" and "fears" of a lasting nature. Short-term expectations arise from events of the recent past which are regarded as a fairly reliable guide to what will happen in the near future. These expectations are based on such recent and "endogenous" influences as prices, profits, the level of employment, the volume of sales, wage rates, interest rates, the money supply, and the availability of credit—influences within the economic system proper. The shorter the period under consideration, the greater is the feeling of certainty that the same conditions will prevail and the smaller the risk in going ahead with the investment plans for that period. Therefore the marginal efficiency of capital based on short-term expectations is likely to be rather stable and the volume of current investment less volatile. But as businessmen look beyond what lies immediately before them, they become less and less certain about the prospective rate of profit and more and more hesitant about undertaking new investments of a long-term nature. For anything can happen in the long run, as the common saying goes.

Long-term expectations arise from such "exogenous" factors as the outbreak of war, the development of an existing war,

[11] For a further study see Keynes, *General Theory*, pp. 147–164 and 194–209; A. G. Hart, "Keynes' Analysis of Expectations and Uncertainty," in *The New Economics*, pp. 415–424; Mabel F. Timlin, *Keynesian Economics* (Univ. of Toronto Press, 1942), pp. 26–37 and 141–149.

probabilities of peace, the size and composition of population, innovations and inventions, the coming into power of certain political parties, trends of the labor movement, and political and economic policies abroad. These factors often impel businessmen to change their investment plans drastically. Hopes of profit and fears of loss are greatly accentuated by the uncertain, unpredictable nature of "exogenous" influences, coming as they do largely from outside the economic system over a period of years. Businessmen must expect all kinds of "surprises" in the long run. Obviously no one can accurately estimate the prospective rate of profit over the distant future. The marginal efficiencies of particular types of capital might be reduced to zero, if, for instance, some great innovation took place in the course of time to render particular enterprises obsolete. Who could have foreseen that the emergence of an automobile industry would wipe out all the investment opportunities associated with the "horse and buggy" enterprise?

Apart from the distinction between short-term and long-term expectations, "the outstanding fact," as Keynes puts it, about businessmen's calculation of the prospective rate of profit is that it is based on the uncertain knowledge of the future.[12] This uncertain knowledge about the future is not an epistemological generalization, but a reflection of the unplanned nature of a market economy. Volatility in investment activity is inevitable whenever and wherever investment decisions are left to the influences of "animal spirits," "wishful thinking," and other subjective reactions of a speculative nature. Fluctuations in the state of business confidence, however caused, also account for the *intensity* of business cycles. Business organization on a corporate basis (separation of ownership and management) only aggravates risk and uncertainty, and therefore exaggerates the "speculative" motive for liquidity and the instability of the propensity to invest.

[12] *General Theory*, p. 149.

CHANGES IN THE TAX STRUCTURE

The private inducement to invest may be affected also by changes in the tax structure. The downward revision of taxes on corporations, corporate income, and business property is believed to be necessary to stimulate "investment incentives." [13] We are not now concerned with whether such taxes *ought* to be reduced; rather we are interested in considering tax changes as a plausible factor in investment decisions. Taxes have many repercussions, some political, some social, and others purely economic, but we shall isolate the repercussion on the inducement to invest. It is said that the corporation income tax, for example, is detrimental to business incentive on the ground that it not only strikes immediately at profits but also increases the risk in new investment.[14] The basis for this argument is that the government shares in prospective corporate earnings but not in losses. In all cases the deflationary effect of taxes on business incentive is stressed.[15]

Take, for example, the possibility of the revision of the present corporation income tax with respect to depreciation charges. It is said that the present method (i.e., "straight-line") of calculating depreciation charges should be replaced by the principle of "accelerated depreciation." According to the "straight-line" method, taxable corporation income is large even if there are small earnings to absorb depreciation. Suppose that a corporation acquires a $1,000 asset with a useful durability of 20 years. Under the existing arrangement, the corporation is allowed to deduct from its annual earnings $50 for 20 years. But under the proposed plan based on the principle of accelerated depreciation, the corporation would be allowed to write off the entire book value of the

[13] *Cf.* J. W. Angell, *op. cit.*, pp. 273–278.
[14] *Cf.* H. R. Bowen, *The Future of the Corporation Income Tax,* Irving Trust Co., New York, April, 1946.
[15] See Committee for Economic Development, *Taxes and the Budget: A Program for Prosperity in a Free Economy* (New York, 1948).

$1,000 asset within the first few years by deducting, say, $200 annually for 5 years. This plan is believed to have the effect of encouraging more prompt replacement of capital assets (by releasing funds for replacing the obsolete equipment) and also of reducing the risk involved in the purchase of new capital assets. The general idea is that such a plan, if adopted, would permit corporations to increase depreciation rates so that the higher depreciation charges allowed would reduce taxable income during the early years of life of durable assets. Whether this plan would actually have a stimulating effect on new investment is of course a matter of conjecture. But it is one of the many possibilities aimed at stimulating investment incentive.

It is difficult in fact to isolate the effect of taxes on the inducement to invest, since other effects are also in operation. If, for instance, the increasing effect of low taxes on investment is offset by the decreasing effect of high taxes on consumption, the net result may be zero as far as aggregate income and employment are concerned. It is quite possible that the government may have to tax low-income groups more heavily for revenue reasons in order to stimulate the private inducement to invest via low business taxes. If we can overlook other effects and implications, we can probably say that low taxes tend to raise the marginal efficiency of capital on new investment. On the other hand, it is also probable that many kinds of investment are tax-inelastic. It is said, for example, that as long as the marginal tax rate (i.e., an extra amount of income paid in taxes) is less than unity, investment decisions based on profit maximization are independent of the income tax structure.[16] The most that can be said for low taxes on business is that in so far as profits after taxes serve as a satisfactory measure of anticipations, such taxes will have the effect of raising the marginal efficiency of capital and therefore of shifting the investment function upward.

[16] On this point see L. R. Klein, *op. cit.*, p. 171.

CHANGES IN WAGE RATES

Changes in money wages, however brought about, may affect the propensity to invest conceivably through their influence on (a) the state of business confidence, (b) the interest rate, and (c) net foreign balances. We have already seen that because of the interest elasticity of the liquidity function any increase in the money supply due to a general reduction of wages (i.e., a reduction in the demand for cash balances) will not lower the interest rate significantly enough to stimulate investment. Nor will a general rise in money wages (i.e., an increase in the demand for cash balances) have the effect of raising the interest rate appreciably to discourage investment. But a general reduction of money wages might lead to lower interest rates if the liquidity function were relatively inelastic due to a preponderance of the transaction and precautionary motives. Investment would be stimulated to this extent.

As for the effect of wage reductions on net foreign balances, there seems to be little doubt that domestic investment will be stimulated at least in the short run. For a general decline in money wages has the effect of lowering costs and prices and therefore of stimulating exports on the one hand and discouraging imports on the other. If a favorable balance of trade follows from the shift of domestic demand from imports to home goods as well as from increased exports—due to the lower costs and prices at home—domestic investment will be expanded. It would not be amiss to add, however, that the supposed benefit of wage reductions on domestic investment presupposes the stability of the foreign exchange market and the absence of foreign retaliatory action.

Wage changes also affect investment via their influence on the marginal efficiency of capital.[17] It is often supposed

[17] Cf. Keynes, General Theory, Chap. 19; S. E. Harris, "Keynes' Attack on Laissez Faire and Classical Economics and Wage Theory," in The New Economics, pp. 549–557; L. R. Klein, op. cit., pp. 106–110; L. Tarshis, "Changes in Real and Money Wages," Economic Journal, March, 1939.

that a "once and for all" decline in money wages may prove stimulating to investment. But such a change in money wages may prove inadequate or impracticable, since a "once and for all" decline is likely to lead in fact to a series of deflationary wage spirals. If a general rise in money wages is expected to continue, businesses are likely to make investment outlays now rather than later. Conversely, a series of downward wage spirals tend to make businesses postpone current investment until wages have hit rock bottom. In this case wage decreases reduce the marginal efficiency of capital, for the prospective rate of profit would be lower the more general the postponement of purchases of capital goods became in anticipation of further wage decreases. Thus it is by no means obvious that downward wage adjustments will necessarily increase the volume of current investment. Even if we make the favorable assumption that general wage reductions have the effect of stimulating investment incentives, we cannot be sure of the *net* result of such wage changes. For it is conceivable that the favorable effect of downward wage adjustments on the propensity to invest may be more than offset by the adverse effect of such wage changes on aggregate demand.

Our discussion of the effect of wage changes on the propensity to invest would be more meaningful if we took into account the effect of wage changes on the propensity to save. For simplicity we may construct two models, one in which wage decreases lead to an *upward* shift of the *investment* schedule and a *downward* shift of the *savings* schedule, and the other in which wage decreases lead to an upward shift of the *investment* schedule and an upward shift of the *savings* schedule. Figure 21 illustrates these two cases. The investment schedules are drawn to be relatively income-inelastic (i.e., more or less "induced"). The savings schedules are assumed to be income-elastic but less than unity (to be compatible with the requirement of stable equilibrium).

In Figure 21 (A) the wage reduction in question has shifted the investment schedule from I_1 to I_2 upward and the savings schedule downward to the right from S_1 to S_2. Before the wage reduction the two schedules intersected at E_1 to give equilibrium income Y_1, but after the wage reduction the savings-investment equilibrium occurs at E_2 to give the Y_2 level of income. If general wage cuts actually had these effects on the propensities to invest and to save, high levels of income and employment could be obtained simply by reducing wages as the classical theory supposed. But there is reason for grave skepticism, for model (B) seems to be more realistic than model (A).

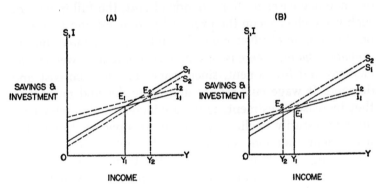

Fig. 21. Possible Effects of General Wage Reductions on the Propensities to Invest and to Save

In Figure 21 (B) we again make the favorable assumption that the wage reductions have shifted the investment function upward to the left as in (A). But this time the savings function is shown to have shifted upward also. The result is lower income Y_2, and inferentially a lower level of employment. Although the upward shift of the investment function may appear plausible, is the upward shift of the savings function a realistic assumption? The answer may be that the

consumption function falls as a result of general wage reductions. A reduction in the total wage bill would certainly
lead to a decrease in the amount of consumption expenditures, but why should the consumption function be supposed
to fall? The consumption function would fall if the general
wage cuts gave rise to a perceptible alteration in the distribution of income. The kind of general wage cuts needed
to raise the investment function could very well involve
such a change in the distribution pattern. For this reason an
upward shift of the savings function is within the bounds of
possibility.

Though there is among businesses a presumption in favor
of wage decreases on the grounds of *cost*, the full impact of
such wage changes on the propensity to invest and therefore
on the volume of investment depends on their effect on *aggregate demand*. There is no simple correlation between wage
changes and investment, since wages are at once cost and
demand. If wage cuts reduce aggregate demand more than
they increase investment, aggregate income and employment
must necessarily decline. In jargon, an upward shift of the
investment function accompanied by an upward shift of
the savings function inevitably leads to underemployment
equilibrium. Until and unless it is demonstrated that wage
reductions lead to an upward shift of the investment function
and a downward shift of the savings function, the supposedly
beneficial effect of wage reductions on investment and employment will remain doubtful. Since investment decisions
depend on many factors besides cost and demand, the net
result of wage changes is indeterminate as far as the inducement to investment is concerned.

CAPITAL ACCUMULATION

Another factor of great importance affecting the inducement to invest is capital accumulation. For the present purpose we mean by "capital accumulation" the *production* of

real physical *fixed* capital, that is, plant and equipment. This is the sense in which Keynes uses the concept of capital accumulation in his long-run analysis. He uses the plural "accumulations" to refer to the *stock* of fixed capital that has grown over time. Capital accumulation in this narrow sense may be taken as a constant in the short run, since the production of new plant and equipment in such a period is supposed to proceed at the same rate as that at which the old ones are wearing out. If, in other words, no more fixed capital is required per unit of final output, capital accumulation makes no difference to the marginal efficiency of capital and therefore to the volume of new investment. But a highly developed economy like the American economy is capable of accumulating capital (in the narrow sense) in the longer period and at full employment to such an extent that the specter of superabundant capital threatens to reduce the "scarcity-value" of capital to zero. Keynes alluded to such a possibility when he asserted that there are no "intrinsic" reasons for the dearth of capital, as classical economists supposed.[18] Available evidence seems to support the view that the capacity to accumulate capital in the United States is so great that the marginal efficiency of capital may fall even below the practical minimum rate of interest.[19] This is the famous theory, in a nutshell, of the declining tendency of the marginal efficiency of capital—a theory often considered common to Keynes and Marx.[20]

The disturbing thing about capital accumulation is that

[18] *General Theory,* p. 376.

[19] *Cf.* S. Kuznets, *National Income and Capital Formation* (New York, 1937). Kuznets' data point to a strong possibility that the capital stock may be easily doubled within a relatively short period of twenty or more years.

[20] Both Keynes and Marx see in capital accumulation "the ultimate barrier" to the development of capitalism, and in the dynamics of capitalist development certain "offsets" to the falling rate of profit. Keynes differed from Marx in regarding these offsets not as historically given but as socially desirable variables. (On this point see Joan Robinson, *An Essay on Marxian Economics,* London, 1942; S. S. Alexander, "Mr. Keynes and Mr. Marx," *Review of Economic Studies,* February, 1940; L. R. Klein, *op. cit.,* pp. 130–134.)

when the stock of capital increases in quantity or changes in composition, the marginal efficiency of capital or the expected rate of profit tends to fall faster and more than the institutionally rigid rate of interest, so that the volume of new investment must decline. Then "abundance of capital" truly interferes with "abundance of output," as Keynes considered inevitable under *laissez faire*.[21] It is therefore in the long run and in the advanced capitalistic economies that capital accumulation tends to wipe out profitable investment outlets for what people wish to save out of full-employment income. For this reason many persons have come to believe that the rate of investment should be publicly regulated, to avoid or minimize the otherwise inevitable conflict between "abundance of capital" and "abundance of output."

It is easy to show diagrammatically how capital accumulation lowers the rate of profit even below the going rate of interest, and how the lower rate of profit leads to a downward shift of the schedule of the marginal efficiencies of all possible types of capital and therefore to a decline in the volume of investment. Figure 22 is such an attempt.

In Figure 22 (A) the vertical axis measures the profit rate and the interest rate, while the horizontal axis measures the growth of the capital stock. The D curve is the investment demand schedule, which is assumed to be relatively inelastic with respect to interest. With a capital stock of OC_1, the rate of profit (the marginal efficiency of capital) is Or_1. When, however, the capital stock doubles, as measured by the horizontal length OC_2, the rate of profit is only Or_2, which is shown to be *below* the going rate of interest, r (probably around 2½ per cent). Unless the interest rate falls to the Or_2 rate, the OC_2 capital stock cannot be maintained; that is, the growth of the stock of capital must stop or else the marginal efficiency of capital will fall farther. OC is the equilibrium output of capital goods, since the interest rate and

[21] *General Theory*, pp. 219–220.

the profit rate (r) are identical, thus indicating that the marginal efficiency of capital has no tendency to change above or below the interest rate. If, however, the interest rate does not fall below Or for some institutional reasons even in the face of the doubling of the capital stock, the investment demand schedule must shift to the left and the volume of investment must decline, as shown in Figure 22 (B).

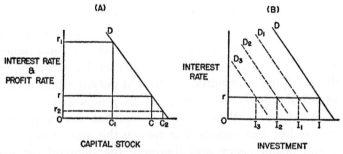

FIG. 22. CAPITAL ACCUMULATION AND THE RATE OF PROFIT

TECHNOLOGICAL DEVELOPMENTS

Technological developments of certain kinds are conducive to the propensity to invest. Historically, technological innovations and inventions gave incessant impulses to investment during the heyday of *laissez-faire* capitalism.[22] We look back nostalgically to that "extraordinary episode" of the electrical and automobile age in the United States, and wonder if such great innovations will occur to open up vast investment opportunities again. In a dynamic economy like that of the United States all kinds of innovations and inventions are taking place all the time, but the crucial question is whether these changes in technology are such as to stimulate the inducement to invest. On this question there is no agreement even among technological experts, not to men-

[22] See J. Schumpeter, *op. cit.*

tion economists. While even the recent past is no accurate guide to future technological advance, the record of inter-war innovations is none too encouraging to the inducement to invest.[23]

The kind of changes in technology that can shift upward the propensity to invest are those of a "capital-using" nature. That is to say, innovations should be such as to require *more capital per unit of output*. This is what some call a "deepening of capital." If, on the other hand, technological developments are of "capital-saving" nature, as they are believed to have been in recent years, then the inducement to invest will not be stimulated. The reason for this is simply that less capital is required per unit of output when innovations result merely in an increase in productivity without making net additions to existing equipment. A case in point is the kind of innovations that reduce the rate of depreciation and obsolescence and therefore the demand for new capital goods which would otherwise be needed to replace the old. Thus it is only those changes in technology that are "capital-using" in character that are relevant to the inducement to invest. Needless to say, the impact of technological developments on investment is felt more in the longer than the shorter period. More will be said about this question in connection with secular investment.

POPULATION GROWTH

Changes in the size and composition of population also affect in the long run the inducement to invest.[24] A growing population is a presumption in favor of expanding investment opportunities, since it calls forth a "widening of capital," i.e., more capital *pari passu* with increasing output. A sta-

[23] *Cf.* Temporary National Economic Committee, Monograph No. 22, Washington, 1941.

[24] *Cf.* Keynes, "Some Economic Consequences of a Declining Population," *Eugenics Review*, April, 1937; Hansen, "Economic Progress and Declining Population Growth," *American Economic Review*, March, 1939; W. B. Reddaway, *The Economics of a Declining Population* (London, George Allen & Unwin Ltd., 1939).

tionary or declining population, on the other hand, signifies a decline in the demand for housing, furniture, and many "capital-using" durable consumer goods. The marginal efficiency of capital will fall if the stock of capital accumulates relative to a stationary population. There is evidence that the rate of population growth is declining, at least in the industrially advanced Western countries. The marginal efficiencies of particular types of capital are affected by the changing *composition* of population. Thus a marked decline in the number of children and a similar increase in the number of the aged will affect the long-term investment plans of those enterprises producing specific goods and services designed for these age groups.

The significance of the effect of a declining population on investment is that the demand for capital goods cannot be maintained at a high level continuously, unless a decline in consumer demand incident to a declining population is more than offset by a higher standard of living, a fall in the interest rate, or some other favorable changes. A higher standard of living implies an increase in the demand for luxuries, but since the demand for luxuries is typically elastic, the demand for new investment cannot depend on this source for a continuous, steady stimulus. Nor can the interest rate be counted on for offsetting a decline in the rate of profit, especially in those countries in which the interest rate has already fallen to what is regarded as an irreducible minimum. Nor yet can technological developments be expected to be always of a "capital-using" nature. In these circumstances therefore a declining population is bound to depress the inducement to invest.

P

12

The Multiplier and Acceleration Theories

~~~~~~

THE MULTIPLIER and acceleration theories are indispensable tools in business-cycle analysis. They are helpful not only for an understanding of the dynamic process of income formation, but also for policy making with respect to the stabilization of aggregate demand. The multiplier theory explains the cumulative effects of changes in investment on income via their effects on consumption expenditures; while the acceleration theory has to do with the expanded demand for capital goods derived from net changes in the demand for consumer goods. These theories together help to clarify much of the mystery surrounding the processes of the expansion and contraction of income.

The Multiplier Theory

The idea of the multiplier originated as an explanation of the favorable effects of public investment on aggregate employment,[1] but it has become part of the general theory of

---

[1] For the original formulation of the multiplier concept, see R. F. Kahn, "The Relation of Home Investment and Unemployment," *Economic Journal,* XLI, 1931.

the dynamic process of income propagation due to any injection of purchasing power coming from outside current income. More specifically, the concept of the multiplier is derived from the concept of the marginal propensity to consume and refers to the effects of changes in capital outlays on aggregate income through their effects on the demand for consumer goods.[2]

CONCEPT OF THE MULTIPLIER

Since the multiplier principle has to do with the effects of changes in investment on consumption expenditures, it is no surprise that the multiplier should be related to the marginal propensity to consume or to its inverse, the marginal propensity to save. The value of the multiplier is in fact determined by the marginal propensity to consume. The multiplier is *the ratio of the change in income to the change in investment.* This ratio will be higher the higher the marginal propensity to consume. If the marginal propensity to consume is equal to one-half, the value of the multiplier is 2. If it is equal to two-thirds, the multiplier is 3. And so on. The general formula for the multiplier is $K = \dfrac{1}{1 - dC/dY}$, where K stands for the multiplier and $1 - dC/dY$ for the marginal propensity to save. In other words, the multiplier is nothing else but the reciprocal of the marginal propensity to save. Thus we can write:

[2] For theoretical discussions of the multiplier principle and its application, see Keynes, *General Theory*, pp. 113–131; Hansen, *Fiscal Policy and Business Cycles*, pp. 265–274; P. A. Samuelson, "Interactions between the Multiplier Analysis and the Principle of Acceleration," *Review of Economic Statistics*, May, 1939; J. M. Clark, "An Appraisal of the Workability of Compensatory Devices," *American Economic Review*, March, 1939; R. M. Goodwin, "The Multiplier," in *The New Economics*, pp. 482–499; A. Smithies, "Keynesian Economics: The Propensity to Consume and the Multiplier," *American Economic Review*, May, 1948; F. Machlup, "Period Analysis and Multiplier Theory," *Quarterly Journal of Economics*, November, 1939; G. Haberler, "Mr. Keynes' Theory of the 'Multiplier': A Methodological Criticism," in *Readings in Business Cycle Theory* (Blakiston, Philadelphia, 1944), pp. 193–202.

Change in total income $= \dfrac{1}{1 - dC/dY} \times$ change in investment

If we know the value of the marginal propensity to consume, it is not difficult to estimate by how much an increase (or decrease) in aggregate investment will increase (or decrease) aggregate income. Although a precise knowledge of the actual value of the marginal propensity to consume is required for accurate forecasting, we may assume various marginal propensities to consume for theoretical purposes.[3] Table II gives the results (logical) of hypothetical marginal propensities to consume and the corresponding multipliers in terms of the initial and ultimate increases in income.

TABLE II. THE MULTIPLIER, CONSUMPTION, AND INCOME

Marginal Propensity to Consume	Multiplier	Investment (Multiplicand)	Induced Consumption	Initial Increase in Income	Final Increase in Income
0	1 (unity)	$10.0 b.	$0	$10.0 b.	$10.0 b.
½, or 50%	2	$10.0 b.	$5.0 b.	$15.0 b.	$20.0 b.
⅔, or 65%	3	$10.0 b.	$6.5 b.	$16.5 b.	$30.0 b.
¾, or 75%	4	$10.0 b.	$7.5 b.	$17.5 b.	$40.0 b.
1, or 100%	infinity	$10.0 b.	$10.0 b.	$20.0 b.	infinity

When the marginal propensity to consume is zero, the multiplier is unity and the induced consumption expenditures are zero. In this case, since nothing is spent out of the extra income from the initial investment, the change in investment has a zero multiplier effect on aggregate income; income increases only by the amount of the change in investment, i.e., $10 billion. Such a case is conceivable when the recipients of the $10 billion pay their bank debts or let the income "leak out" some other way instead of spending most or part

[3] The actual value of the multiplier in the United States has been estimated to be 2.7 for 1921–25, 2.2 for 1926–30, 3.1 for 1931–33, 2.6 for 1934–37, and 1.7 for 1938–41. (See L. Tarshis, *The Elements of Economics*, Houghton Mifflin, Boston, 1947, p. 407.)

of it. If the marginal propensity to consume is equal to one-half, that is, if the income recipients generally spend half of the extra income earned, the multiplier is 2, the induced consumption expenditures $5 billion, the initial increase in aggregate income $15 billion ($10 + 5$), and the final income, over time, is $20 billion ($10 \times 2$). The multiplier of 3 is perhaps the most realistic figure for the United States in normal times. If so, every dollar considered as a new injection of purchasing power will increase income three times that initial outlay through the process of respending on a two-thirds basis. In the above example the $10 billion increase in investment leads to the $30 billion increase in aggregate income.

If the marginal propensity to consume is assumed to be 1, or 100 per cent, the result may prove "explosive." For the initial dollar invested will emerge and re-emerge as $1 of consumption expenditures, and result in an infinite increase in income, given sufficient time. Such a situation is quite conceivable during a hyperinflation, since income recipients try to spend money as soon as they receive it and since consumption is increased by as much as income increases. But fortunately this explosive situation is an exception to the general rule. In the actual world, people ordinarily spend somewhat less than the increment in income, so that the final increase in income due to a sequence of respendings is finite.

PROCESS OF INCOME PROPAGATION

Thus far we have neglected time lags by assuming instantaneous adjustments. We must now investigate how the initial investment leads, *over time*, to an increase in income many times that initial outlay. For this purpose the step-by-step or "sequence analysis" is useful; but this method of analysis is not to be taken for a description of the actual change in income resulting from the change in investment. The sequence analysis is simply an analytical device to show a "motion picture" of income propagation under certain assumptions.

The first thing to recognize is the fact that it takes time for the impact of the initial investment to make itself felt throughout the whole economy. Suppose that $10 billion is newly injected into the spending stream. Those producing investment goods receive incomes equal to $10 billion, and spend most of those incomes on consumption, the amount of additional spending depending on their marginal propensity to consume. Suppose that all income recipients have the same marginal propensity to consume, say, one-half, or 50 per cent. In the first "round" $5 billion is spent by those producing the $10 billion investment goods, as they receive an equivalent amount of income in the forms of wages, interest, rents, profits, etc. Now the consumption-goods industries get the $5 billion to pay out again in the forms of wages, interest, etc., to those producing the consumer goods which were bought in the first round. In other words, the $5 billion spent on consumption in the first round has re-emerged as an equal amount of income. The recipients of the $5 billion income will by hypothesis in turn spend half of that income on consumption, namely, $2.5 billion.

The transition from one round to another may well take two or three months. This interval of time between consumption respendings is the *multiplier* or *propagation period*. As we move from one round to another, the initial expenditures give rise to a dwindling series of successive additions to income, as long as the marginal propensity to consume is between zero and one. With a marginal propensity to consume of one-half, the initial $10 billion investment will give rise to an income of $5 billion in the first round, $2.5 billion in the second, $1.2 billion in the third, and so on, until the final increase in aggregate income amounts to $20 billion. Table III shows the process of income propagation in its simplest form.

TABLE III. PROCESS OF INCOME PROPAGATION
$$(dC/dY = \tfrac{1}{2})$$

Initial Investment	Successive Consumption Respendings					Final Increase in Income
	0	1	2	3	4	
$10.0 b.	+$0	+$5.0 b.	+$2.5 b.	+$1.2 b.	+$0.6 b.	=$19.3 b

Table III shows that after the fourth round the $10 billion investment has increased aggregate income by nearly $20 billion, given a marginal propensity to consume of one-half. If each round consists of 2 months and 4 rounds are involved, it will take about 8 months for a capital outlay of $10 billion to increase income by nearly $20 billion. If the multiplier is 3, the average respending period 2 months, and 5 rounds are involved, the needed adjustment period will be about 10 months. It goes without saying that in order to maintain the new level of income, i.e., $19.3 billion plus income from the previous period, investment must be increased continuously at the rate of $10 billion. Otherwise income will return to the old level.

The multiplier effects of investment on income can also be shown diagrammatically, that is, in terms of equilibrium adjustment. Figure 23 illustrates such an adjustment. The C curve is drawn according to our assumed marginal propensity to consume of one-half (a curve with slope of 0.5 at all levels of income). The investment schedule (the C + I curve) is merely superimposed on the C curve. The old equilibrium level of income is Y_1. We now make the assumption that the propensity to invest rises for one reason or another so that an amount equal to the vertical distance between the C + I and C' + I' curves can be invested continuously. The C' + I' curve represents this new investment schedule. This new consumption-plus-investment curve intersects the 45° line at E_2 to give new income Y_2, which is greater than the old income by Y_1Y_2, which is in turn twice the difference between the C + I and C' +I' curves. Thus, given a marginal propensity to consume of one-half and therefore the multiplier of 2, the increase in investment (the vertical distance between the C + I and C' +I' curves) leads to the increase in income from Y_1 to Y_2, or twice the initial outlay.

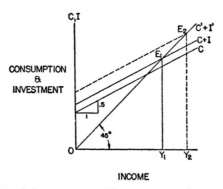

FIG. 23. MULTIPLIER EFFECT OF INVESTMENT
ON INCOME

THE MULTIPLIER AND PUBLIC INVESTMENT

Although the multiplier refers to any type of investment considered as an injection of new purchasing power, it applies to *loan-financed* public investment with unequaled force. In the nature of the case public investment is "autonomous" of the profit-maximization principle. This does not, of course, mean that public investment is never self-liquidating, but it does mean that public investment is free from the restricting influence and vagaries of the profit motive. Since a steady and adequate "injection" is necessary for the multiplier to have positive and sustained effects on income and employment during depression periods, considerations other than profit maximization are essential to the unimpeded operation of the multiplier.

There is no reason why public investment should not be wealth- as well as employment-creating, but in bad years the community may consider the latter aspect of public investment more important. It is often feared that public investment may have such adverse "tertiary" effects on private investment as to offset the beneficial repercussions of the multiplier on private consumption. A large and growing public debt, unbalanced budgets, and wasteful, foolish, or extravagant spending attributed to public investment, whether right or wrong, may nevertheless impair business confidence and therefore lower the marginal efficiency of capital. It is difficult to determine the net "leverage" effects of loan-financed public investment, because of the complex repercussions it may have on consumption and private investment. Perhaps the acceleration theory may help elucidate this point.

The amount of public investment is not only controllable, but also capable of expansion to such an extent as to make the multiplier operate with greater force than would otherwise be possible. The government is in a better position to inject new purchasing power into those channels which will have the greatest multiplier effect on income and employment, namely, those strategic spots of the income stream where the marginal propensity to consume is high (or the marginal propensity to save is low). For if a large portion of public investment became income of people with low marginal propensities to consume, the multiplier effect of such public investment on income and employment would be correspondingly smaller. By directing new purchasing power into the proper channels the government can prevent it from "leaking out" of the spending stream. Furthermore, the government is capable of *timing* public investment in such a way as to let the multiplier principle have its full and free play. The following considerations might be useful for the counter-cyclical timing of public investment in general and of public works in particular.

Countercyclical public investment, if it takes the form of

public works, should be postponed until the economy is out of inflationary full-employment conditions. Otherwise the multiplier effect of public investment on effective demand would be dissipated in higher prices. At less than full employment, on the other hand, an increase in investment has the effect of increasing output and employment not only in the capital-goods industries but also in the consumption-goods industries. How much less than full employment should the economy have before starting fruitful public investment projects? Experience suggests that antidepression public works projects should be started as soon as employment has declined below an objectively defined minimum that is unavoidable for frictional reasons. In conservative terms this might mean that compensatory public investment should be started as soon as the unemployment figure has reached 3 million, or 5 per cent of a labor force of 60 million, with 2 million or so taken as an adequate allowance for "frictional unemployment." Humanitarian considerations and political pressures may in some countries force the government to launch antidepression public investment on the basis of a smaller minimum figure, that is, less than 5 per cent of a labor force.

Most business cycle students seem agreed on the desirability of concentrating a vigorous program of public investment projects during the first years of a recession, on the ground that such timing would avert a serious depression or protracted mass unemployment that might result from the reverse operation of the multiplier, as shown in the following section. The thing to avoid in this regard is a "wait-and-see" attitude that would only enhance the danger of "missing the boat" while debating whether the recession is serious enough to warrant a bold program of public investment; or that at best might lead to an anemic "shot-in-the-arm" on the way to chronic unemployment. To get around such dangers, it may be wise to maintain a permanent "shelf of public-works projects" ready to be set into motion whenever needed, or to set up an "extraordinary budget" to take care of counter-cyclical public expenditures without depending on a regular budget geared to long-range welfare and developmental public projects. These, however, are matters for technical research. These and other considerations concerning the proper timing of public investment should be studied for the maximum effect of employment-multiplier operations.

Thus, though there is no difference in principle between the multiplier effect of public investment and that of private investment, there may be significant differences between them in fact. It is a matter for empirical research, however, to discover what the multiplier for any particular public investment project is in a given period. Whatever the multiplier may happen to be, public investment policy will be guided increasingly by the multiplier as well as by accelera-tion analysis. For it is in the field of public investment that the multiplier analysis serves as a most fruitful and effective guide to policy. This does not, of course, preclude the applica-tion of the multiplier principle to other fields in which in-vestment is instrumental in injecting new purchasing power into the spending stream.

REVERSE OPERATION OF THE MULTIPLIER

The multiplier operates backward or forward, depending on the direction of the initial change in investment. If, for example, investment *decreases* by $10 billion, those engaged in the production of consumer goods will have that much less income than before. With a marginal propensity to con-sume of one-half and a multiplier of 2, consumption expendi-tures would keep declining on a 50 per cent basis in each round until aggregate income decreased by $20 billion. Thus the initial reduction in investment precipitates the reverse operation of the multiplier. With a marginal propensity to consume of four-fifths, or 80 per cent, the ultimate decline of income would be $50 billion. Thus the higher the marginal propensity to consume, the greater the value of the multiplier and the greater also the cumulative decline of income. In other words, a community with a high propensity to save is hurt less by the reverse operation of the multiplier than one with a low propensity to save. The effects of the decrease in investment on income in these two cases are shown in Figure 24.

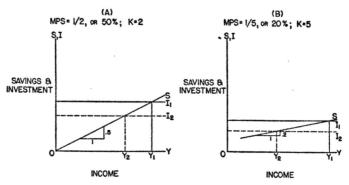

FIG. 24. EFFECTS OF THE DECREASE IN IN-
VESTMENT ON INCOME, WITH DIFFERENT
MARGINAL PROPENSITIES TO SAVE

In both (A) and (B) the investment schedules are drawn to be horizontal straight to indicate the autonomous nature of investment. In (A) the savings curve slopes upward in such a way as to indicate a marginal propensity to save of one-half, and in (B) it is flatter to designate a marginal propensity to save of one-fifth. In both cases the decline in investment is assumed to be the same, as measured by the distance between the two investment curves, I_1 and I_2. The equilibrium level of income given by the intersection of the savings curve and the new (dotted) investment curve is much lower down *from the initial level* in (B) than in (A). With a marginal propensity to consume of four-fifths, or

80 per cent (inverse of the marginal propensity to save of one-fifth), the ultimate decline of income would be $50 billion. On the other hand, with a marginal propensity to consume of one-half, or 50 per cent (inverse of the marginal propensity to save of one-half), the ultimate decline of income would be $20 billion. The $50 billion decline in income corresponds to the horizontal length Y_1Y_2 in (B), and the $20 billion decline in income is reflected in the distance between Y_1 and Y_2 in (A). These declines in income are on the assumption that the initial decline in investment is $10 billion in both cases, as measured by the distance between the old, solid investment curve and the new, dotted investment curve. The horizontal length Y_1Y_2 in (A) will be found to be exactly twice the vertical distance between the two investment curves. This conforms to our previous explanation that, with a marginal propensity to consume of one-half and therefore with the multiplier of 2, a $10 billion investment outlay leads to an ultimate income of $20 billion. Similarly, the horizontal length Y_1Y_2 in (B) equals five times the vertical distance between the two investment curves. This is so because the marginal propensity to consume involved is equal to four-fifths and the multiplier involved is 5.

Thus we can say that the initial decline in investment will have a more devastating effect on the levels of income and employment when the marginal propensity to consume is high (or when the marginal propensity to save is low) than when the marginal propensity to consume is low (or when the marginal propensity to save is high). It follows that the cumulative decline of income is likely to be greater, with a given decline in investment, when and where the marginal propensity to consume exhibits an upward trend than when and where it tends to fall. If, for instance, people in the United States should form the habit of spending more out of a given increment of income, say, four-fifths instead of three-fifths, the value of the multiplier would rise from

2.5 ($= 1/.4$) to 5 ($= 1/.2$), and thus would subject the economy to a more shocking decline of income whenever aggregate investment declined.

But there is one redeeming feature in all this dismal picture, namely, the fact that the marginal propensity to consume is normally less than unity. The fact that people ordinarily spend less than the full amount of extra income means in this case that they do not reduce consumption expenditures as much as the decrement of income. Thus the marginal propensity to consume of less than 1 serves as a floor against the downward cumulative decline of income when investment declines. If it were not for this fact, the reverse operation of the multiplier principle would imply a complete collapse of economic activity.

LEAKAGES

We have seen that the magnitude of the multiplier is determined by the marginal propensity to consume or by its inverse, the marginal propensity to save. The marginal propensity to save in this context refers to all kinds of "leakages" which influence the multiplier effect via their influence on consumption. In general, the higher the marginal propensity to save, the smaller the value of the multiplier, and the smaller also the cumulative effect of the initial change in investment on income. Thus a marginal propensity to save of one-fifth gives a multiplier of 5, and a marginal propensity to save of two-fifths gives a multiplier of 2.5, according to the formula $K = \dfrac{1}{1 - dC/dY}$. In other words, the greater the amount of "leakage" the smaller the beneficial effect of the initial investment on income. In our example, one dollar of new investment will give rise to "leakages" of 20 cents if the marginal propensity to save is one-fifth, and 40 cents if it is two-fifths.

It does not much matter to theory what forms "leakages" assume, but it may be useful for policy to know how the initial investment may "leak out" of the income stream. The increase in investment may be prevented from having a significant multiplier effect on consumption, and therefore on income, if that increase leaks out in each respending round through (a) debt cancellation, (b) accumulation of idle cash balances, (c) net imports, and (d) price inflation. Each of these forms requires elucidation in some detail.

If recipients of the initial investment outlays use a part of the income earned to pay debts, say, to the banks, instead of spending it for further production or consumption, as the case may be, that part of the income disappears from the income stream. It is of course arguable that the banks may use the repayments by relending them. If the banks relend the repayments to businesses, we must consider the subsequent effects as belonging in acceleration analysis, not in multiplier analysis. If they relend them to consumers, then the cancelled debts reappear as income to someone else. If the banks fail to find willing borrowers, the repayments must remain idle and stay out of the income stream. The same holds true if the debts in question are due to individuals.

If people happen to have a strong liquidity-preference to satisfy the transaction, precautionary, and speculative motives, they will certainly try to accumulate idle cash balances in the form of inactive checking accounts or inactive savings accounts. To the extent that they do so, a part of the initial expenditure will leak out of the spending stream. Unless events reverse the liquidity-preference, consumption respending must suffer the consequences.

In an open system there is always the possibility that a part of the initial expenditure may leak out of the domestic income stream to the benefit of foreign exporters or creditors. If import outlays fail to return as an increased demand for exports in the short run, the resulting net imports must be considered as a "leakage." Unless a "leakage" incident to net imports is offset by the multiplier effect of expanding exports, which net imports make possible in the longer period, we must reconcile ourselves to a temporary "leakage" on this score.

Finally, the multiplier effect of the increase in investment on income and employment may be somewhat offset by price inflation, if and when the increase in question takes place at or near full employment. For at full employment an increase in investment has the effect of reducing rather than increasing the demand for consumer goods and therefore the demand for employment in the consumption-goods industries. This is so because an increase in the demand for investment in conditions of full employment involves a diversion of labor from the consumption-goods industries to the investment-goods industries, and therefore the bidding up of the factor as well as commodity prices in the former industries to the detriment of the demand for consumer goods. In these circumstances an increase in money income is partly dissipated in higher prices instead of increasing output and employment.

To the extent that any of these "leakages" can be stopped, the initial increase in investment will have greater multiplier effects on the levels of income and employment. In fine, the marginal propensity to consume must be sufficiently high to let the multiplier principle have its full effect on income.

FOREIGN–TRADE MULTIPLIER

Income due to exports is in the nature of an "injection," and has the same multiplier effects on domestic income and employment as any other injections of new purchasing power.[4] Foreign expenditures on our exports become income of our exporters, which in turn becomes income of those producing export goods, which in turn becomes income of those producing consumer goods in the first round, and so on down the line, the final increase in income depending on the value of the

---

[4] Cf. F. Machlup, *International Trade and National Income Multiplier* (Blakiston, Philadelphia, 1943); J. J. Polak, "The Foreign Trade Multiplier," *American Economic Review*, December, 1947; S. Enke and V. Salera, *International Economics* (Prentice–Hall, New York, 1947).

multiplier. It is convenient to derive the value of the foreign-trade multiplier from the domestic marginal propensities to save and to import which constitute a "leakage." Suppose that the combined value of the marginal propensities to save and to import is one-fifth, or 20 per cent. Then we get the multiplier of 5, according to the formula $K = \dfrac{1}{1 - dC/dY}$, or $\dfrac{1}{0.20}$. Suppose that our exports increase by $1 billion. Then the final increase in domestic income will be $5 billion, given the multiplier of 5. If the marginal propensities to save and to import are equal to one-third, or 30 per cent, the multiplier will be 3 and the final increase in domestic income $3 billion. Thus the higher the domestic propensities to save and to import, the smaller the multiplier effects of the increase in exports on domestic income. We can write the general formula thus:

Change in domestic income $= \dfrac{1}{(1 - dC/dY) + (dM/dY)} \times$ change in exports

where $(1 - dC/dY)$ stands for the domestic marginal propensity to save and (dM/dY) for the marginal propensity to import

Increased foreign expenditures for our exports are not likely to affect significantly in the short period our marginal propensity to save, but they may raise in the longer period our marginal propensity to import. If so, each successive respending of initial foreign expenditures will be correspondingly smaller. It is of course possible that foreign prices or foreign exchange rates may be such as to prevent our marginal propensity to import from rising appreciably with rising domestic income incident to increased exports. But import expenditures (M), though not necessarily their ratio to income (M/Y), will rise with rising domestic income, given the propensity to import $(M(Y))$. Another thing we must note is the possibility that the beneficial multiplier effects of increased exports on domestic income and employment may be somewhat offset by a decrease in domestic aggregate demand

Q

due to a shift of demand toward imports induced by the initial increase in domestic income. In the absence of import restrictions our propensity to import is likely to rise as domestic money incomes increase. The main difficulty with the foreign-trade multiplier lies in the fact that the very process of income expansion, due to an initial increase in exports, involves a higher propensity to import (in the schedule sense) and therefore a possible "leakage" from the domestic income stream.

If it were not for these and other adverse repercussions (e.g., repercussions on foreign marginal propensities to save and to import and therefore on export expenditures), the foreign-trade multiplier would have as beneficial effects on domestic demand as would the income multiplier of domestic investment. The benefits of the foreign-trade multiplier should never be so exaggerated as to inspire "beggar-my-neighbor" trade policies for achieving export surpluses. But the foreign-trade multiplier is a useful tool for analysis of the effects of a net change in the balance of payments on domestic income and employment. This point will receive further attention in Part III.

The Acceleration Theory

We have thus far assumed that an "injection" of new purchasing power via investment channels induces only consumption expenditures. This assumption must now be dropped, to allow for the possibility that the induced consumption may in turn induce further investment. It has long been recognized that the demand for some capital goods is "derived" from the demand for consumer goods. It is also a matter of common observation that capital-goods industries are subject to volatile fluctuations. The acceleration theory is an attempt to explain the nature of the instability and vulnerability of capital-goods industries in general and the exaggerated effects of change in consumption expenditures upon investment in particular. For this reason the acceleration theory is a helpful tool for business cycle analysis.[5]

ACCELERATION COEFFICIENT

Just as the change in consumption expenditure is functionally related to the change in investment via the multiplier, so is the change in investment outlays related to the change in the rate of consumption expenditures via the acceleration coefficient. This latter function measures the "leverage" effect of an increment (or decrement) in the rate of consumption on the volume of investment. The acceleration coefficient is *the ratio between a net change in consumption outlays and the induced investment.* It is a factor of proportionality to measure the functional relation between two marginal magnitudes, between a net change in consumption outlays (or national income representing final sales) and a net change in investment outlays. For example, if we find that a net increase in the rate of consumption expenditures equal to $5 billion leads to a net increase in investment outlays equal to $10 billion, we shall conclude that the acceleration coefficient involved is 2. If a $5 billion increase in consumption gives rise to a $5 billion increase in investment, the acceleration coefficient must be 1 or unity. There is always some such relation, for technical and other reasons, between the production of final goods and services and that of capital goods.

As far as fixed capital is concerned, the acceleration coefficient may be regarded as a technological factor of proportionality between the production of consumer goods and that

[5] For further discussion see Hansen, *Fiscal Policy and Business Cycles*, pp. 274–283; P. Samuelson, *op. cit.;* J. M. Clark, "Business Acceleration and the Law of Demand: A Technical Factor in Economic Cycles," *Journal of Political Economy*, March, 1917; S. Kuznets, "Relations between Capital Goods and Finished Products in the Business Cycle," in *Economic Essays in Honour of Wesley Clair Mitchell* (Columbia Univ. Press, 1935); J. Tinbergen, "Statistical Evidence of the Acceleration Principle," *Economica*, May, 1938; R. Frisch, "The Inter-relation between Capital Production and Consumer Taking," *Journal of Political Economy*, October, 1931.

of capital goods, including additions to the existing stock of equipment as well as replacement. As for inventories, the acceleration coefficient may be considered as a customary ratio between the rate of sales and orders for additional holdings. In either case it is a matter for empirical investigation to discover just what the correct value of the acceleration coefficient is for the economy as a whole. For the purposes of analysis we can merely assume certain values.

The acceleration coefficient may be zero, if the production of consumer goods involves little or no capital equipment or if the production of consumer goods calls for no "deepening" of capital. The former is conceivable where "roundabout" capitalistic production is unknown or rare, as in a predominantly handicraft economy or in an undeveloped area. The latter case is possible when technological innovations are typically of a "capital-saving" nature, as is believed to be the recent trend in the advanced economies. If, on the other hand, a great deal of new capital is required per unit of output, then the acceleration coefficient must be positive and perhaps greater than unity. The acceleration coefficient may be positive but less than unity, if the durability structure is such as to render replacement demand insignificant.

The acceleration coefficient would be far less than unity, if not zero, and have little or no "accelerated" effect on investment if (a) there is excess equipment, (b) the new demand for consumer goods is expected not to last, and (c) the demand for capital depends largely on "exogenous" factors. Less than full employment of equipment enables additional output to be produced without producing additional capital goods. More bread, for example, can be produced with the existing breadmaking equipment. In this case, not even the normal replacement demand, let alone additions to the existing stock of breadmaking capital, is affected—a case of zero gross investment. This is the typical case during the initial period of the recovery phase of the business cycle, in which there is much idle equipment or capacity for potential full utilization. Moreover, if the demand for consumer goods is expected not to last long, that is, if the producers as a whole suspect that an increase in the rate of consumption expenditures is only temporary, the producers will hesitate to commit themselves to long-term capital outlays involving either replacement or net additions to the existing stock of capital. The anemic recovery during the New Deal period is attributed partly to this kind of entrepreneurial reaction to the stimulus to consumption expenditures given by "deficit spending." As has already been shown, "autonomous" investment does not depend on consumption expenditures. Some types of capital outlays may go on regardless or in spite of the level of income, that is, for welfare, political, and other noneconomic reasons. Similarly, some types of investment may not be forthcoming even though consumption sales will warrant capital expansion. Long-term investment in the field of public utilities, for example, is often carried on well in advance of an expected change in the rate of consumption. There are always some "exogenous" factors in operation to affect investment decisions independently of the level of income or of the economic system proper. Assuming that none of the above conditions exists, we can say that the greater the value of the acceleration coefficient, the greater the induced investment. We shall now turn to the operation of the acceleration principle under some assumptions.

OPERATION OF THE ACCELERATION PRINCIPLE

The acceleration principle may be illustrated by a simple example. Suppose that 100 of capital equipment is needed to maintain the constant flow of 1,000 consumer goods. Suppose, further, that 100 of capital equipment wear out in 10 years and therefore require 10 replacements every year. Finally, suppose that the acceleration coefficient is 1. This means that a 10 per cent increase in consumption, say, from 1,000 to 1,100, calls for a 10 per cent increase in the production of capital goods, in addition to the normal replacement, or 20 of new capital goods, 10 for replacement and 10 additions to the existing stock. Table IV summarizes the results of the operation of the acceleration principle under those assumptions regarding capital equipment, consumption, and the acceleration coefficient.

TABLE IV. ACCELERATION EFFECTS ON INVESTMENT

Period	Change in consumption	Capital equipment	Gross Investment			Percentage change in gross investment
			Additions	Replacements	Total	
0	1,000	100	0	10	10	——
1	1,100	110	10	10	20	+100%
2	1,100	110	0	10	10	—50%

Table IV shows that a 10 per cent increase in the rate of consumption, from 1,000 to 1,100, calls for a 10 per cent increase in the production of new capital goods, in addition to the normal replacements of 10, making a total gross investment of 20, according to the assumed acceleration coefficient of 1. The remarkable thing to note is the 100 per cent increase in gross investment resulting from the initial 10 per cent increase in the rate of consumption. This, however, is not the end of the story. If it were, the acceleration principle might be considered quite one-sided. But note what happens when the rate of consumption remains constant. A zero increase or a drop of zero per cent in consumption (i.e., no change from 1,100) gives rise to a 50 per cent fall in gross investment, and this on the favorable assumption that the replacement demand remains intact. If the entrepreneurs decided that it would not pay to produce new capital goods even for replacement, gross investment would fall 100 per cent, with disastrous effects on aggregate employment. This is the familiar case of capital consumption or "disinvestment"—a process of letting the existing stock of capital wear out or existing inventories deplete without replacement.[6] Thus, for example, during the Great Depression the workers who would otherwise have been employed in the production of replacement capital goods found themselves either employed to produce consumers' goods or completely unemployed.

Thus the so-called "derived" demand for capital goods is a highly precarious sort of demand, for it depends on the change in the rate of consumption which in turn depends on highly unpredictable, capricious investment in the short period, at any rate. As long as the basic conditions favorable to investment (i.e., technological and structural conditions) prevail, the acceleration principle serves as an inducement to investment. If activity in the capital-goods industries is to be stabilized, that is, freed from the adverse influence of change in the consumption demand, investment will probably have to be geared more and more to "autonomous" considerations (i.e., other than the volume of current sales, the level of income, and the like—in other words, welfare or political considerations). For those types of investment which depend primarily on technical inventions, innovation, population growth, wars, and such other "exogenous" factors are just as precarious as those depending on the current rate of consumption.

LEVERAGE EFFECTS OF ACCELERATION AND MULTIPLIER
INTERACTIONS

In order to measure the *total* effect of initial expenditure on national income we must combine the acceleration and multiplier analyses. First let us consider a single dose of initial expenditure. The results of such a single "injection" via the multiplier and acceleration coefficients are shown in Figure 25.

It goes without saying that if the total increase in national

[6] In the longer period it is possible that an increase in the replacement demand may compensate for a drop in the demand for gross capital formation.

income is to be maintained, $100 must be injected continuously. Moreover, the result would be very different if we assumed the values of the multiplier and the acceleration coefficient to be other than in the diagram below (i.e., other than 2 and 1). This greatly simplified model nevertheless gives us a crude idea of the leverage effects of initial expenditure on national income.

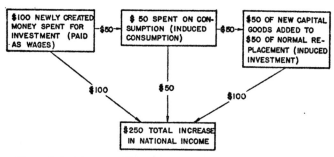

FIG. 25. TOTAL EFFECT OF SINGLE INJECTION
ON INCOME
Assumptions: 1) The marginal propensity to consume of ½
2) The acceleration coefficient of 1

Let us now introduce the time lags, to see the process of income propagation via the multiplier and acceleration principles. We shall assume the marginal propensity to consume to be one-half and the acceleration coefficient to be 2. Table V shows this process. We obtain the third column, induced consumption, by dividing each total increase in national income by 2, according to our assumption of the marginal propensity to consume of one-half. We obtain the fourth column, induced investment, by multiplying a successive net change in consumption by 2, according to our assumed acceleration coefficient of 2. The fifth column, total increase in national income, represents the sum of initial expenditures, induced consumption, and induced investment in each multiplier period. It is interesting to observe that after the third multiplier period the total increase in consumption is too small to induce a favorable change in investment. A total injection of $50 for the five periods considered has given rise to a total increase in national income equal to $146.75, or nearly 3 times the initial expenditures of $50. Here again the results would be very different, if we assumed the marginal propensity to consume and the acceleration coefficient to be other than in this model.

TABLE V. MULTIPLIER AND ACCELERATION EFFECTS ON
INCOME (SEQUENCE ANALYSIS)

(1)	(2)	(3)	(4)	(5)
Multiplier period	Initial outlay	Induced consumption	Induced investment	Total increase in Nat'l income
1	$10	$0	$0	$10
2	10	5	10	25
3	10	12.50	15	37.50
4	10	18.50	12	40.50
5	10	20.25	3.50	33.75

Assumptions: 1) The marginal propensity to consume of $\frac{1}{2}$
2) The acceleration coefficient of 2

The acceleration principle before Keynes was based on Say's law and therefore explained the dependence of the demand for capital goods on the demand for consumer goods without showing the stabilizing influence of the marginal propensity to consume of less than 1. Thus an increase in the rate of consumption would give rise to a proportional increase in investment, and a decrease in the rate of consumption would lead to a similar decline in investment—a cumulative expansion or contraction without limit (that is, unless credit policy or price-cost rigidities reversed the process). The pre-Keynesian theory of the acceleration factor therefore gave an exaggerated picture of instability. But with the introduction of the concept of the consumption function of less than unity, the long-sought-for "limit to the fluctuations short of zero" was at last discovered. As was explained earlier, it is now clear that the marginal propensity to consume of less than unity provides the key to the question, why does the cumulative process come to a stop before a complete collapse or before full employment? Thus, as one writer puts it, the Keynesian notion of a consumption function has revealed "the true significance of the acceleration principle" for business cycle analysis.[7] For, as J. M. Clark observed even before the appearance of Keynes' *General Theory*, "the challenging problem is not why there are cyclical fluctuations but why there is a limit to the fluctuations short of zero, on the one side, or the full capacity of existing productive equipment, on the other."[8] Clark's own answer was essentially the same as Keynes', namely, the marginal propensity to consume of less than unity, though not in this Keynesian terminology.

It is therefore in conjunction with the multiplier analysis based on the concept of the marginal propensity to consume that the acceleration principle serves as a useful tool for business cycle analysis and as a helpful guide to stabilization policy.[9]

[7] See L. A. Metzler, "Keynes and the Theory of Business Cycles," in *The New Economics*, pp. 436–449.

[8] *Cf.* J. M. Clark, "Capital Production and Consumer Taking: a Further Word," *Journal of Political Economy*, October, 1932, p. 693.

[9] Harrod, Hansen, and Samuelson are credited for having brought the modern significance of the acceleration principle to the fore. Keynes himself did not include the acceleration principle in his formal analysis.

13

Secular Underemployment Equilibrium

SINCE THE Great Depression of the 1930's there has been a growing feeling in Britain and the United States that the advanced economies of these nations may be confronted with not only cyclical mass unemployment but also with chronic depression or "secular stagnation." [1] This feeling has found formal expression in the thesis that mature capitalistic economies are incapable, under *laissez faire,* of continuously maintaining such a high level of employment as is warranted by technical conditions. The policy counterpart of this thesis has been evidenced by the perceptible shift of emphasis from monetary policy to fiscal policy in general and from "pump

[1] For positive views see Keynes, *General Theory,* pp. 217–221, 272–284, 307–308, 347–348, 353; "Some Economic Consequences of A Declining Population," "National Self–Sufficiency," and "The United States and the Keynes Plan," *New Republic,* July 29, 1940; Hansen, *Full Recovery or Stagnation?* (Norton, New York, 1938), Chap. 19; "Economic Progress and Declining Population Growth," "Some Notes on Terborgh's 'The Bogey of Economic Maturity'," *Review of Economic Statistics,* February, 1946; A. Sweezy, "Declining Investment Opportunity," in *The New Economics,* pp. 425–435; B. Higgins, "To Save or Not to Save," *Canadian Journal of Economics and Political Science,* February, 1948; L. R. Klein, "Review of Swanson and Schmidt," *Journal of Political Economy,* April, 1947.

priming" to "compensatory spending" in particular. The stagnation thesis has been dismissed as a "bogey" by some and discounted as an overstatement by others.[2] Without entering this controversy we shall content ourselves with treating the hypothesis of "secular stagnation" as a part of formal analysis, so that we may be in a better position to minimize or avoid the danger of such devastating chronic mass unemployment as we experienced between 1929 and 1939.

Statement of the Problem

The theoretical possibility of secular underemployment equilibrium arises from (a) the propensity to invest, which is not high enough to offset *full-employment* savings, and (b) the propensity to save (or its inverse, the propensity to consume), which remains more or less stable relative to the unstable propensity to invest. Given these propensities to invest and to save, the economy may be in equilibrium far short of full employment for an indefinite period of time. This theoretical possibility of secular underemployment equilibrium is illustrated in Figure 26 below.

Beginning with the position of equilibrium at full employment, we can see that the investment schedule, which is superimposed on the consumption schedule, is just high enough to offset full-employment savings (as measured by the vertical distance between the C curve and the C + I curve at the Y_0 level of income). In other words, the economy finds itself in the position of full-employment equilibrium because it is will-

[2] For negative or critical views see J. H. Williams, "Deficit Spending," *American Economic Review*, February, 1941; J. M. Clark, "An Appraisal of the Workability of Compensatory Devices," *American Economic Review*, March, 1939; J. W. Angell, *Investment and Business Cycles*, Chap. 13; W. Fellner, *Monetary Policies and Full Employment*, Chap. 3; G. Terborgh, *The Bogey of Economic Maturity* (Machinery and Allied Product Institute, Chicago, 1945); W. I. King, "Are We Suffering from Economic Maturity?" *Journal of Political Economy*, October, 1939; E. W. Swanson and E. P. Schmidt, *A Critique of Recent Doctrines on the Mature Economy, Oversavings, and Deficit Spending* (McGraw–Hill, New York, 1946).

ing and able to invest at the same rate as that at which it is disposed to save out of full-employment income. If, for example, the full-employment savings amount to $40 billion a year (in terms of the value of current dollars), the economy must keep on investing at the rate of $40 billion annually to remain in the position of full-employment equilibrium. But suppose that investment opportunities are not so inexhaustible as to warrant investing at the continuous rate of $40 billion. The propensity to invest must then inevitably fall, the degree

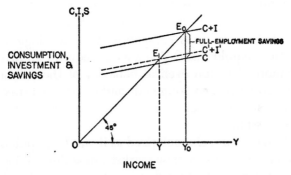

FIG. 26. SECULAR UNDEREMPLOYMENT
EQUILIBRIUM

of the decline depending on the remaining profitable investment opportunities. It may fall as low as shown in Figure 26, that is, the dotted C' + I' curve which is just above the C curve. In terms of our example, this new rate of investment could be around $7 billion at all possible levels of income, leaving an oversaving gap of $33 billion annually.

With the favorable assumption that the consumption function does not fall even in the face of the downward shifting investment function, the C' + I' curve intersects the 45° line to give the Y level of income, which is considerably below the full-employment level of income Y_o. If "sixty million jobs" are associated with full-employment income Y_o, the fall in the level of income from Y_0 to Y (the horizontal length Y_0Y) can

surely cost the economy a loss of several million jobs. Therefore, in order for the economy to remain in the position of
full-employment equilibrium, either the propensity to invest
must be kept stable at a level high enough to offset the absolute
amount of full-employment savings, or the propensity to save
must be made to fall to raise the propensity to consume to a
level high enough to reduce those savings to be offset by investment. Otherwise the economy will be confronted with
the inevitable result of chronic mass unemployment. The
practical question is: are there any reasons for supposing that
the propensity to invest and the propensity to save would not
actually behave in ways compatible with the logic of full-
employment equilibrium? The answer requires an investigation of more than the cyclical behavior of those functions.
Here the abstract theorizing ends and a historical survey begins. Let us take a look at history in the light of the foregoing discussion.

The 19th century, characterized as it was by population increases, new inventions, new markets, new discoveries of resources, and wars, bestowed upon the advanced industrial
countries almost unlimited investment opportunities for all
the savings the economies of those countries were capable of.
Under those circumstances, "to save and to invest," to borrow
Keynes' eloquent phrase, became "at once the duty and the
delight of a large class," and "the morals, the politics, the
literature, and the religion of the age joined in a grand con-
spiracy for the promotion of savings." [3] There was then a
tendency for investment to outrun savings—so much so that
economists took the scarcity of capital for granted. Beginning with the turn of the century, the rate of investment in
the advanced countries began to slow down. Yet mentality
lagged behind reality; economists, let alone laymen, were still
inclined to the notion that unlimited investment opportunities

[3] *Monetary Reform*, pp. 9–10.

were ahead.[4] As late as 1936 Keynes found it necessary to remind his fellow economists that "nothing short of the exuberance of the greatest age of the inducement to investment" could make one "lose sight of the theoretical possibility of its insufficiency." [5]

Secular underemployment is believed to arise from certain historical tendencies peculiar to the advanced capitalistic economies. In the course of their development these economies reach a stage in which, for technological, institutional, psychological, and other reasons, they find themselves with a chronic excess of savings over investment. The problem of "secular stagnation," in other words, is supposed to originate in the constant tendency of savings to outrun investment. When the rate of savings outstrips the rate of technical application of those savings, the marginal efficiency of capital tends, under *laissez faire*, to fall to zero; and capitalism may break down with it. Such is believed to be the dismal destiny of modern private capitalism. This belief, right or wrong, is the basic reason why many, including Keynes and Hansen, the two principal proponents of "the stagnation thesis," are strongly inclined to rely upon the government as "the balancing factor" for averting the complete breakdown of capitalism or, more positively, for preserving and developing the best features of the capitalistic system. Keynes and Hansen differ, in this connection, from Marx in believing that capitalism need not "dig its own graveyard," as Marx would have it. This difference of opinions is due to the fact that Keynes and Hansen, unlike Marx, place boundless confidence in the workability of monetary-fiscal compensatory devices for economic stabilization. This confidence is shared by many economists who may disagree with Keynes and Hansen on the causes of "secular stagnation."

---

[4] Malthus, Sismondi, and Marx were outstanding exceptions.
[5] *General Theory*, p. 353.

To avoid confusion, it is necessary at this juncture to distinguish between the Hobsonian version of "oversaving" and the Keynesian theory of secular underinvestment. It is true that both Hobson and Keynes stress the danger of oversaving, but their concepts of oversaving are not the same. As was explained earlier, Hobson and other underconsumptionist theorists regard "oversaving" as synonymous with "overinvestment." They are concerned with "oversaving" because they tacitly assume that excessive savings actually flow into proportional investment to produce more capital goods than can be profitably used to maintain the flow of final goods and services. With them "underconsumption" is at once the cause and the effect of "oversaving." It is a cause because it gives rise to excessive savings, and an effect because it brings about excessive investment *relative to the consuming power of the community.* The crucial flaw in the Hobsonian theory of "oversaving" is found, as Keynes has shown, in its underlying assumption that excessive savings are actually invested, whereas the real problem of modern capitalism is *how to make full-employment savings flow into investment.*[6] With Keynes, on the other hand, oversaving is a fundamental tendency for the propensity to save to be stronger in conditions of full employment than the inducement to invest. Thus viewed, oversaving reduces itself to *underinvestment.* In other words, it is believed to be a characteristic of modern capitalism to exhibit "a constant tendency to oversave" *relative to investment opportunities.*

Factors of Secular Oversaving

There are two ways of approaching the problem of secular underemployment: namely, (a) from the standpoint of "a constant tendency to oversave," and (b) from that of declining investment opportunities. It is useful to analyze sep-

[6] *General Theory,* pp. 367–368.

arately the principal factors of secular oversaving and those of secular underinvestment. Such an analysis, however, is not to be taken as a substitute for empirical research; it is meant to be merely a broad outline of those institutional and psychological factors that are believed to be responsible for chronic mass unemployment and prolonged depression. We shall begin with the factors of secular oversaving.

PARADOX OF THRIFT

Keynes has pointed out that "the primary evil" of thrift lies in the fact that the propensity to save in conditions of full employment produces more savings than can be easily offset by investment to maintain the full-employment level of income. But for this fact, thrift would be rightly considered to be an unmitigated virtue. The high propensity to save characteristic of a wealthy capitalistic economy would be no cause for alarm if the propensity to invest was equally high at all times. But suppose that the community persists not only in saving a portion of current income but also in wanting to save more at all possible levels of income (i.e., an upward shift of the entire savings schedule) even though investment opportunities are zero. Suppose, further, that the investment function is inelastic with respect to income and does not rise as it should. This income-inelastic investment function, it will be recalled, is plausible when the private inducement to invest is influenced largely by "autonomous" factors outside the economic system proper. Under those circumstances "the paradox of thrift" would assert itself, as shown in Figure 27.

Should the community raise its propensity to save from S_1 to S_2 over a period of time, the result (the propensity to invest remaining equal) would be not only a diminution of aggregate income, from Y_1 to Y_2, but also a decline in savings, from Y_1E_1 to Y_2E_2. Thus the community's attempt to save more than

R

is being invested actually results in decreased savings, if investment opportunities remain unchanged. This is the famous "paradox."

The result would be just as dismal if, instead, the propensity to save declined over time and the propensity to invest declined even more, as is believed to have been actually the case in the United States for the past few decades (except the war period).[7] The decline in the statistical propensity to save (rise in the actual consumption function) is attributed to such

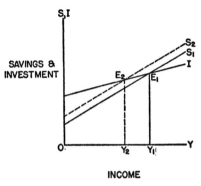

FIG. 27. PARADOX OF THRIFT

factors as changes in consumer tastes, the growth of the advertising industry, urbanization, educational opportunities, progressive taxation, and more and more extensive social security. Yet we had a prolonged period of oversavings relative to investment during the 1930's because the propensity to invest declined much faster than the propensity to save. The result of equilibrium adjustment of the declining propensity to save and the even more rapidly declining propensity to invest is shown in Figure 28.

In Figure 28 the intersection of the S_1 and I_1 curves gives the Y_1 level of income. If the investment function falls more rapidly than the savings function, there will be oversavings

[7] L. R. Klein, *The Keynesian Revolution*, p. 175.

relative to investment and therefore lower levels of income and employment. Thus the intersection of the dotted S_2 and I_2 curves gives the Y_2 level of income. This is exactly what happened in the United States during the 1930's. The Y_1 level of income would have been maintained if people had realized the "evil" of thrift at less than full employment and lowered the savings function to S_3 (with I_2 remaining equal), or if investment opportunities had been such as to lower the investment function only to I_3 (given the S_2 schedule).

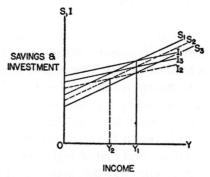

FIG. 28. OVERSAVINGS RELATIVE TO
INVESTMENT

INEQUALITY IN INCOME DISTRIBUTION

Another factor contributing to secular oversaving is an unequal distribution of income. Quite apart from the desirability of income redistribution, the fact remains that the greater the degree of inequality in the distribution of income, the greater is the amount of aggregate income saved. This may be illustrated by a simple example. Suppose that there are two income brackets, which together receive a total income of $10,000 annually. Suppose, further, that each bracket receives the same amount as the other, or $5,000 each. This is of course an extreme case of 100 per cent equality in income distribution. Now the marginal propensity to save, under those circumstances, is likely to be identical for both brackets. Let us assume that both brackets have the marginal propensity to save of 0.2, or 20 per cent. Accordingly, each group will save $1,000 out of $5,000, making a total of $2,000. If, on the other hand, one bracket receives $9,000 and the other $1,000, the resulting amount of income saved may be quite different from what it is when income is equally divided. For the high-income bracket is likely to have a higher marginal propensity to save than the low-income bracket. Suppose that the former bracket has the marginal propensity to save of 0.4, or 40 per cent, and the latter's marginal propensity to save is zero (i.e., the marginal propensity to consume equal to unity). The $9,000 bracket will, accordingly, save $3,600 and the $1,000 bracket none, making a total of $3,600. This sum of savings is larger than the previous savings by $1,600 (= $3,600 — $2,000).

Thus the amount of savings is greater when income distribution is unequal than when it is equal. This is based on the fact that there is a gap between the marginal propensity to save of lower income groups and that of higher income groups. If the industrial countries move farther in the direction of greater equality in income distribution, as they seem to be moving for both welfare and stability reasons, the gap between the two extreme marginal propensities to save will be narrowed and the amount of aggregate savings out of full-employment income will become smaller relative to available investment opportunities.

The question of income redistribution properly belongs to policy discussions and will be dealt with later. The distribution of income being what it is, most industrial countries have "a constant tendency to oversave" relative to profitable investment outlets.[8] Although the existing system of income distribution is being modified by gradual changes in the tax structure, the social security program, public welfare expenditures,

[8] For an interesting comment on this question see M. Kalecki, "The Maintenance of Full Employment after the Transition Period: etc.," *American Economic Review*, June, 1947.

the interest structure, etc., it is unlikely that the marginal propensities to save of various income groups will alter drastically
enough to make a significant difference to the amount of income saved in any foreseeable future. For the saving habits
are too deeply ingrained in the minds of higher-income and
middle-income groups to change right along with institutional
changes.

CORPORATE AND OTHER INSTITUTIONAL SAVINGS

The corporate form of business organization has been on
the increase, and the amount of corporate savings with it.
In good years a large part of aggregate gross savings is made
up of corporate savings. Corporate savings consist of depreciation reserves for replacement purposes and retained earnings
for expansion purposes, and are reflected in the amount of undistributed profits of corporations. In the relatively pros-
perous years 1923–29 corporate savings in the United States
averaged $7.9 billion annually.[9] In the postwar "boom" year
1947 corporations retained five-eighths of their profits after
taxes, that is, at the annual average rate of $9.6 billion, or twice
the amount saved by corporations in the war years and four
times that of 1929.[10] These data indicate a rather stable corporate policy of plowing back a fairly constant portion of
corporate income into surpluses or reserves for *potential* re-
investment. A continuous flow of corporate savings at full
employment presents an additional problem of finding or providing profitable outlets to maintain that full employment.

The rapid growth of private life insurance is another important contributing factor in our "constant tendency to oversave." In the absence of a comprehensive program of social security people find it necessary or desirable to save for "the
rainy day," and insurance companies and other private savings
institutions are instrumental in accumulating such personal

[9] *Cf.* Hansen, *Fiscal Policy and Business Cycles* (London, George Allen &
Unwin Ltd.,) p. 241.
[10] The President's *Economic Report,* January, 1948.

savings. In 1947, for example, the amount of income saved via insurance firms, mutual savings banks, savings and loan associations, and savings departments of commercial banks in the United States amounted to nearly $7 billion, or 62 per cent of personal savings.[11] It is possible that the amount of income saved through insurance companies and other similar institutions may decrease in the future, if, for instance, the coverage of the existing social security programs is enlarged. In the meantime institutional savings present yet another problem of finding appropriate savings outlets. One writer has made the observations that "the record of nearly fifty years seems to show that the savings institutions have not been passive in the investment process," and that "the operations of the intermediary institutions have played a substantial role in our failure to maintain that stable rate of investment which would equal the amount which people want to save at high employment." [12]

It may be that in the future the insurance and other savings institutions will reduce their liquidity-preference, that is, decrease the proportion of cash held to funds received, if their portfolios consist increasingly of high-grade securities (including not only conventional bonds but also equities) that can be readily converted into cash. In the meantime institutional savings will continue to strengthen our tendency to oversave relative to available investment opportunities.

Factors of Secular Underinvestment

EXISTING CAPITAL ACCUMULATIONS

A constant tendency to oversave would be no problem for wealthy industrial countries were it not for a chronic deficiency of private investment. To complete our analysis of the secular-underemployment problem we must now turn to

[11] *Cf.* H. Jones, "The Optimum Rate of Investment, the Savings Institutions, and the Banks," *American Economic Review*, May, 1948, p. 324.
[12] H. Jones, *op. cit.*, p. 330.

an examination of the principal factors of underinvestment. Keynes made the observations that the propensity to save had historically exhibited a chronic tendency to be stronger than the propensity to invest, and that the extent of existing accumulations might largely account for the weakness of the propensity to invest.[13] Thus he considered the extent of existing capital accumulations as the crucial factor in the secular-underinvestment tendency of advanced industrial countries. Technological progress facilitates the growth of capital, which in turn facilitates increased productivity to satisfy the requirements of a rising standard of consumption. For this reason classical economists favored maximum savings for maximum capital formation. What they failed to realize, however, is that the accumulation of capital might reach a point where the marginal efficiency of capital was too low to induce further capital formation. Here lies what Kalecki calls "the tragedy of investment." [14]

As the wealth and capital equipment of the community increase, the amount of income people wish to save at high employment tends to increase, while on the other hand the growth of capital tends to lower the marginal efficiency of capital. This declining tendency of the marginal efficiency of capital is due to the fact that every addition to capital equipment competes with the existing stock of capital to lower the prospective rate of return on new investment. Now the declining tendency of the marginal efficiency of capital would not upset the secular savings-investment equilibrium at the full-employment level of income, if the interest rate could be lowered to the level of the fallen marginal efficiency of capital or if the propensity to save could be drastically reduced. Our analysis of the liquidity function and the consumption function indicates that neither of these alternatives is easy. Barring public investment, the falling marginal ef-

---

[13] *General Theory*, pp. 347–348.
[14] Cf. *Essays in the Theory of Economic Fluctuations*, pp. 148–149.

ficiency of capital seems difficult to avoid, unless the production of new capital goods is supposed to be proceeding at the same rate as that at which the old ones are wearing out. This latter supposition would be realistic in the short run or in stationary society, but would hardly hold valid for the long run and in dynamic society. If, then, "the show must go on," as it must in dynamic society, increasing capital may wipe out the scarcity-value of capital sooner than we imagine. Thus every investment considered as an addition to the existing stock of capital lowers the marginal efficiency of capital and so reduces new investment, even though every investment as expenditure is the main source of prosperity.

UNCERTAIN TECHNOLOGICAL ADVANCE

Thoughtful students of secular economic trends have all emphasized the important role which technological developments play in capital formation. It has been observed that the 19th century was favored by such technological developments, population growth, and territorial expansion as to bring about both "deepening of capital" and "widening of capital." Schumpeter attributes the last long period of prosperity (1897–1920) to the emergence of the electrical, chemical, and automotive industries, which were all of a capital-using nature.[15] Since then innovations may have been less capital-using in effect. The transition from a handicraft economy to a "roundabout" capitalistic economy necessarily involved the increasing use of capital per unit of output, but the further development of the capitalistic method of production involved technical perfections along capital-saving lines. This tendency was reinforced by the growth of monopolies, since monopolies made greater use of large-scale equipment in order to economize capital outlay, labor, fuel, etc., per unit of capacity or of output.[16]

[15] J. A. Schumpeter, *op. cit.*
[16] Temporary National Economic Committee, *op. cit.*, p. 197.

In recent years technological developments have been characterized by capital-saving inventions.[17] For example, the development of safeguards against breakdowns and excessive wear and tear has greatly diminished the continued demand for capital goods incident to rapid obsolescence. In many instances such equipment has been installed as to increase productivity by merely speeding up the operation of existing equipment. The Temporary National Economic Committee, after an extensive investigation of the technological aspect of the American economy, concludes that "new industries can develop and greatly increase their production by using capital-saving innovations," that "the production of new and different products can often be effected merely by minor changes in existing techniques," and finally that "the emergence of new industries does not necessarily create a great demand for capital goods with a resultant expansion of activity throughout the entire economic system."[18]

On the other hand, some writers are much more optimistic with respect to technological developments. One writer, for example, insists on the crucial importance of "the total flow of technological development" in expanding investment opportunities.[19] In other words, if we have enough innovations, some capital-saving and some capital-using in character, we are supposed to have an abundance of investment opportunities, so that we may safely dismiss the stagnation thesis as a mere "bogey." By contrast, Schumpeter and Hansen emphasize the capricious, discontinuous, and unpredictable nature of modern innovation, let alone an increasing tendency toward capital-saving inventions. When one stops to ponder over the implications of atomic power for future investment opportunities, one may be impressed with the great possibility of *capital-saving* innovation. The application of atomic power would,

[17] *Ibid.*, p. 179.
[18] *Ibid.*, p. 181.
[19] G. Terborgh, *op. cit.*

for instance, probably minimize the need for the construction of capital-using hydroelectric works. Though recent technological developments along capital-saving lines do not warrant the prediction that capital-using industries will not spring up in the future, it is obvious that a program of full employment cannot be based on so uncertain a prospect as favorable changes in technology.

A DECLINING POPULATION

When it is realized that population growth accounts for nearly half the total demand for new capital in the 19th century,[20] the economic significance of a declining population is not difficult to understand. And statistical evidence shows that in many of the countries industrially advanced the natural rate of population increase (apart from migration) is now negligible. The United States is no exception to the rule. Sociologists have long recognized that there is a high correlation between the rising standard of living and the declining rate of population growth. If the drive to maintain a high standard of living at the expense of the size of families continues, it will only aggravate the problem of a chronic deficiency of investment.

A declining population may affect in several ways the inducement to invest. The most obvious way in which such a population discourages new investment is of course its decreasing effect on the sheer number of consumers. A smaller or stationary number of consumers is a presumption against expanding markets, and therefore against "widening of capital" associated with expanding final output. It is therefore no accident that some of the highly developed economies with declining populations look hopefully upon the undeveloped areas with "teeming millions" for additional markets. To what extent a drop in the number of consuming units is responsible for a chronic deficiency of private investment is difficult to

[20] Keynes, "Some Economic Consequences of a Declining Population."

assess even in the light of statistical evidence (e.g., American experience in the 1930's), but it is fairly certain that such a drop can cause a sharp downward trend in the demand for particular capital goods.

The single most important field of real investment so affected is residential construction. This is most disturbing because private residential construction makes up a quantitatively significant part of gross investment in all advanced economies. To make the matter worse, a declining population also diminishes the demand for such associated outlays as furniture, domestic appliances, roads, schools, railways, and public utilities. For these reasons a retardation of population growth may reduce the aggregate demand for fixed capital and consumer durables only to add to the instability of the durable-goods industries. This implies that the demand for new investment must come from other sources, that is, other than from a growing number of consuming units.

It is sometimes argued that investment can be stimulated by producing more of the better things which a stationary population may want.[21] It is true that as the proportion of children in the population becomes smaller, the demand for necessities decreases and the demand for luxury or semiluxury goods increases, but the demand for the latter is typically so elastic as to make it highly precarious to depend on that source for a steady stimulus to investment. The argument is plausible to the extent that luxury or semiluxury goods become necessities, as they tend to do in the American economy, and so render the demand for them relatively inelastic. Apart from the debatable elasticity of demand for better things, it is possible, in modern technical conditions, to produce more of them to satisfy a rising standard of living without increasing capital per unit of final output. A more promising line of argument is that a rising standard of living may raise the entire historical consumption function, or (which is the same) lower

[21] See, e.g., J. H. Williams, "Deficit Spending."

the savings function, as is believed to have happened in the American economy in the past several decades. This implies that there need not be expanding investment opportunities relative to *individual* savings. The difficulty is that while the amount of disposable income saved by individuals may be smaller at all levels of income, as implicit in a rising consumption function, the amount saved by *corporations* at all levels of income seems to be on the increase. This weakens the argument that investment may be stimulated by a rising standard of living even with a stationary population, or that the derived demand for capital may be sustained by a possible fall in the propensity to save on the part of individuals and particularly on the part of the aged sector of the stationary population.

Some writers have advanced the view that secular stagnation is due, among other things, to the limiting effect of a stationary population on the labor supply.[22] They reason that the unplanned rate of the growth of capital will call for more labor per unit of output than is available or can profitably be used to continue the production of final goods and services indefinitely. Thus "sooner or later . . . the point is reached where all the available labour is absorbed in production," and "current production cannot be increased much further." [23] This shortage of labor is regarded as "ultimately responsible" for "temporary exhaustion of investment opportunities." It is concluded from this that the rate of the growth of capital must be so regulated as to be compatible with a stationary population. J. M. Clark expresses a similar idea when he says that "while money income might increase without limit, physical product is more restricted; and investment demand depends on physical product." [24] He does not tell us what physical limitations he has in mind, but it may not be amiss to say

[22] Cf. N. Kaldor, "Stability and Full Employment," *Economic Journal,* December, 1938; also A. Sweezy, *op. cit.*

[23] Kaldor, *op. cit.*

[24] Cf. *American Economic Review* (Book Reviews section), March, 1949, p. 505.

that Clark, no less than Kaldor, is trying to stress the importance of such "exogenous" factors as population growth, technological change, and other nonmonetary variables for long-run analysis. And the shortage of labor implicit in a declining population may well be as significant a variable as the technical difficulty of substitution between capital and labor in the production function.

The same conclusion regarding the need for the regulation of the growth of capital is reached by Hansen, Kalecki, Harrod, and others, on the basis of population considerations, though somewhat differently from the labor shortage argument.[25] Here the main idea is that the cyclical objective of maximizing investment in fixed capital for full employment should not be allowed to come in conflict with the secular objective of maintaining that rate of capital growth which is compatible with a stationary population and technical progress. Spelled out, this idea means that an advanced economy is confronted with the danger of stagnation, because, on the one hand, its propensity to save is so high as to call for a high rate of capital growth, and because, on the other hand, the growth of capital justified by such a propensity to save tends to be greater than is warranted by population trends and technical advance. More concretely, a declining population tends to limit the production of capital goods in the aggregate (less widening of capital), while technological uncertainties set a limit to the production of capital goods per unit of output (less deepening of capital), thus diminishing investment opportunities to absorb the very volume of fixed capital dictated by a high propensity to save. The implication is that the growth of capital should be so regulated as to generate full employment continuously by maintaining a proper ratio between the rate of capital growth and the rates of population growth and technical progress.

[25] Hansen, *Economic Policy and Full Employment*, Chap. 15; R. F. Harrod, *Towards a Dynamic Economics*, Lectures 2, 3, and 5; M. Kalecki, *Economics of Full Employment* (Blackwell, Oxford, 1944).

LIMITED INVESTMENT AREAS

How much the discovery of new territory and resources accounted for "the exuberance of the greatest age of the inducement to investment" is difficult to say, but it is generally recognized that there is no easy substitute for "free land." In so far as free international trade serves to make up for the absence of "the frontier," aggregate home investment need not decline as much as it would in a closed economy. Yet in view of increasing trends toward state trading, "bulk purchasing," and other forms of controlled trade, it is unlikely that "free trade" in the classical sense will be extensive enough to be a substitute for "the frontier." Moreover, with the increasing industrialization of undeveloped areas, coupled with rising political and economic nationalism in all those areas, it will not be easy for the advanced industrial countries to find either profitable investment outlets or new sources of cheap raw materials outside their national borders. Nor can we count on the continuous and timely discovery of new resources (e.g., minerals and forests) within the national borders for expanding investment opportunities.

Technological progress will possibly create new resources and so open up some investment opportunities, but it is clear that no technological advance can recreate "the frontier" that once upon a time accounted for a vast "widening of capital." The only hopeful outlet for the excessive savings of the wealthy industrial economies in the absence of such a frontier seems to lie in the gradual restoration of multilateral trade in general and in the promotion of multinational developmental investment particularly.[26] Private lending through the International Bank for Reconstruction and Development is doubtless a step in the right direction. Apart from this possibility, which will be dealt with in detail in Part III, the future of "widening of capital" will be considerably handicapped by limited investment areas. J. R. Hicks, in an in-

[26] For an extended discussion of foreign investment see Chapter 21.

teresting footnote, joins with Keynes and Hansen in saying that "the practical cessation of geographical discovery," coupled with a declining population and uncertain techno-logical developments, throws a pessimistic light on the future of capitalist society as a whole.[27] Yet, in a peaceful and friendly world we are entitled to hope that international trade and finance will serve as an effective substitute for "the frontiers" or past territories of imperialistic conquest, so that both the capital-rich and the capital-poor countries may no longer suffer from the consequences of oversaving and undersaving.

The foregoing discussions of the various factors affecting secular oversaving and underinvestment may be useful for the appraising of measures necessary to insure continuous full employment. Such long-run measures will be discussed along with short-run measures necessary to prevent cyclical depression.

[27] *Value and Capital,* p. 302.

14

Measures to Promote Investment

EARLIER WE considered some of the important measures called for by inflation, and called attention to the need for flexible measures to cope with both inflation and deflation. In this chapter and the next we shall concentrate on measures to minimize the danger of cyclical and chronic depressions. Certain "trend forces" are at work to change the propensities to consume, to save, and to invest, but we cannot rely upon those forces for solving the problem of periodic or chronic depression. For it takes time for those forces to make their impact felt, apart from the uncertainty in the direction of their change. Our analysis of effective demand indicates that conscious public-policy measures are required to promote the private inducement to invest, and to raise the consumption function in order to maintain full employment continuously. We shall begin with those measures designed to promote investment.

Modification of the Corporate Income Tax

Much attention has of late been directed to the discouraging effects of the corporation income tax on private investment or on "venture capital." Not a few economists and others have come out for the drastic modification, if not complete elimination, of the existing corporation income tax.[1] The argument is essentially that by taxing away a part of the corporate profits without sharing in the losses the government discourages *risk* enterprise and new investment. Therefore it has been proposed that incomes from profits should be left untaxed or taxed in such a way as not to stifle new investment. The main idea seems to be that if the government is a *de facto* part owner of corporations and enjoys a share of corporate profits in the form of taxes (in effect, dividends), it should be made to share the losses as well. Otherwise, it is argued, corporations alone risk all the losses incurred. For this reason it has been suggested that losses be permitted to be carried over from year to year so that uneven incomes may be averaged over several years.[2] Some, while accepting this suggestion in principle, consider it practically unacceptable on the ground that it entails wasteful accounting, with greater opportunities for improper manipulations, and that the carry-over of losses would relieve corporations only partly because there might be little or no profits in the subsequent years.[3]

An interesting proposal is to permit gross investment actually undertaken during the current year to be subtracted from gross corporation income to calculate taxable income,

---

[1] *Cf.* H. M. Groves, *Production, Jobs and Taxes* (McGraw–Hill, New York, 1944); K. Buters and J. Lintner, *Effects of Federal Taxes on Growing Enterprise* (Boston, 1945); H. R. Bowen, *The Future of the Corporation Income Tax;* W. Fellner, *op. cit.;* J. W. Angell, *op. cit.;* A. H. Hansen and H. S. Perloff, *State and Local Finance in the National Economy* (Norton, New York, 1944); M. Kalecki, *The Economics of Full Employment* (Oxford, 1944); R. A. Musgrave, "Federal Tax Reform," in *Public Finance and Full Employment* (Federal Reserve Postwar Economic Studies, No. 3, December, 1945); H. Simon, "Federal Tax Reform," in *Planning and Paying for Full Employment;* The Committee for Economic Development, *op. cit.;* A. P. Lerner, "An Integrated Full Employment Policy," in *Planning and Paying for Full Employment.*

[2] R. A. Musgrave suggests that the averaging provision be so formulated as to "permit the taxpayer to recompute his tax liability on an average income basis at, say, five-year intervals, and to claim refunds for the difference between aggregate taxes paid on annual incomes and revised liabilities on an average income basis." See his article, *op. cit.,* p. 34.

[3] *Cf.* A. P. Lerner, *op. cit.*

S

instead of depreciation being subtracted from gross income.[4] This proposal would have the effect of completely offsetting business losses. It would have the double advantage of encouraging current investment on the one hand and discouraging corporate savings on the other, since the retained earnings of corporations would pay no tax if invested but would pay the full tax if uninvested. Whether current investment should be abated from taxable income in whole or in part depends on the adequacy of consumption expenditures, the government's need for so much revenue, and many other considerations.

Reduction or elimination of corporation income taxes is typically anticyclical in effect. Even here some economists have expressed considerable skepticism over the supposed stimulating effects of modified business taxes on investment. It has been argued, for example, that a reduction in the tax rate from 40 per cent to 10 per cent would not alter an entrepreneur's investment decisions, and that the profit-maximizing decisions of business firms are independent of tax rates as long as the marginal tax rate is always less than unity. But a zero rate would be something else. In the long run taxation of uninvested retained earnings to discourage corporate savings may turn out to be more important than reduction or removal of corporation income taxes to stimulate investment.[5] The former type of tax reform would minimize the chronic tendency of capital to go on "strike," whereas the latter would be self-defeating if reduction or removal of corporation income taxes necessitated such increases in other taxes as to lower the propensity to consume more than the propensity to invest increased.

Apart from specific tax reforms to stimulate investment, the *tax* approach to investment as compared with the classical

---

[4] M. Kalecki is the main advocate of this proposal. The proposed principle of "accelerated depreciation" has already been touched upon and will not therefore be repeated here.

[5] *Cf.* L. R. Klein, *The Keynesian Revolution*, pp. 171–172.

interest approach is a reflection of the failure of automatic forces to equilibrate savings and investment except at less than full employment. And experience has shown that the manipulation of tax rates is a more powerful anticyclical weapon than that of interest rates. One writer has suggested that the community might prefer a combination of low private investment and higher consumption to one of higher investment and lower consumption, and that such a preference would require removal of regressive taxes rather than reduction of corporation income taxes.[6] The reason offered for such a preference is that greater equality in income distribution may be deemed more desirable than social progress associated with capital formation. A more cogent argument against "higher investment" would be to show the depressing effects of capital accumulations on the marginal efficiency of capital, as Keynes, Kalecki, and others have done. In the shorter period the encouragement of private investment via the manipulation of business-tax rates seems wise, in view of the fact that the inducement to invest is far more unstable than the propensity to consume, and income from risky investments far more volatile than consumer income.

"Pump Priming"

The stimulating effects of tax reductions on private business outlay may not raise the level of aggregate spending adequately, if public expenditures remain unchanged or do not increase as well. The kind of public spending which is associated with a recovery program is known as "pump priming," which presupposes that private investment is periodically deficient and therefore needs to be stimulated by public investment. This type of public spending is stimulating to private investment in two respects, i.e., both as a method of financing and as a method of spending.

---

[6] O. H. Brownlee, "The CED on Federal Tax Reform," *Journal of Political Economy,* April, 1948.

During a period of depression the banks and the general public tend to accumulate idle cash balances rather than assume the risk of investment. If the government borrows from banks and individuals with an excess of cash which they would not otherwise spend themselves, such borrowing provides an outlet for idle cash balances (i.e., investments in gilt-edged government securities). Moreover, by borrowing from the banking system the government enables bank assets and deposits to expand and so create "new money" to be spent by the economic system. Thus the very method of financing "pump priming" is conducive to recovery. "Pump priming" as a method of financing not only facilitates investments by institutional savers but also supplements monetary policy by stimulating credit expansion and general business recovery.[7]

"Pump priming" stimulates private investment mainly through its magnifying effects on income via the multiplier principle. Once consumption expenditures are enlarged by the initial public outlays, the rest is taken care of by the operation of the acceleration principle, provided that excess capacity and other offsetting conditions do not exist. The sequence of events leading to recovery is "pump priming," increased consumption, increased induced investment, and increased total spending. Actually the process of expansion is not as simple or as smooth as all that. The "tertiary" effect of public investment ("pump-priming" effect of government outlays on private investment) during the 1930's was rather disappointing. The usual reasons offered are that the net increase in public expenditures (after allowing for offsetting moves by state and local governments) was insignificant, that business did not expect the increased consumption outlays to last, and that a general antibusiness attitude, labor relations, foreign economic policies, tax measures, and other de-

---

[7] On this point see J. H. Williams, "Deficit Spending," *op. cit.*

velopments did not favor private investment.[8] There is, more-over, some reason to believe that the confusion among the stabilization and other aspects (e.g., revenue and reform) of public finance prevented the adoption of a bold and consistent program of "pump priming" during the 1930's.

But there is no reason why "pump priming" in the future should not be made more consistent and effective in stimulating private investment, especially in the light of the lessons of the 1930's. Our analysis of the multiplier and acceleration principles indicates that unless induced private spending (new investment and consumption outlays by those whose anticipations are changed by public investment) is positive and large, "pump priming" will have no significant "tertiary" effects. But the main reason that "pump priming" has lost much of its charm is the realization that we are confronted not merely with cyclical disturbances but also with the secular tendency of private investment to be deficient, however stimulated. Nevertheless, "pump priming" will remain an important anticyclical weapon as long as central bank policy remains less effective in stimulating credit expansion, and therefore general activity, than in arresting credit expansion.

"Compensatory Spending"

Along with secular structural changes in the advanced economies there has occurred a shift of emphasis from the traditional business cycle analysis to the new emphasis on the *levels* of income and employment, and a parallel change in policy from monetary policy and "pump priming" to "compensatory" fiscal policy. Business cycle policy no longer consists of "eliminating" the causes of cyclical disturbances so as to render government intervention unnecessary, but rather

---

[8] *Cf.* G. Colm and F. Lehmann, "Public Spending and Recovery in the United States," *Social Research*, May, 1936; also A. Smithies, "American Economy in the Thirties," *American Economic Review*, May, 1946.

of letting public investment fill the inevitable cyclical and secular gaps created by a deficiency of private spending.[9] Thus "compensatory" public spending is based on the assumption that private capitalism, left to itself, is no longer capable of maintaining aggregate spending at a level compatible with full employment either in the short run or in the long run. On the basis of his analysis of persistent tendencies toward underemployment equilibrium, Keynes stressed the need for public investment as a "balancing factor."[10] This he believed to be a *sine qua non* of the continuation of the capitalist system in a new dynamic and stable form.

Hansen and others have emphasized the need for bold, long-range programs of public investment for stabilization as well as welfare reasons.[11] One writer envisages increasing public investment in all democracies for the following reasons.[12] First, the public interest requires government ownership and operation of public utilities to an increasing extent. Second, private enterprise based on the self-liquidating or profit-maximization principle is unequal to the task of undertaking such nationally important projects as the TVA. Third, public authorities can partly provide improved public health, education, and other social amenities which technical progress makes possible but which cannot be wholly provided by private enterprise. These reasons, when added to the overall requirement of long-run economic stability, present a formidable argument for public investment on a large and continuous scale. These long-range objectives are also reflected in American public policy.[13] Thus "compensatory

[9] *Cf.* B. Higgins, "Keynesian Economics and Public Investment Policy," in *The New Economics*, p. 477.

[10] *General Theory*, p. 220 and pp. 319–320.

[11] *Cf.* Hansen, *Economic Policy and Full Employment;* League of Nations, *Economic Stability in the Post–War World* (Geneva, 1945); International Labor Office, *Public Investment and Full Employment* (Montreal, 1946).

[12] D. B. Copland, "Public Policy—The Doctrine of Full Employment," in *The New Economics*, p. 216.

[13] See the President's *Economic Report, op. cit.*

spending" is an integral part of a general policy of guaranteeing full employment (Britain, etc.) or of guiding the national
economy along the lines of maximum output, employment,
and purchasing power (U.S.).

There are some implications of "compensatory spending"
which cast some doubt on the feasibility of large-scale, continuous public investment even as a balancing factor. The
first implication brought out by some is that "compensatory
spending" tends to *supplant* monetary policy, whereas "pump
priming" *supplements* the weakness of central bank policy.[14]
It is feared that a large and growing public debt incident to
"compensatory spending" will render the traditional monetary controls (variations in the interest rate and the money
supply) ineffective as "instruments of control of economic
fluctuations." A large and growing public debt has the effect
of increasing excess reserves of banks for potential excessive
credit expansion on the one hand and of reducing interest
rates on the other. Now, large excess reserves of banks make
these banks independent of central bank credit controls, and
this in turn renders anti-inflation monetary policy considerably
ineffective. This criticism would be valid if the economy were
subject to more inflations than depressions.

As for lower interest rates, although public investment is
undoubtedly facilitated by low interest *cost* (i.e., interest on
long-term government bonds), some types of private investment will be discouraged by the low "interest *return* from investment." It is feared that "compensatory spending" will
eventually require borrowing at a zero rate of interest and so
wipe out the incentives of "a wide range of institutions and
individuals" depending on fixed-income-yielding investments.
It is conceded, however, that these short-run effects of a long-
range program of "compensatory spending" could perhaps be
"dismissed as part of the necessary cost of a successful mone-

---

[14] *Cf.* J. H. Williams, "The Implications of Fiscal Policy for Monetary Policy
and the Banking System," *American Economic Review*, March, 1942.

tary policy," provided that "the low interest rates did actually achieve an adequate recovery of investment, output, and employment." [15]

It is unlikely that interest rates will, for risk and administrative reasons, go down to zero. Unless the government resorts to the printing press to finance continuous full employment, it is safe to assume that "compensatory spending" will continue to be financed by issuing and selling interest-bearing securities largely to the banking system and so provide banks with stable interest income and a large source of liquidity. But then it is argued that long-continued government spending would make the central bank more and more an agency to preserve a stable government bond market, and the private banking system an *investing* rather than *lending* mechanism. The first is considered objectionable because it implies a weaker exercise of monetary control, and the second is found even more objectionable because it implies "eventual government ownership" of banks. These implications may or may not be warranted, but as long as there persists traditional faith in the quantity theory and in its policy counterpart, or in the successful operation of automatic forces—as evident in all these arguments against "compensatory spending"—long-continued government spending, however desirable and necessary from the standpoint of long-run economic stability, will be difficult of realization. A refusal to let the government assume the main responsibility of stabilizing the economic system may well "set men free but . . . make them slaves to chance." [16]

Wage Reduction

Whether wage reduction is conducive to investment is not easy to determine, since the question is complicated by the dual nature of wages, i.e., the income aspect and the cost as-

[15] Williams, *op. cit.*
[16] A. P. Lerner, *op. cit.,* p. 192.

pect. It is highly misleading to concentrate on the one aspect to the neglect of the other. For example, it is a common error to apply the case of an individual firm or industry, whose output and employment are favorably affected by wage reduction, to the whole economy. For aggregate demand—and particularly consumer demand—may not remain constant when a general reduction in money wage rates occurs. Therefore any realistic antidepression wage policy needs to be guided by the principle that if the wage reduction should give rise to a corresponding decline in aggregate demand there would be no increase in aggregate output and employment.

As for the direct effects on investment of a general reduction in money wage rates, we have already discussed three principal ways in which the marginal efficiency of capital may be affected by a change in money wages: (a) via its effect on the interest rate, (b) via its effect on anticipations, and (c) via its effect on the balance of payments in an open system. We have found that in case a general reduction in money wage rates is expected to continue, current investment is likely to be postponed until wages have hit rock bottom, and that only when the wage reduction is permanent (i.e., not expected to fall further) is the marginal efficiency of capital favorably affected. We have also found that the stimulating effect of low interest rates incident to a smaller total wage bill may be offset by a possible rise in people's liquidity-preference due to a feeling of insecurity and uncertainty which low money wages usually induce. For this reason the lowering of interest rates by monetary and fiscal methods rather than by wage reductions is generally considered more expedient. But we have conceded that in countries depending on foreign trade a general reduction in money wage rates may affect domestic investment favorably via its favorable influence on the balance of payments of those countries.

In all these cases, however, the inflationary impact of wage reduction on investment is likely to be offset by its deflation-

ary effect on consumption expenditures—the other compo-
nent of aggregate demand. For this reason most economists
today are disposed to let money wages remain stable to prevent them from decreasing; or in some cases to increase them
during depression.[17] In an economy with strong monopolistic
tendencies the proportion of the national income going to
nonwage earners tends to be larger than that going to wage
earners during depression, ignoring other periods for the moment. In these circumstances a shift of income from wage
groups to nonwage groups resulting from a general reduction
in money wages would have the effect of reducing consumption and of increasing savings, unless the latter groups are
assumed to have a higher marginal propensity to consume.
The fact that nonwage groups have a lower marginal propensity to consume is itself a presumption against general
wage reductions, unless such wage reductions are supposed
to preclude a shift of income from wage groups to nonwage
groups. The adverse effect on aggregate demand of the transfer of income from wage groups to nonwage groups would
lower the marginal efficiency of capital and therefore deter
current investment. Even though businesses should expand
their output and employment in response to wage reductions,
the results would prove disappointing as long as the actual
marginal propensity to consume for the economy as a whole
remained less than unity. For a decrease in consumer demand
incident to wage reductions would not be offset by a corresponding increase in nonwage groups' demand, given the marginal propensity to consume of less than unity.

It is not without significance that Professor A. C. Pigou,
who had long believed in and upheld the employment-
stimulating effect of wage reduction, came out recently with

---

[17]*Cf.* Keynes, *General Theory*, Chap. 19; Hansen, *op. cit.*, Chap. 13;
Kalecki, *Essays in the Theory of Economic Fluctuations*, Chap. 3, (London,
George Allen & Unwin Ltd.); Klein, *op. cit.*, pp. 106–110; League of Nations,
op. cit., pp. 128–130; Harris, " Keynes' Attack on Laissez Faire and Classical
Economics and Wage Theory," in *The New Economics*, pp. 549–557.

the confession that he no longer considered the manipulation of wages as effective or practical a method of attacking the problem of unemployment as the manipulation of demand.[18] He concurs with Keynes in the belief that in modern conditions wage reductions are unfeasible, if not unplausible. It is likely that in the future antidepression wage policies will aim at stabilizing or increasing consumer demand rather than at stimulating investment. This point will be elaborated in connection with the measures to raise the consumption function.

Credit Policy

We have already appraised the role of cheap-money policy in cyclical and secular stabilization; but it is a mistake to dispense with monetary policy as irrelevant even though it is admittedly less effective in combating depression than fiscal policy. For credit policy does affect aggregate spending via its influence on private investment and the demand for durable consumer goods. Moreover, it must be remembered that cheap-money policy is indispensable to loan-financed compensatory spending. Although the experience during the Great Depression justifies skepticism about the effectiveness of monetary policy in achieving recovery, monetary policy still has a modest role to play in the general scheme of economic stabilization. It has been pointed out that in the industrially and financially less-developed countries credit and banking policies are much more than a mere "brake" on undue credit inflation.[19] Even in industrially advanced countries there is scope for effective antidepression credit policy as long as real estate credit, consumer installment credit, and other particular types of credit remain restricted by high interest rates. Even if credit policy is incapable by itself of turning the tide

[18] See his preface in *Lapses from Full Employment* (Macmillan, New York, 1945).
[19] *Cf.* League of Nations, *op. cit.*, p. 154.

of depression, it can increase overall liquidity via open-market operations and other conventional methods, thereby creating the monetary atmosphere necessary for the successful operation of more effective measures of fiscal and other policies.

The proper credit and banking policies during depression include the lowering of interest rates to a practical minimum or the prevention of interest rates from rising, the increasing of general liquidity and particularly the improvement of commercial banks' liquidity positions, the prevention of bank failures and panics, and the putting of idle savings at the disposal of government investment.[20] The monetary authorities have various instruments to implement these general objectives of antidepression credit policy. Although interest rates in the United States and some other wealthy industrial countries have already reached an "irreducible" minimum which barely covers the overhead costs of lending institutions, the Federal Reserve authorities still can make use of rediscount policy to influence short-term business borrowing and consequently long-term borrowing. Just how much rediscount policy can influence business borrowing depends on the extent of the downward change in the induced bank rates, and on the proportion of short-term borrowing to total business borrowing. In this respect a depression in a wealthy industrial country is not likely to get much help from low rediscount rates, since interest rates in such a country are already very low and since its total business borrowing is more long-term than short-term, given the increasing use of fixed capital in modern production. Moreover, in advanced industrial countries much of long-term investment is financed out of the accumulated profits of corporations themselves. Even the financing of inventories, which usually depends on short-term bank loans, is increasingly facilitated by retained profits.

Open-market operations are perhaps more effective than

[20] *Cf.* H. S. Ellis, "Monetary Policy and Investment," *American Economic Review*, March, 1940; K. R. Bopp, "Three Decades of Federal Reserve Policy," in *Federal Reserve Policy*, Postwar Economic Studies, No. 8, 1947.

rediscount policy. By purchasing securities (mostly government) on the open market the Federal Reserve authorities can increase the cash reserves of the commercial banks and therefore their ability to expand lending and to acquire investments. Open-market operations can supplement rediscount policy in influencing not only short-term but long-term interest rates, especially if open-market operations over long maturities and a variety of securities are permitted. Open-market operations, however, help to combat depression mainly because they increase the cash reserves of commercial banks. An increase in the liquidity of commercial banks has the effect of preventing these banks from taking such deflationary actions as selling assets, calling in loans, accumulating idle funds, etc., which may be "sound" from the standpoint of each individual bank but which are clearly detrimental to the whole economy during depression. Moreover, the increase of banks' liquidity via open-market operations enables the banks to purchase government and other securities and so to contribute to a lowering of long-term interest rates and therefore to capital expansion, both private and public.

Through these and other appropriate monetary measures the private inducement to invest may be increased and the conditions favorable to recovery created. As an adjunct to fiscal policy, monetary policy can help prevent depression.

The Reservoir Plan

Another scheme to provide effective incentives to enterprise is the so-called "reservoir plan." [21] This plan claims to supersede all other antidepression and antistagnation plans, because it is supposed to provide "full employment without public debt, without taxation, without public works, and without inflation." Before entering into an appraisal of the plan we must review briefly the principles involved. The

---

[21] The plan is advocated principally by B. Graham (see his *Storage and Stability,* New York, 1937) and F. D. Graham (see his "Full Employment without Public Debt, etc.," in *Planning and Paying for Full Employment*).

plan accepts the Keynesian premise that the instability of aggregate demand is due largely to unstable private investment,[22] but it rejects the Keynesian emphasis on fiscal policy for full employment. Instead, the plan would have open-market operations in commodities, that is, government purchases and sales of certain "storable" commodities in order to "adjust supply to demand." This type of open-market operations differs from those over government securities in that it involves no interest-bearing public debt, but is similar to the latter in the respect of generating purchasing power (or contracting it). In both cases the emphasis is on *supply*, that is, the supply of commodities in the one case and the supply of money in the other. This is a fundamental difference between the reservoir plan and the Keynesian income-expenditure approach which emphasizes the *demand* side.

How does the reservoir plan work? Whenever "sagging markets" appear, that is, whenever there is the danger of "overproduction," the government must, according to the plan, purchase either producers' or consumers' goods at a price sufficient to cover the "out-of-pocket expenses" involved in the production of those goods. In other words, the government is supposed to guarantee markets to private businesses so that the latter would be induced to expand output and employment or not to contract them. How would the government pay for the goods purchased? The answer is "newly issued Federal Reserve deposit credit," that is, *interest-free* currency issues in effect. This is an interesting method of financing, but one that can hardly escape all sorts of questions.[23] As has already been indicated, it might be necessary to provide banks and other institutions with interest-bearing government securities not only as an outlet for idle reserves during depression but as a source of earnings just when interest

[22] F. D. Graham's analysis runs largely in terms of "hoarding" instead of those of underemployment savings-investment equilibrium.

[23] For an interesting criticism of interest-free financing see Hansen, *Economic Policy and Full Employment*, pp. 145–151.

income from loans and private securities is negligible. Moreover, if total spending is to be increased via interest-free financing, it seems more sensible to finance more hospitals, schools, highways, and other needed projects than to take off the glutted market and store away commodities which could otherwise be used by the community.

Even if the stored commodities were to be repossessed by their original producers by the repurchasing of "liens" on them, there is no assurance that those commodities would not have become obsolete by the time "private demand revives." Barring, for example, a commodity such as women's hats subject to rapid obsolescence, some of the stored goods would probably have to be sold at such a discount as might not even cover the repurchase price. But a more serious criticism is that the reservoir plan fails to recognize the crucial importance of stabilizing the demand for capital goods.[24] Even though the plan includes, among the storable commodities, both consumer goods and capital goods, it fails to distinguish the cyclical significance of these different types of commodities. It is in the *capital-goods* industries that demand is most unstable. This means that an antidepression reservoir plan would have to face the necessity of piling up all kinds of fixed capital at a rate which would be compatible with full employment but which would develop "a vast stock of utterly unusable goods." [25] It is for this reason, among others, that some writers suggest that the reservoir plan is less appropriate to industrially developed economies than to agrarian economies,[26] or that it can more fruitfully be applied to the international stabilization of primary products.[27]

Moreover, it has been pointed out that the very act of guar-

[24] Hansen, *op. cit.*, pp. 220–221.
[25] *Ibid.*
[26] C. D. Calsoyas, "Commodity Currency and Commodity Storage," *American Economic Review*, June, 1948.
[27] *Cf.* R. F. Harrod, *Towards a Dynamic Economics*, pp. 122–124; also League of Nations, *op. cit.*, pp. 81–86 and 265–271.

anteeing markets via the reservoir plan would increase aggregate output and income and therefore savings more than an increase in investment.[28] If savings increased in this way, demand would increase less than supply, so that overproduction would again confront the economy. Thus it is argued that a system of government guarantees of markets to business firms is no guarantee that an increase in investment will be just such as to offset the increased savings. A tendency to underestimate an excess of savings over investment in conditions of full employment is therefore considered by some to be a fundamental flaw in the reservoir plan. The reason for this tendency to underestimate the danger of full-employment oversaving is to be found in the familiar classical assumption that the interest rate automatically equilibrates savings and investment regardless of the level of income.[29] It has already been shown that there can be no such savings-investment equilibrium where the liquidity function is interest-elastic, the savings function interest-inelastic, and the investment function also interest-inelastic.

Thus, even with a system of government guarantees of markets, there would still be a strong possibility that investment opportunities might not be permanently large enough to offset the full-employment savings that such a system would help generate. The main difficulty with subsidy and other artificial methods of stimulating private investment lies in the fact that every increase in private investment by such methods lowers the marginal efficiency of capital and repeats "the tragedy of investment, "while at the same time those methods merely aggravate oversaving.[30] On the asset side, however, must be listed interest-free financing as an economizer of public debt, and the stock-piling of raw materials as a stabilizer of the world market.

[28] Lerner, *op. cit.*, p. 190.
[29] See, e.g., F. D. Graham, *op. cit.*, pp. 58–59.
[30] See Keynes, *General Theory*, Chaps. 11, 12, and 16.

15

Measures to Raise the

Consumption Function

~~~~~~

IN CONNECTION with our discussion of Keynes' psychological law of consumption we suggested that in the short run it is logically sound and practically wise to concentrate our effort on increasing investment, for the reason that the consumption function does not change and cannot be changed quickly, given the existing psychological-institutional complex. We alluded, however, to the desirability of maintaining full employment via promoting *both* consumption and investment *in the long run.* In the short run it is easier to change a single point on the consumption-function curve by increasing income than to change the position or shape of the curve itself. This was made clear in our analysis of the multiplier effect of the increase in investment. A public-works program, for example, has the effect of changing the income variable and therefore the amount of consumption outlays without affecting the position of the consumption schedule. Such a cyclical policy is different from a long-range policy of changing the position and shape of the entire consumption function. Given the stable consumption function, it is realistic to rely upon the

T

measures to increase investment for combating cyclical depression and to relegate the measures to raise the consumption function to a longer term policy of maintaining the full-employment savings-investment equilibrium. We are therefore largely concerned with the measures to "educate" the consuming public to change its fundamental habits of saving and consumption.

Income Redistribution

We have seen that the manner in which income is distributed is one of the institutional factors affecting the propensity to consume. We know that a measure of inequality in income distribution is conducive to rapid economic *progress* because it facilitates savings and therefore capital formation. Poor countries, with the exception of those depending on industrial countries, are generally less subject to cyclical disturbances, and may therefore attach more importance to economic progress than to economic *stability*. In this case the problem of income redistribution is largely academic. On the other hand, for wealthy industrial countries, in which the existing stock of capital is already large, income redistribution is a practical issue. For in such countries the main problem is not one of promoting economic progress via more savings but one of promoting economic *stability*, upon which progress itself depends. The theoretical justification for greater equality in income distribution is therefore based on the fact that with the existing capital accumulations, the growth of wealth, which the unequal distribution of income facilitates, not only impedes the further growth of wealth but also increases economic instability. But the practical question is: How and to what extent would a redistribution of income raise the propensity to consume or lower the propensity to save? [1]

[1] Without exception, all modern theoretical full-employment discussions and policy measures for full employment include income redistribution as an

If a redistribution of income affects total consumption expenditures significantly, it must be an important variable in income and employment analysis. Since consumption is typically the function of the poor and savings the function of the rich, it is widely believed that an appropriate transfer of income from the rich to the poor will increase total consumption and decrease total savings to the benefit of aggregate income and employment. This belief, it should be noted, has to do with the *amount* of income spent on consumption, not necessarily with the consumption *schedule*. The validity of this belief depends entirely on the kind of the marginal propensities to consume assumed for different income groups, or, more specifically, for the rich and for the poor, so to speak.

Suppose that the marginal propensity to consume is the same at all levels of income. In this instance, each dollar shifted will reduce consumption in the high-income brackets by exactly the same amount by which it increases consumption in the low-income brackets, with the result that the effect of the redistribution on total consumption is zero. Now suppose that the marginal propensity to consume is higher in the low-income than in the high-income brackets. In this case, each dollar transferred will increase consumption in the low-income brackets by a larger amount than it reduces consumption in the high-income brackets, so that there is a net increase in aggregate consumption. Thus aggregate consumption is an increasing function of income redistribution only when low-income consumer units (households) are in the habit of spending more of an increment of income than high-income groups. These two situations are implicit in Figure 29.

In the diagram, C_1 is the consumption function that is straight all the way through, indicating that the marginal

---

important variable. But greater equality in income distribution may actually be brought about by a desire to promote social welfare or justice rather than by a desire to promote economic stability.

propensity to consume is constant for all income levels. This is approximately the actual situation prevailing in the United States. The C_2 curve has a slightly convex curvature, indicating that the marginal propensity to consume at lower income levels is higher than at higher income levels. Whenever and wherever the actual distribution of income exhibits this latter characteristic, income redistribution will have a positive effect on total consumption. Figure 29 leads to the conclusion that the wider the gap between the marginal

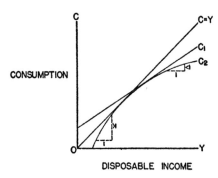

FIG. 29. TWO MARGINAL PROPENSITIES TO
CONSUME

propensities to consume of high and low income groups, the greater the influence of income redistribution on total consumption. It is estimated that, with the consumption function being what it is in the United States, income distribution toward equality to the extent of 10 per cent would increase total consumption by an amount equal to .52 per cent of total income, a 50 per cent redistribution by 2.87 per cent, and a 100 per cent redistribution by 5.82 per cent.[2]

The above short-run analysis, however, does not preclude the possibility of changing the marginal propensities to consume and to save via distributive reform in the long run. But

[2] See H. Lubell, "Effects of Redistribution of Income on Consumers' Expenditures," *American Economic Review*, December, 1947.

it does show that if the marginal propensity to consume is a constant over a wide range of income levels (between $2,000 and $5,000 in the United States), an increase in consumption expenditures resulting from an additional dollar acquired by someone in, say, the $2,000 bracket will be exactly offset by a decrease in consumption resulting from the loss of that dollar by someone in the higher income bracket. Nevertheless, there is still scope for redistribution as long as there is a wide gap between the marginal propensities to consume of those receiving below $2,000 and those receiving above $5,000.

A greater equality in income distribution may be brought about by (a) increasing the productivity of lower income groups, (b) increasing the purchasing power of lower income groups, and (c) transferring purchasing power from the rich to the poor. The first method involves measures to improve economic opportunity, public health, working conditions, housing, educational facilities, etc. The second requires measures to reduce the cost of living, particularly the prices of necessities, i.e., measures involving better organization of production and distribution, antimonopoly legislation, lower tariffs, and many others. The third method depends on a combination of progressive taxation and relief-welfare public expenditures. The first and second methods are likely to promote both stability and progress, since these methods are conducive to a rise in the propensity to consume without significantly affecting the propensity to save. The third method may lower the propensity to save more than the propensity to consume.[3] This last method requires amplification.

[3] Here the two functions are regarded as two independent activities of lower income groups as consuming units and higher income groups as saving units. In this regard, L. A. Metzler has shown that, if the marginal propensity of lower income groups is greater than unity, the multiplier spending of those groups will increase total income to such an extent as to benefit the higher income groups which are taxed to subsidize the former groups. See his article "Effects of Income Redistribution," *Review of Economic Statistics*, XXV, 1943.

A progressive tax structure means that the burden of taxation falls more heavily on the portion of income saved than on that which is spent. Such a tax structure has the effect of raising the consumption function and of lowering the savings function. For this reason, and in view of the practical limitations of antidepression public spending, Keynes, for example, regarded progressive taxation as a means for redistributing income and raising the consumption function. A gradual removal of regressive consumption taxes and increasing reliance on progressive income taxes, coupled with expanding welfare expenditures, would probably bring about such a redistribution of income as to shift substantially the consumption function upward and the savings function downward. In all countries where the incidence of taxation as a whole is progressive, the chances are great that the consumption function will rise so high as to serve as a cushion against the shock of cyclical depression and as an offset to secular underinvestment.

In advanced economies a greater equality in income distribution would probably promote economic stability more than it would check progress. Moreover, a more equal distribution of income through progressive taxation, relief and welfare expenditures, and other measures, while somewhat retarding progress, would nevertheless lead to full employment and a better allocation of resources.[4] This is not to say, however, that a better distribution of income can by itself cure unemployment; it can *contribute* to a long-range full-employment program by lowering the savings function relative to limited investment opportunities.

Wage Policy

It is necessary to distinguish, at the outset, between those measures of wage policy which are designed to increase con-

---

[4] A better allocation of resources is likely because free consumer choice would not be distorted by an unequal distribution of income as it is at present. See B. Higgins, "To Save or Not to Save?" *op. cit.*

sumption expenditures with a given consumption function and those aimed at raising the consumption function itself. The former are typically an anticyclical policy, and have to do with money wage *rates*. The latter are essentially a long-range wage policy which has to do with the *distribution* between labor income and nonlabor income.

Higher money wage rates can, in principle, increase consumption outlays to make up for any decrease in investment outlays to maintain the desired level of income. But given the short-run constancy of productivity, labor would simply price itself out of the market if it demanded higher money wages. On the other hand, given the deflationary implication of wage reduction for aggregate demand and the institutional fact of trade unionism, the downward adjustment of money wage rates is clearly out of the question. For these reasons *stable* wages are considered essential to short-run stability. An anticyclical wage policy will therefore have to be content to prevent consumer demand from falling. Such a policy is the joint responsibility of labor and management, to be sure, but it cannot be maintained unless the government adopts more effective measures of antidepression *monetary-fiscal* policy. Otherwise the depressed economy would revert to the mistaken classical policy of attacking unemployment mainly by manipulating wage rates.

A long-range wage policy is concerned with the possibility of raising the entire consumption schedule. As such it is an integral part of public policy designed to effect a transfer of income from nonwage groups to wage groups. As has been indicated, public measures to increase the purchasing power of wage groups and to transfer income from nonwage groups to wage groups are defensible, if these measures raise the consumption function without at the same time lowering the investment function. As far as a wealthy economy is concerned, progressive taxation as a means of redistributing income has the double advantage of raising the consumption

function and of lowering the savings function without im-
poverishing the economy.

A system of "guaranteed wages" has of late been given wide
publicity as a supplementary measure to prevent the consumption function from falling, if not to raise that function
substantially.[5] Such a system is merely the generalization of
those existing isolated cases of "job security." Security of
tenure enjoyed by some professional groups is a case in point.
The general idea is that the employers should assume some
part of the risk of unemployment by guaranteeing minimum
annual wages, that is, steady employment at some appropriate
proportion of regular wages for a minimum period, the
length of the period depending on the ability of each firm or
industry to maintain the working force on its payroll. The
period of unemployment not covered by such a guarantee
plan is to be taken care of by a social security program. A
system of "guaranteed wages" is considered as a useful adjunct to the existing social security program, the coverage
and benefit payments of which are obviously inadequate.
It is doubtful, however, that guaranteed-wages plans will
create such a great sense of security as to reduce people's
liquidity-preference in the short run or to lower their propensity to save significantly in the long run. Even if some
enlightened employers appreciate the· beneficial effects of a
general gain in security of income and adopt guarantee plans,
as they indeed have adopted them in the United States,[6]
their efforts may well be offset by the myopia of other employers. It would therefore seem more realistic to concen-

[5] *Cf.* Hansen, *Economic Policy and Full Employment,* pp. 158–160; Office
of War Mobilization and Reconversion, *Guaranteed Wages: Report to the
President* (Washington, 1947); J. L. Snider, *The Guarantee of Work and
Wages* (Harvard Univ., 1947); A. D. H. Kaplan, *The Guarantee of Annual
Wages* (Brookings Institution, Washington, 1947); H. Feldman, "The Annual
Wage—Where Are We?" *American Economic Review,* December, 1947;
Rita Ricardo, "Annual Wage Guarantee Plans," *American Economic Review,*
December, 1945.

[6] *Cf.* J. E. Chernick and J. G. Helickson, *Guaranteed Annual Wages* (Univ.
of Minnesota Press, 1945).

trate on the extension of social security and minimum wage legislation.

Social Security

All advanced countries are committed to some kind of social insurance, and are rapidly moving in the direction of more extensive systems of social insurance. A system of social security is significant, apart from its humanitarian merits, partly as an anticyclical measure but mainly as a long-range stabilization measure. In the short run a system of social security serves as an offset to a cyclical decline in investment. We know that consumption expenditures fall with falling investment, partly because of the reduced spending of those who become unemployed and of their dependents. Social security will therefore contribute to the prevention of consumption expenditures from falling too low during depression. Moreover, a social security program helps to sustain the accustomed level of spending among employed workers during depression, since it creates a sense of security conducive to such spending. It should be noted, however, that if the benefit payments are smaller in amount than the employment taxes collected, the net result will be deflationary.[7]

In the wealthy industrial countries there is increasing recognition that an extensive system of social security is needed for achieving a high-consumption or low-saving economy. A social security program is regarded as a solution to "the paradox of thrift" common to all the wealthy capitalistic economies. Thus viewed, a system of social security is an attempt to remove some of the primary causes of the need for savings, such as are characterized by the phrase "saving for the rainy day." This emphasis on the long-run aspect of social security is based on the growing conviction that a high-consumption economy is "the long-run hope for capitalism."[8]

[7] On this point see Hansen, *op. cit.*, pp. 124–127.
[8] *Cf.* L. R. Klein, *op. cit.*, p. 117 (the phrase is his); Keynes, *General Theory,* p. 325; Hansen, *op. cit.*, pp. 48–49; B. Higgins, "Keynesian Economics and

By diminishing the fear of insecurity a comprehensive program of social security (involving not only unemployment compensation but also old-age pensions and health insurance) would raise the consumption function and reduce the propensity to save to such an extent that a chronic deficiency of private investment might well cease to disturb the secular savings-investment equilibrium at full employment.

Adoption of a comprehensive program of social security might be more feasible where people tend to prefer outlays on social security benefits to public investment than where the idea of "subsidizing mass consumption" is generally considered more repugnant than that of public investment.[9] This is not to suggest that social security and public investment are simple alternatives, for they can be promoted simultaneously, as the recent British experience indicates. Apart from the question of feasibility, it is clear that no industrially advanced country subject to chronic mass unemployment can really afford to minimize the importance of a comprehensive program of social security for stabilization as well as for welfare purposes.

Easy Consumer Credit

Consumer credit control is part of any integrated anticyclical policy. Experience has shown that consumer credit control is capable of arresting excessive installment buying.[10] There is no intrinsic reason for supposing that this type of selective control is incapable of stimulating the demand for strategically important consumer durables, such as automo-

---

Public Investment Policy," in *The New Economics*, p. 476; J. H. Williams, "Deficit Spending" *American Economic Review*, February, 1941; See, e.g., Lord Beveridge, *Full Employment in a Free Society* (London, George Allen & Unwin Ltd., 1945), pp. 336–341.

[9] In this regard see M. Kalecki, "Political Aspects of Full Employment," *Political Quarterly*, October–December, 1943.

[10] For example, installment credit fell to about $1.8 billion during World War II, owing to "Regulation W," but the removal of the latter control led to installment credit amounting to some $7 billion in 1948 (before the new control went into effect in September of that year).

biles, household equipment, and perhaps television sets. During depression, "Regulation W" should be reversed to reduce the cost of consumer credit and to increase its availability, that is by reducing down payments, by lengthening the period of amortization, and by liberalizing other terms of lending.

In view of the fact that an increasing proportion of the total sales of durable consumer goods is effected on credit,[11] and since the demand for those goods is one of the most unstable elements of aggregate demand (demand for consumer durables being postponable in favor of more urgently needed necessities), easy consumer credit is an important part of an effective antidepression policy. During a period of depression and mass unemployment, the monetary authorities, with the co-operation of the producers of durable consumer goods, can and should reduce down payments, etc., in order to sustain the demand for those goods or to increase that demand. The lowering of interest rates is considered undependable, since such a change exercises only a small influence on the size of short-term installment credit. Easy consumer credit to stimulate the demand for durable consumer goods would be of no avail if the producers of those goods were unwilling to adjust their prices to the demand. Price flexibility in these lines of production would of course be difficult to obtain should they be dominated by monopoly interests. It would be to the long-run interest of the producers concerned to co-operate with the monetary authorities by co-ordinating their price policy with the latter's consumer credit policy.

As for the long-run effects of easy consumer credit, they will be reflected in the extent to which durable consumer goods are sold on credit in the future. In the United States, at any rate, the propensity to consume is likely to rise and the propensity to save likely to fall, if the present trends in

[11] *Cf.* G. Haberler, *Consumer Instalment Credit and Economic Fluctuations* (National Bureau of Economic Research, New York, 1942).

installment buying continue. It is not without significance that the percentage of all consumer durables sold on credit increased in the United States from 40 per cent in 1929 to nearly 60 per cent in 1938. This percentage can be increased over time by the progressive liberalizing of the conditions of consumer credit, including interest rates. The secular significance, let alone the cyclical significance, of a substantial increase in the proportion of durable consumer goods sold on credit for private investment as well as for private consumption must not be overlooked. According to Kuznets' investigation, the average annual output of consumer durables (e.g., passenger automobiles, household equipment, and radios) in the period 1919–38 amounted to $7,100 million, or about 20 per cent of gross capital formation.[12] A long-range consumer credit policy must, therefore, be guided by the stimulating effects of an enlightened system of installment credit on both the consumption and the investment functions. Here is a fruitful field of co-operation among the Federal Reserve authorities, Federal credit agencies, private consumers' research organizations, and many other public and private groups interested in the promotion of consumer demand.

Other Measures for a Higher Consumption Function

We have noted that there are certain "trend forces" which naturally tend to raise the propensity to consume and to lower the propensity to save. A conscious attempt to tinker with some of those forces may be made with a view to supplementing the major lines of attack outlined above. First, we may try to expand educational opportunities along the lines recommended by the President's Commission on Higher Education, thereby increasing the percentage of the American youth going to college from the present figure of 16 to at

[12] Cf. *Commodity Flow and Capital Formation* (National Bureau of Economic Research, New York, 1938).

least 32.[13] The existing low standard of educational opportunities—an anomaly in the world's richest nation and an
anachronism in this day and age—is attributed to the fact
that the Federal government has assumed no responsibility
for the education of its citizens.[14] The President's Commission recommends, among other things, that the Federal government should annually spend a third of the $3.2 billion
necessary for an effective higher education program as "an
investment in human talent, better human relationships, democracy and peace." There is doubtless much in such a
program that is intrinsically valuable, but the relevant point
here is that education serves to develop an expensive taste
and so helps to raise the propensity to consume.

Another roundabout method of raising the consumption
function is to facilitate urbanization. Family-budget studies reveal, among other things, the interesting fact that city
people have a much higher propensity to consume than do
"country folks." It is sometimes suggested that the government should help mechanize agriculture so that the surplus
population can migrate into cities.[15] A Federal long-range
program of urban redevelopment (i.e., slum clearance, low-
cost housing, etc.) would also contribute to further urbanization and incidentally to the lowering of the savings function. Unless, however, continuous full employment is maintained in urban areas, a "back-to-the-farm" movement may
counteract an influx of agricultural families into cities. Urbanization, though helpful in raising the consumption function, is not a dependable method. It would perhaps be more
to the point to "educate" the country folk to make greater use
of mail-order buying, etc., and so to lower their propensity
to save.

We have also noted that the development of an advertis-

[13] The President's Commission on Higher Education, *Higher Education for
American Democracy* (Harper, New York, 1948).
[14] See *Hansen, op. cit.*, p. 173.
[15] Klein, *op. cit.*, p. 176.

ing industry was a contributing factor in the downward shift of the savings function over the last few decades. In view of this historical experience the suggestion has been made that "truthful advertising" be publicly subsidized to raise the consumption function.[16] Such a policy might prove difficult of administration. Moreover, it would be self-defeating if the government paid a large part of advertising costs by allowing corporations to deduct them from taxable income and thus unwittingly encouraged larger corporate savings, or if the subsidy policy merely encouraged the growth of monopolistic competition (product differentiation) and thus let monopoly prices stand in the way of effective consumer demand. It is likely that in view of increasing tendencies toward monopolistic competition the advertising industry will develop further without government subsidies, to raise the consumption function over time.

[16] Klein, *op. cit.*

16

Epilogue on Full Employment
Policy

~~~~~~

THE ANTIDEPRESSION measures that have been presented in the preceding chapters are means to an end, namely, continuous full employment. The validity, adequacy, appropriateness, effectiveness, and feasibility of these and other means depend basically upon value judgments with respect to social objectives, including full employment and many others. Disagreement on general or *ad hoc* antidepression measures stems partly from differences of theoretical diagnosis but principally from differences of normative judgment as to what *kind* of a full-employment society we ought to have.[1]

The sort of a full-employment society contemplated here is one in which the following social objectives are promoted concomitantly:

---

[1] On this question see Keynes, *General Theory*, Chap. 24; Hansen, *Economic Policy and Full Employment*, Chap. 2; D. H. Robertson, *Essays in Monetary Theory* (King & Son, London, 1940), Chap. 8; A. Halasi, "Toward a Full Employment Program: A Survey," in *Planning and Paying for Full Employment*, pp. 1–33; H. R. Bowen, *Toward Social Economy* (Rinehart, New York, 1948), Parts 4 and 5; D. B. Copland, *op. cit.*; L. R. Klein, *op. cit.*, Chap. 7.

1. The continuous full employment of productive resources, both human and material, beyond an irreducible minimum which must necessarily exist for frictional and dynamic reasons;
2. The maximum real income compatible with technological progress, that is, the fullest possible output of goods and services with given conditions of arts and sciences;
3. The allocation of available resources such that the primary needs of the population (e.g., food, clothing, shelter, medical care, and education) are satisfied first of all and as completely as possible;
4. Greater equality in the distribution of the fruits of full output and full employment among the factors of production, i.e., as equitable a distribution of incomes and wealth as is compatible with the maximum efficiency and progress in conditions of full employment;
5. The maintenance of the basic political and economic liberties, such as the representative form of government, free consumer choice, and free occupation choice;
6. The freest possible exchange of goods, services, and ideas among nations in an atmosphere of continuous universal peace and full employment.

This is a formidable challenge to modern society, to be sure, but it is the kind of a full-employment society that the logic of the modern monetary analysis requires. It provides a perspective which the policy makers of any free society can scarcely afford to lose sight of. There is general agreement on the desirability of those social goals, but there is no such agreement on particular means to those ends. But this latter area of disagreement is being rapidly narrowed, owing largely to a better understanding of the nature of the basic social and economic problems of our times. It is possible, therefore, to make some generalizations concerning full employment policy.

1. First, all modern full employment policies are premised on the firm conviction that depression and mass unemployment are *dispensable.* This intellectual assent is in itself a great advance over the traditional concept of business cycles, and represents prima facie evidence of the correctness of the

theoretical diagnosis of the instability of aggregate demand as well as of the effectiveness of the practical cure that logically follows from that diagnosis. Instead of leaving our material well-being to "the workings of blind forces," as we were inclined to do under *laissez faire*, we now find ourselves more determined than ever to control those blind forces in such a way as to enjoy continuous full output and employment without sacrificing essential liberties. Thus there is an increasing realization that there can be no genuine welfare and freedom without conscious control, without the deliberate manipulation of demand.

2. There is now wide agreement that only the government is capable of pursuing a *consistent* full employment policy. There are two obvious reasons for this agreement. First, no one economic group, whether it be a group of businessmen, workers, or farmers, is interested in promoting the public welfare and economic stability at the expense of its immediate, narrow sectional interests. Thus we find managements, labor unions, and farmers pursuing conflicting policies at the expense of one another and often to the utter neglect of the public interest. This state of affairs is an inevitable concomitant of an unregulated market economy. Second, as one economist so aptly puts it, "no other organization possesses the power necessary for the task." [2] For these reasons the main responsibility for achieving and maintaining full employment and continuous prosperity rests with the national government and its agencies. But there is also a fundamental reason for it.

Increasing reliance on the government for a consistent full-employment policy is really a reflection of the failure of "individualistic capitalism" to "deliver the goods." [3] This failure expresses itself in the inability of the price system to insure full output, full employment, continuous stability, and

[2] F. D. Graham, *op. cit.*, p. 40.
[3] Keynes, "National Self-Sufficiency."

U

even an optimum allocation of resources.[4] Keynes was one of the few economists even before the onset of that devastating Great Depression to recognize the self-destroying nature of *laissez faire* and the shocking inadequacy of the unregulated price mechanism.[5] His *General Theory* put the last nail in the coffin of *laissez faire*, as far as economists are concerned. The question is no longer whether the government should intervene in private enterprise, but rather to what extent public control is necessary to achieve full employment and other equally desirable social objectives. Keynes would leave such matters of detail to "the particular conditions of the time," as any realistic economist would. At any rate, there is now widespread recognition of the need for a greater degree of public control than was contemplated by classical economists, that is, the need for a "mixed system" in which economic life is guided in part by free market forces but largely by deliberate public policy, and in which the government guarantees, or creates a favorable political and economic environment for, maximum output, employment, and purchasing power.[6] To implement such a policy the United States, for example, established the Council of Economic Advisers in accordance with the 1946 Employment Act (American counterpart of the 1944 British White Paper on employment policy).

3. All the full employment measures have this in common, that they are aimed at maintaining *aggregate demand* at a level sufficient to insure full employment. Past emphasis on the stabilization of the price level has given way to new emphasis on the stabilization of the volume of income and

---

[4] For cogent explanations of why the pricing principle and the unregulated price mechanism fail to meet the requirements of the age, see H. R. Bowen, *op. cit.*, Parts 4 and 5, and J. E. Meade, *Planning and the Price Mechanism*, Chap. 1 (London, George Allen & Unwin Ltd., 1948).

[5] Keynes, *The End of Laissez-Faire* (London, 1926), and *Monetary Reform* (New York, 1924).

[6] On a "mixed system" as a desideratum, see Hansen, *Fiscal Policy and Business Cycles*, Chap. 20.

expenditure, since the principal demand factor determining general prices is national income. Furthermore, the choice of national income as the central variable and the choice of such aggregates as consumption expenditures and investment outlays characterize modern full-employment analysis and policy as essentially monetary. The simple income equation $Y = C + I$ underlies even the most complicated full-employment policy conceivable. This simplest model of Keynes has served to provide us with the clarity of purpose necessary for effective full-employment measures. If the level of employment is found to depend on aggregate spending, the stabilization of that level is possible through measures to stimulate consumption expenditures, investment expenditures, or both, the choice depending largely upon the cyclical or secular nature of the employment in question. Our theoretical analysis suggests that we should concentrate on the effort to promote investment in the short run, given a stable consumption function, and that continuous full employment can best be maintained by stimulating both investment and consumption. In either case it is monetary expenditures that determine the level of employment.

If the maintenance of adequate aggregate demand turns mainly on investment, as it does in the short period, then we have a choice to make between stimulating private investment and increasing public investment or exports. This choice depends on a number of economic and noneconomic considerations, such as the interest elasticity of private demand for capital, the existing stock of capital, a general attitude toward public investment, the proportion of foreign trade to total trade, etc. If private investment is merely deficient, "pump priming" will provide the necessary stimulus. If, on the other hand, private investment is lacking, as it tends to be, relative to savings, in wealthy capitalistic economies, "compensatory spending" is what is needed. In both cases, however, public investment should not take the form of "spending for spending's sake"; it is desirable and possible to combine the employment-generating and wealth-creating aspects of public spending. In this regard, Keynes' allusion to pyramid building is a valid didactic argument for income-creating public spending in conditions of less than full employment, but it is not to be taken for policy recommendation. It is well to remember that, as Keynes himself pointed out, employment-generating public investment need not have harmful "tertiary" effects on business confidence, provided that it does not consist of "obviously wasteful, foolish, or extravagant projects." [7]

4. As to the financing of public investment. Popular emphasis on the possible disturbance to the economy from the additional taxation necessary to service a large and growing public debt is misplaced. One way to get around the tax burden of deficit financing is to resort to the printing press or interest-free financing, as some are disposed to suggest. But then banks and institutional investors would be deprived of a profitable outlet for their idle cash balances during depression and an opportunity to acquire riskless earning assets (i.e., interest-yielding, gilt-edged government securities) for stable income. If the printing press is undesirable or unfeasible, the government can service the debt by additional borrowing from the banking system. This is considered by some to be a better way of avoiding the tax burden involved in deficit financing. Additional borrowing to service the debt would be unnecessary, if the loan-financed public investment actually led to such a high level of national income as to create a budgetary surplus. If, however, deficit financing and spending gave rise to full employment, additional borrowing and taxation would become necessary to minimize the accompanying inflationary pressure anyway. The point of all this is simply that public investment conducive to full employment should not be opposed on the

[7] Cf. *Macmillan Report of the Committee on Finance and Industry*, 1931.

ground that it entails a large and growing public debt, unless those opposing it are prepared to accept interest-free financing or the consequences of deficient private investment.[8]

Some types of public expenditure, however financed, are certainly defensible on grounds other than those of full employment. Development projects, slum clearance, public health, education, and the like are cases in point. If therefore public investment is directed into channels through which both full employment and welfare are promoted concurrently, there will be fewer objections to deficit financing. In the long run, it is possible to promote both full employment and social justice by placing increasing reliance upon the greater progressivity of income taxes for financing additional public expenditures. For this method of financing would help finance full employment, while at the same time facilitating a greater equality in the distribution of income. Although it is doubtful that taxation alone, however progressive in incidence, can finance "compensatory spending," it is at least a worthwhile supplement to borrowing. The promise of financing public expenditures via progressive taxation lies mainly in the field of combating secular oversaving or underinvestment. For such a method of financing would help to compensate for the lack of private investment, while simultaneously lowering the propensity to save which is too high relative to available investment opportunities.

5. Of all the measures aimed at stimulating consumption, the most important single measure from a long view is a redistribution of income. We have shown that a more nearly equal distribution of income has the effect of raising the consumption function, not to mention the amount of consumption expenditures with a given consumption function.

[8] For controversial discussions see Hansen, *Economic Policy and Full Employment*, Chap. 18; A. P. Lerner, "Functional Finance and the Federal Debt," *Social Research*, February, 1943; E. D. Domar, "The Burden of the Debt and the National Income," *American Economic Review*, December, 1944.

The extent to which income should be redistributed toward equality depends on (a) the existing stock of capital, (b) the community's choice between stability and progress, and (c) the further development of welfare economics. A stronger case for greater equality in income distribution exists in wealthy industrial countries than in undeveloped countries, since the growth of wealth, which an unequal distribution of income is supposed to promote, is more likely to contribute to economic instability than to social progress in the former countries. By showing "the paradox of thrift" Keynes removed the chief social justification for great inequality in the distribution of wealth and income.[9] In undeveloped countries a measure of inequality in income distribution may still find some justification in the fact that in those countries social progress via capital formation is needed more than economic stability.

In democracies, the principal means for redistributing income is a combination of progressive taxation and welfare expenditures. It has been shown that the extent to which such a redistribution of income will increase total consumption expenditures depends on the actual marginal propensities to consume of lower and higher income groups. The fiscal measures for income redistribution are the more effective the greater the above difference in the marginal propensities to consume of those income groups. Since lower income groups generally have a high marginal propensity to consume, a transfer of income to these groups will result in a net increase in total consumption. In the longer period, the consumption function can be raised by gradually increasing the progressivity of income taxes as well as by gradually removing all the regressive taxes now in existence, particularly in the State and local field. Although greater equality in income distribution may be defended on many grounds, it cannot by itself solve the problem of cyclical or chronic depression, con-

[9] See *General Theory*, p. 373.

trary to an underconsumptionist tendency to regard it as the panacea.

6. As to the relative effectiveness of monetary and fiscal policies. Although all the significant variables chosen in income analysis, except employment, run in monetary terms, it does not follow that traditional monetary and banking policies are more effective than fiscal policies in achieving and maintaining full employment. Deliberate changes in the cost and availability of credit, as the traditional analysis would suggest, are no longer considered adequate in stimulating investment, in promoting consumption, or in discouraging savings, as far as the industrially advanced countries are concerned.[10] Our observation of the actual liquidity, investment, and savings functions obtaining in the United States seems to support the above conclusion. This is not to deny the desirability of a cheap-money policy to facilitate low-cost public investment or to stimulate particular types of investment (e.g., construction, public utilities, and other long-term capital outlays). Nor is it implied that the traditional central bank credit controls, especially rediscount policy and open-market operations, are of no avail to a recovery program. But it does imply that monetary policy cannot make a significant contribution to the maintenance of full employment and continuous prosperity *except in conjunction with fiscal policy.* For while monetary policy is still justifiable on its own merits, fiscal measures are no longer contemplated without reference to their impact on the stability of the whole economy and aggregate employment in particular, even though policy decisions may be made on political and other noneconomic grounds.

But there is nothing to be gained by drawing an exaggerated dichotomy between monetary and fiscal policies, i.e.,

---

[10] Monetary policy may still be defended as an effective means for preventing a "boom" from developing into a "bust." See J. R. Hicks, *Value and Capital*, p. 301.

by relying exclusively on one or the other. In view of the present institutional setup it seems more realistic to consider monetary policy better adapted to the short run and to depend on fiscal policy for combating mainly persistent deflation or inflation. For the Federal Reserve authorities already have the necessary powers to change rediscount rates and reserve requirements or to initiate open-market operations; whereas potentially more effective measures of fiscal policy require Congressional approval after a long period of controversy for political and other reasons, and thus may come to the rescue of less effective measures of monetary policy too late. To the extent, however, that greater flexibility in fiscal policy is achieved, that policy will become actually more effective than monetary policy even in short periods. Nevertheless, the real promise of fiscal policy lies in the field of maintaining secular stability and continuous full employment, since compensatory spending for stabilization purposes can be reinforced by long-range welfare and developmental public expenditures and by a gradual shift to a progressive tax structure.

7. Price flexibility (i.e., absence of price-cost rigidities) as a *general* solution for instability is now considered inadequate for a number of reasons.[11] First, downward price and wage adjustments might increase output and employment in particular industries with *elastic* demands for their products, but these adjustments would have no such effect on the whole economy in which elastic demands for particular goods and services are offset by *inelastic* demands for others. And "product differentiation" so prevalent in this age of colossal advertising is a strong presumption in favor of inelastic demand for many goods and services. Second, if prices of goods and factors were to fall together, the price-cost relation would

[11] For some of these and other reasons, see Hansen, *Fiscal Policy and Business Cycles*, pp. 313–338; O. Lange, *Price Flexibility and Employment* (Principia Press, Bloomington, 1944), pp. 83–90; H. R. Bowen, *op. cit.*, p. 302; L. R. Klein, *op. cit.*, p. 90.

remain intact to the detriment of the inducement to invest, and the value of money would rise to the benefit of the propensity to save, thus leaving aggregate income and employment virtually unaffected. Third, a rise in the marginal efficiency of capital due to a reduction in factor prices without a corresponding reduction in commodity prices is offset by a fall in aggregate demand, with the result that there is no significant change in aggregate employment. As has been shown, if higher factor prices led to higher commodity prices, the increase in aggregate demand due to the higher factor prices (e.g., wages) would be dissipated in higher general prices instead of leading to an increase in aggregate output and employment. Lastly, "sticky" wages, which are often considered to be a cause of depression and mass unemployment, may in fact have a stabilizing effect on the economy, since such wages serve to deter an otherwise possible deflationary spiral.

Even if price flexibility could change aggregate output and employment, such a change would be short-lived unless proper monetary-fiscal measures were in operation to translate the gains of price flexibility into terms of stable monetary expenditures. Plausible assumptions regarding the parameters of the Keynesian functions cast doubt on the possibility of insuring stability by merely eliminating price-cost rigidities. As has been shown, underemployment equilibrium is still possible even in the complete absence of price-cost rigidities —as long as the liquidity, investment, and savings functions respond the way they do to interest changes. This is not to deny, however, the usefulness of promoting price-cost flexibility in those particular sectors of the economy whose price movements may be of strategic importance to general economic stability.

8. Finally, it is important to stress that the lasting success of any national full-employment policy rests on effective monetary, trade, and political co-operation among nations,

especially among the major industrial nations on which so many countries depend for their internal prosperity via their foreign trade relations. In an open system, fluctuations in the levels of income and employment in one country tend to spread to another, as will be shown in a later chapter. For this reason nations are more conscious today than ever before of the international character of the modern problem of deficient aggregate demand, and therefore of the need for multinational monetary and commercial co-operation for world prosperity. The existing international monetary and other agencies (United Nations affiliates) are prima facie evidence of a world desire to maintain lasting economic stability through co-operative efforts rather than through "beggar-my-neighbor" policies.

PART III

Domestic vs *International Equilibrium*

17

The External Value of Money—
The Gold Standard

~~~~~~

INTERNATIONAL as well as domestic economic stability presupposes stability in the value of money as a *sine qua non*, among other requirements. The external value of money or the domestic price of foreign currencies on the foreign exchange market is determined diversely under different monetary standards, and the way in which it is determined affects domestic and international economic welfare differently. It is therefore necessary to examine both the theoretical basis and the practical implications of various international currency systems. We shall consider three typical monetary standards, namely, (a) the gold standard, (b) the paper standard, and (c) the mixed standard—the International Monetary Fund. Our discussions in this chapter and the two following may serve as a background for an understanding of the more complex problems of international and domestic equilibrium presented in the last two chapters. We shall begin with the gold standard.

Stable Exchange Rates

It seems useful to begin with a definition of the gold standard. A country is said to be on the gold standard (a) when its monetary authority is committed to a policy of buying and selling gold at a fixed price in unlimited amounts, (b) when the purchasing power of a unit of its currency is kept equal to the purchasing power of a given weight of gold, and (c) when the external value of its currency is fixed through the medium of gold. Practically all major trading nations were on gold in the above sense before 1931, and gold served as a principal international means of payment and as an important reserve of international liquidity.

Under an international gold standard exchange rates are fixed, since each national currency is convertible into gold at a fixed rate and therefore into another currency at a fixed rate. If, for example, $4 and £1 can both be exchanged for the same amount of gold, it follows that the exchange value of £1 cannot be above or below $4. In reality exchange rates under the gold standard do fluctuate but only within the narrow limits set by the gold export and import points, that is, by the cost of sending gold from one point of the system to another. The *gold export point* is the upper limit beyond which the domestic price of a foreign currency may not rise, while the *gold import point* is the lower limit beyond which the domestic price of a foreign currency may not fall. It goes without saying that one country's export point is another's import point. These gold points are illustrated below.

Gold Export Point		*Gold Import Point*	
Mint par	$4.80 = £1	Mint par	$4.80 = £1
Exchange rate	$4.90 = £1	Exchange rate	$4.70 = £1

In the case of the gold export point the dollar price of the pound sterling will not rise beyond $4.90, since $4.90 is the point beyond which it becomes less costly to ship gold than to purchase a draft on London. That is to say, if the domestic price of a sterling draft on the foreign exchange market (e.g., a New York bank engaged in foreign exchange transactions) is higher than the mint price of gold, Americans would naturally rather pay English creditors more cheaply by sending gold than by buying sterling drafts. In the case of the gold import point it is more profitable for Americans to have gold shipped to them than be paid with drafts, since they can sell the gold to the mint and receive $4.80 instead of the $4.70 which they would otherwise get by converting the drafts into dollars. Hence $4.70 is the gold import point.

Thus under the international gold standard the external value of a national currency is determined by (a) the mint par of the standard monetary unit relative to that of foreign currencies, and (b) the limits set by the gold export and import points. The stability of exchange rates is the *raison d'être* of the gold standard, since it promotes international trade and finance by eliminating risks involved in otherwise unstable exchange rates. Yet it was partly rigid adherence to fixed exchange rates that eventually made the gold standard countries go off gold in protest during the 1930's. The main fault of the gold standard was that the external value of a national currency was kept stable at the expense of the stability of its internal value. That is precisely why the entire world today is disposed to share Keynes' conviction that the *de jure* external value of a national currency should be adjusted to conform to its *de facto* internal value instead of the other way around.[1] How was the stability of the internal value of a national currency sacrificed on the altar of stable exchange rates? The answer requires a brief examination of the specie-flow-price mechanism.

The Specie-Flow–Price Mechanism

The beauty of the gold standard is that it provides a self-regulating, automatic mechanism for economic adjustments

[1] *Cf.* Speech in the House of Lords, May 23, 1944.

among trading nations. Gold inflow or outflow, as the case may be, automatically leads to equilibrium in the country's balance of payments.[2] Let us first take the case of a debtor country which loses gold to others as a result of an adverse balance of payments. The sequence of events leading to equilibrium via internal deflation is shown below.

1. An excess of debits over credits on current account (disequilibrium in the balance of payments).
2. Gold outflow.
3. A decrease in gold reserves to support central bank credit and note issue as well as in commercial bank reserves to support demand deposits (the latter effect being due to the loss of reserves involved in customers' payment for the gold).
4. Credit contraction by both the central bank authorities and commercial banks (i.e., a "tight" money market).
5. A deflation of domestic prices, money incomes, money costs, and employment.
6. A fall in imports and a rise in exports.
7. Equilibrium in the balance of payments.

Confronted with an actual or probable outflow of gold, the central bank could attempt to offset the deflationary impact of gold outflow by increasing MV (i.e., not observe the "rules" of the gold standard game in order to avoid internal

[2] In this connection it is useful to recall certain fundamental concepts involved. First, *balance of payments* refers to the difference between *all* debit and credit items (current transactions, gold movements, and capital transactions), while *balance of trade* signifies the difference between commodity exports and commodity imports in terms of value. Second, an *adverse* balance of payments (or simply a "deficit") indicates that a country's visible and invisible imports (current transactions) exceed in value its similar exports. An excess of visible and invisible exports over similar imports, on the other hand, signifies a *favorable* balance of payments (or simply a "surplus"). Balance-of-payment *difficulties* arise when nations cannot export enough on current account to pay for imports, or when they lose gold or exchange reserves to a critical extent without entirely wiping out the deficits. Third, for accounting purposes the *total* balance of payments (with all trading nations) is always in balance, since capital or gold movements are entered in the balance-of-payments statement to balance debits and credits on current account. Thus a deficit nation, for example, may "settle" an adverse balance of payments *on paper* by entering on the credit side gold exports equal to the amount of the deficit.

deflation). But then such an attempt could not last, since increased MV would lead, among other things, to more imports and therefore to more gold outflow. *At less than full employment*, increased MV would increase the demand for domestic and foreign goods and services *without necessarily increasing domestic prices*. Hence the central bank would have to take deflationary steps, as shown above, to decrease MV and therefore imports. The decreased imports thus effected, coupled with increased exports due to lower domestic prices and costs, would lead to an export surplus and therefore to gold inflow. Thus the adverse balance of payments is overcome automatically. Until this long-run adjustment takes place, the gold-losing country has to sacrifice internal economic stability, including the stability of the internal value of its currency, for the sake of the stability of the external value of that currency. Otherwise a debtor country could overcome its adverse balance of payments by depreciating the exchange value of its currency, but then such a method of adjustment is in violation of the rules of the game.

The reverse is true of the effects of gold inflow, that is, an inflation of domestic prices and incomes. There is no point in trying to offset the inflationary impact of gold inflow by decreasing MV, since the subsequent fall in domestic prices and incomes would only increase exports on the one hand and decrease imports on the other. Accordingly, the gold-receiving country presumably lets domestic prices, incomes, and costs rise until the reverse disequilibrium in its balance of payments is overcome. An increase in domestic MV resulting from gold inflow leads to an increase in the demand for imports and in the amount of import expenditures because of (a) larger domestic incomes, and (b) higher domestic prices relative to foreign prices. For these reasons part of the increased MV will flow out and the "multiplier" effect of gold inflow on domestic incomes and employment will be partly offset. This point will receive further attention in the subsequent chapters. In the short run, therefore, a gold-receiving country has no choice but to suffer from the inflationary impact of gold inflow, if it is to stay on gold. At less than full employment, such an inflationary impact is welcome; but it is well to remember that part of the beneficial effect of gold inflow on domestic employment "leaks out" to the benefit of employment in foreign countries.

The central bank of a gold-receiving country might try to reduce the inflationary pressures accompanying the gold inflow, but could do so only by deviating from the rules of the game. In other words, a gold-receiving country is supposed to take inflation for granted just as fatalistically as a gold-losing country is expected to take deflation and like it. Yet there is reason to believe that the gold standard mechanism generally works to the advantage of gold-receiving countries. The gold standard mechanism has, in Joan Robinson's words, "an inherent bias towards deflation." [3] This is plausible for the following reasons.

First, a gold-losing country must deflate credit, prices, and incomes in order to arrest gold outflow, or, to put it differently, to get out of disequilibrium. By contrast, a gold-receiving country is under no equal pressure to inflate credit in order to check gold inflow, since more gold is always welcome for purposes of accumulating gold reserves and since the kind of disequilibrium that results from gold inflow (i.e., a "favorable" balance of payments) is, more often than not, beneficial to domestic employment, though harmful to long-run international equilibrium. This means that a gold-losing country must observe the rules of the game at the expense of domestic stability, whereas a gold-receiving country is in no hurry to do so simply because a continuing disequilibrium would result only in more gold reserves and, at worst, in more

---

[3] *Cf.* "The International Currency Proposals," *Economic Journal,* June–September, 1943.

domestic inflation. And from the purely domestic point of view inflation is always easier to bear than deflation.

Second, central bank policy is usually more effective in offsetting the inflationary impact of gold inflow than in counterbalancing the deflationary effect of gold outflow. That is to say, in so far as the rules of the gold standard game are not followed strictly, the traditional central bank controls (e.g., rediscount policy, reserve requirements, and open-market operations) can be used by a gold-receiving country to avert undue credit expansion much more successfully than by a gold-losing country to stimulate credit expansion. For once the gold-losing country's domestic activity has been depressed by its adverse balance of payments and by the subsequent loss of gold reserves, central bank actions to stimulate general economic expansion will not suffice, as the monetary experience of the 1930's clearly indicated. Fiscal and other nonmonetary measures are required to pull the economy out of depression, as has been shown already. In a period of the generally inelastic demand for credit a gold-losing country cannot very well take advantage of central bank credit devices to combat depression, even though it is willing to ignore the rules of the gold standard game.

There may of course be other reasons for the one-sidedness of the gold standard mechanism, but the recognition of "an inherent bias" toward deflation is strongly suggestive of increasing skepticism about automatic forces in general and about the gold standard mechanism in particular.

Devaluation

Devaluation is one way to evade the strict rules of the gold standard game. A country which wishes neither to deflate nor to forgo the advantage of stable exchange rates may elect to devalue its currency, that is, to reduce its gold parity. This it can do by simply fixing a higher price for gold in terms of its own currency. The consequent rise in the nominal value of monetary gold stocks makes possible an expansion of bank credit without lowering the ratio of gold reserves to money income. The United States, for instance, devalued its currency in 1934 by raising the fixed price of gold from $20.67 to $35 per ounce. It left gold in 1933 and returned in 1934 at a lower parity (somewhat below 60 per cent of the old gold parity). A country may devalue overnight without going off gold temporarily, as France did in 1936, when it made a nominal profit of some 17 billion francs. It is not difficult to see that if all gold standard countries devalue their currencies simultaneously, exchange rates among them will remain unchanged. But if only one country devalues its currency, that country stands to gain export advantages since the lower exchange value of its currency will stimulate exports on the one hand and check imports on the other, given the elasticity of international demand (given by the familiar formula: $E = (dQ/Q)/(dP/P)$) as a constant. The domestic and external effects of devaluation are as follows:

Internal Effects	*External Effects*
1. Higher income for gold producers.	1. An increase in exports due to lower export prices in terms of foreign currencies.
2. Maintenance of national income in terms of domestic currency via enabling exporters to receive more dollars for each unit sold.	2. A decrease in imports due to higher import prices in terms of domestic currency.
3. A stimulus to domestic manufacturing due to higher prices of imports in terms of devalued domestic currency.	

The beneficial effects of devaluation on domestic trade and employment are highly dubious, but there seems to be little question about the export advantages which it makes possible. Suppose, for instance, that before the devaluation of the dollar the exchange rate was $4 = £1 (£ representing the currencies of the rest of the world). Now suppose that the rate becomes $5 = £1 as a result of the devaluation of the dollar. This means that American exporters receive $5 instead of $4 for the same amount of exports, while American importers must now give up $5 instead of $4 for the same amount of imports. Looking at it from the standpoint of foreign buyers, the latter now find the American market a cheaper place in which to buy, inasmuch as they can get $5 worth of American goods and services in exchange for the same amount of their currencies.

Some important qualifications and refinements are in order. (1) The export advantages of devaluation presuppose no immediate retaliation on the part of others, whether in counterdevaluation or any other retaliatory measures. (2) The export advantages of devaluation are likely to be offset by any appreciable rise in the domestic cost of production, particularly in the export industry. In the short run, in which no significant increase in productivity can be expected, this means that the cost of production in the export industry can be kept down largely by resisting money-wage increases and monopoly-price increases. If the country in question is experiencing general inflation, many persons would rather see inflation overcome first than agree to devaluation for the same purpose of cheapening exports in terms of foreign currencies. For they argue that as long as inflation is going on, export prices cannot be low enough even in terms of the lower exchange value of domestic currency to stimulate the volume of exports significantly. Yet the policy makers are likely to prefer devaluation to internal deflation, if the choice is between devaluation and anti-inflation policy. This choice, however, cannot be made only with reference to political expediency. An ideal policy would be one of combining devaluation and anti-inflation policy, but such a combination may prove utterly unfeasible for political reasons.

(3) Devaluation will not stimulate exports if the price-elasticity of foreign demand for our exports is low, that is, less than unity. Some writers consider this to be the decisive factor.[4] For example, if a country's exports consist largely of luxuries for which the foreign demand is generally elastic, a 20 per cent reduction in its export prices would lead to a 20 per cent increase in the volume of its exports or even better, the precise percentage increase in exports depending on whether the foreign demand has a coefficient of elasticity equal to or greater than 1. Great Britain is a case in point. On the other hand, a country which mainly exports necessities stands to gain little by devaluation, since the foreign demand for such exports is generally inelastic. Brazil is an example of such a country. In longer periods the possibility of substitution becomes so strong that the criterion of elasticity loses much of its force; but in short periods, in which consumer tastes and substitutability remain constant, the responsiveness of foreign buyers to export prices may well be a compelling argument for or against devaluation. The *income* elasticity of demand is relevant to some internationally traded goods. For example, the American demand for foreign raw materials is more sensitive to a domestic income change than to a foreign export-price change. Thus devaluation would not necessarily stimulate exports if the devaluing country's exports consisted partly of goods for which the world demand was more elastic with respect to income than with respect to price.

(4) The export advantages of devaluation will be more than offset by its import disadvantages, if the devaluing country happens to depend very heavily on imports. This has two implications. First, a rise in the price of imports in terms of devalued domestic currency would cause the domestic cost of living to rise to the extent that necessities are imported, thus lowering real wages. Second, terms of trade would turn against the devaluing country if devaluation caused a greater

---

[4] E.g., J. E. Meade, *op. cit.*, p. 96.

fall in the price of exports than in the price of imports in terms of foreign currencies, so that less real imports per unit of exports could be obtained. In other words, the physical quantity of exports needed to pay for imports of equal value is thereby increased, thus necessitating increased production or a lower standard of living. But there is this to be said in favor of devaluation, namely, that devaluation, though restricting imports and therefore reducing real domestic consumption, does help to stimulate exports. By contrast, import quotas and other forms of "import austerity" do nothing to stimulate exports. Against this must be set the argument that while devaluation discourages all imports from all sources without discrimination, discriminatory import restriction (e.g., import quotas) enables the government to import the necessary goods and services cheaply and on favorable terms by playing off one exporting country against another.[5] Thus viewed, devaluation is a modification of the free-pricing mechanism, whereas import restriction is an instrument of state trading.

(5) Devaluation has the effect of shaking international confidence in the devalued currency and therefore of jeopardizing the very trade which the devaluation is intended to stimulate. Anticipations regarding dollar devaluation, for example, might make the foreigners hesitate to purchase American goods or to hold dollars, since they could get more dollars in exchange for their currencies by buying our goods and holding our money later. It is not therefore difficult to understand why some countries confronted with the urgent need for export expansion take a rather cautious attitude toward the question of devaluation. Such an attitude is all the more understandable when viewed in the light of all the other ramifications of devaluation discussed above. One must, how-

[5] J. E. Meade, *op. cit.*, pp. 94–95. An exception is to be found in a system of multiple exchange rates which discriminates against particular sources of foreign exchange by fixing a lower official price of foreign exchange for exporters of domestic products deemed necessary for home consumption. This system is discussed in the next chapter in some detail.

ever, avoid the extreme of dismissing devaluation as an altogether outrageous proposal regardless of particular problems confronting a country, as the orthodox gold standard theorist seems inclined to do.

18

The External Value of Money—
The Paper Standard

THE GOLD STANDARD imposes on the gold standard countries the alternatives of inflation and deflation. The internal price level and the internal value of a national currency, under that standard, are left to the vagaries of the yellow metal. In other words, the external value of a national currency is kept stable at the expense of internal economic stability. Irving Fisher in the United States and John Maynard Keynes in England did most to convince the world that the traditional policy of maintaining exchange stability should be abandoned in favor of internal economic stability (Fisher emphasizing price stability and Keynes income stability). Only under the pressure of the world-wide depression of the 1930's, however, did nations realize the wisdom of exchange flexibility. Flexible exchange rates are generally associated with autonomous, local monetary systems. A local monetary system is usually a paper standard, but need not be so. In the absence of an international gold standard the external value of national currencies may be made flexible (a) by leaving automatic market forces free to influence it, or (b) by letting the monetary authority deliberately adjust it.

The Purchasing Power Parity Theory

Under a system of autonomous paper standards the external value of a currency is said to depend "ultimately and essentially" on the domestic purchasing power of that currency relative to that of another currency. In other words, exchange rates tend under such a system to be determined by the relative purchasing power parities of different currencies in different countries. This is the essence of the parity theory which underlies the observable fact of fluctuations in exchange rates in a period of volatile international price movements. A numerical example will perhaps help.

Suppose that in a given period the exchange rate between the dollar and the pound is $4 = £1. Now suppose that the general price level in the United States goes up twice as high as in the base period, while general prices in Britain increase three times as much as in the base period. (Particular causes of such price increases are irrelevant to the present analysis.) With the American price index increasing to 200 and the British price index increasing to 300, the internal purchasing power of the dollar is now one-half its original level and that of the pound one-third its original level. In these circumstances the dollar price of the pound should fall to two-thirds of the original price, that is, to about $2.66, according to the purchasing power parity theory. Otherwise, it is argued, trade relations between the two countries would be out of balance. We can generalize by writing

Foreign exchange rate = (domestic price of a foreign currency in the base year) × domestic price index/ foreign price index

In our example the domestic price of a foreign currency in the base year is $4, the ratio of the domestic price index to the foreign price index 200/300, or 0.66, and $4 times 0.66

equals $2.64, which is about two-thirds of the original dollar price of the pound—a correct purchasing power parity rate.

Effects of a change in the domestic purchasing power of the dollar on the exchange value of that currency are illustrated in the following diagrams. In Figure 30 (A) we have elastic demand curves (greater than unity) to indicate that the rest of the world has substitutes for American exports or alternative markets in which to purchase similar goods and services. This means that the rest of the world is rather sensi-

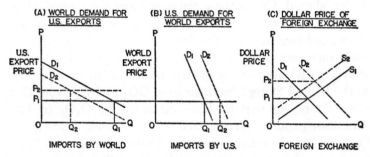

FIG. 30. EFFECTS OF A CHANGE IN THE
PURCHASING POWER OF THE DOLLAR
ON ITS EXCHANGE RATE

tive to slight changes in American export prices. It is assumed that inflation has already occurred in the United States to send up general prices, including export prices. Before the inflation American export prices were P_1 and American exports to the rest of the world (i.e., imports by others) were OQ_1, given the initial world demand for American exports, D_1, as shown in Figure 30 (A). After the inflation American export prices go up to P_2, in response to which the world demand for American exports decreases to D_2, that is, a downward shift of the demand curve to the left. As a consequence American exports (or imports by the rest of the world) decrease to OQ_2. This means that the world demand for dollar exchange (e.g., drafts on New York) also declines, for the simple reason that the rest of the world now has less payments to make to American exporters or creditors. From the American point of view this means that the supply of foreign exchange decreases. Note the leftward shift of the supply curve in Figure 30 (C).

In Figure 30 (B) the demand curves are drawn so as to have a price elasticity of less than unity, on the assumption that the United States does not find close substitutes for those goods and services offered by the rest of the world. It is also assumed that world export prices remain unchanged—no inflation abroad. Under these circumstances the United States finds the rest of the world a cheaper place in which to purchase, and consequently the American demand for world exports increases from D_1 to D_2 at the old price level P_1, as shown in (B). Imports by the United States (or world exports to the United States) increase from OQ_1 to OQ_2. Note that, while American *imports* have *increased* by Q_1Q_2 in (B), American *exports* have *decreased* even more, namely, by Q_2Q_1 in (A). In other words, the United States has a larger import surplus (an export surplus from the standpoint of others). This excess of imports over exports is reflected in the upward shift of the demand curve in (C), that is, in the rise of American demand for foreign exchange.

The American demand for world exports and therefore for foreign exchange far exceeds the world demand for American exports and therefore for dollar exchange. Accordingly, the domestic price for foreign exchange rises from P_1 to P_2, as shown in (C). A rise in the dollar price of foreign exchange means a fall in the external value of the dollar, since Americans must now give up more dollars to get the same amount of foreign exchange. The low exchange value of the dollar will stimulate American exports and discourage American imports until equilibrium is restored in the American balance of payments. Thus a change in the purchasing power of the dollar due to domestic inflation can affect the external value of the dollar, and the balance-of-payments position will change with it. In reality, the reverse is more likely—that is, a great world demand for dollar exchange due to price inflation in the rest of the world and to the generally inelastic nature of the world demand for American exports, as well as a great rise in the entire demand schedule (i.e., an increase in the quantity demanded as well as an increase in demand, as indicated by the steepness of the demand curve and by the upward shift in its position).

Gustav Cassel, J. M. Keynes, and others used the purchasing power parity theory after World War I to show that the fall in the external value of some European currencies was largely the result of postwar inflation in Europe. The theory is also useful in demonstrating the consequences of a possible discrepancy between the internal and external purchasing power of a national currency. The concepts of overvaluation and undervaluation are based on purchasing power parities. A currency is *overvalued* when its external value is kept at a level higher than its internal purchasing power. The overvaluation of a currency may come about via (a) price inflation, given stable exchange rates, or (b) foreign exchange stabilization or control.

The overvaluation of the pound and the undervaluation of the dollar are illustrated in the following example.

The Overvalued Pound and the Undervalued Dollar
Actual Rate $5 = £1
Parity Rate $4 = £1

In the foreign exchange market the pound is clearly overvalued relative to the dollar, indicating a higher price level or lower purchasing power in Britain than in the United States. This means that $5 will buy only $4 worth of goods in Britain. Hence one can say that the pound is "overvalued" and expensive relative to the dollar. It follows that *an overvalued currency,* other things equal, *leads to an increase in imports and to a decrease in exports.* On the other hand, the dollar is "undervalued" and cheap relative to the pound in the above example, thus indicating that the general price level in the United States is lower than in Britain. The dollar is undervalued and cheap in terms of sterling, since Americans must give up $5 instead of $4 to get £1 worth of goods. It follows from this that *an undervalued currency tends to stimulate exports and to reduce imports.* It is possible that the dollar is "undervalued" relative to the pound sterling but "overvalued" relative to other currencies, depending upon relative price levels in those countries. If, for example, prices remain constant in the United States but are rising in Britain, while hyperinflation is going on in the rest of the world, the dollar is likely to be undervalued in terms of sterling but overvalued in terms of all other currencies.

From the policy standpoint it is important to know in terms of what particular currency or currencies it is that the national currency is overvalued or undervalued. If Britain, for example, depended on imports from America more than from a combination of all other countries, the undervaluation of sterling relative to the dollar would be to the great disadvantage of Britain. For the sterling price of imports from the United States might be so high as to offset Britain's export earnings considerably, if not completely. Such a consideration is significant for a nation's balance-of-payments position, and therefore also for its domestic income and employment. An overvalued-currency country can achieve an import surplus if full employment is maintained by domestic policy, or else must suffer from unemployment and an adverse balance of payments. If imports are the main objective, the overvalued rate of exchange may be kept up by limiting the demand for foreign exchange relative to supply. If, on the other hand, export surpluses are desired, the overvalued rate should be "undervaluated" (i.e., depreciated) by allowing the demand for foreign exchange to increase relative to supply; otherwise the country in question must deflate to the possible detriment of domestic income and employment.

This suggests that deviations from the parity rate in the form of overvaluation or of undervaluation should not be criticized as incompatible with the equilibrium rate without reference to particular nations' balance of payments and their income and employment conditions. For natural or deliberate deviations from the parity rate are now often considered necessary to maintain internal economic stability and preferable to an adjustment of domestic prices. Such deviations doubtless do violence to the classical notion of keeping exchange rates "neutral" and of relying on internal price deflation or inflation for external equilibrium, as under an international gold standard. This leads us to a consideration of some relevant criticisms of the purchasing power parity theory.

Basic Defects of the Parity Theory

Before developing the "balance-of-payments theory" of exchange rates, Keynes suggested two basic defects of the parity theory, namely, (a) its failure to take into consideration the elasticities of reciprocal demand, and (b) its failure to consider the influence of capital movements.[1] In Keynes' view, foreign exchange rates are determined not only by price movements but also by capital movements, the elasticities of reciprocal demand, and many other forces affecting the demand for and supply of foreign exchange.

THE ELASTICITIES OF RECIPROCAL DEMAND

By the elasticity of reciprocal demand is meant the responsiveness of one country's demand for another country's exports with respect to price or income. As for the price elas-

[1] Cf. J. M. Keynes, *A Treatise on Money* (Harcourt, New York, 1930), Vol. 1, p. 336.

ticity of demand for exports, the price change which is relevant here might be considered to be due to exchange depreciation or appreciation, not to general price movements. With international price movement remaining constant, whether the external value of a national currency will change depends, among other things, on the responsiveness of the foreign demand for a nation's total exports to a slight change in that nation's export prices in terms of foreign currencies. Take, for example, the world demand for British exports, which is generally elastic with respect to price—luxuries and semiluxuries making up the bulk of those exports. Suppose that the pound sterling becomes depreciated as a result of an appreciation of other currencies, thus making British exports cheaper in terms of foreign currencies and British imports more expensive in terms of sterling. Since the world demand for British exports is assumed, and perhaps safely, to be elastic, there would be a shift of demand in the world market in favor of British exports. Since, also, the depreciation of the pound sterling has the effect of discouraging imports into Britain, the probable result would be a net increase in the world demand for pounds sterling, or what is the same, in the British supply of foreign exchange. This increase in the derived world demand for sterling exchange would result in an appreciation of sterling. Thus a change in the external value of the pound sterling has been brought about without any international price changes.

In general, it can be stated that a country's demand for another country's exports or for foreign exchange is the more elastic the greater the proportion of luxuries and semiluxuries in the exports demanded, the greater the number of alternative markets in which to buy, and the longer the period in which to produce effective substitutes for the goods imported. It is interesting to note in this connection that a world shortage of dollars and its depressing effect on the external value of many currencies other than the dollar is explainable partly in terms of a highly inelastic world demand for American exports relative to a highly elastic American demand for world exports—as in a postwar period—quite apart from relative price levels. Needless to say, in the longer period the elasticities of reciprocal demand can change significantly as a consequence of changes in international consumer tastes.

As for the income elasticity of demand for imports, the change in the demand for foreign goods and services and in the derived demand for foreign exchange is functionally related to the change in national income. The income elasticity of demand $(E = (dM/dY)/(M/Y)$; see Chap. 20) may be regarded as the responsiveness of a country's demand for another country's exports to changes in the domestic money incomes of the former country. In other words, it is the character of the propensity to import out of a given income that is supposed to affect exchange rates independently of international price movements. Suppose, for example, that because of some "trend" factors the income elasticity of demand for imports is high in the United States, while that of world demand for American exports is low in the rest of the world for similar reasons. Under these circumstances there would be a shift of demand in the world market in favor of non-American goods and services, as well as a shift of demand in the American economy from home goods to imports. The probable effect on exchange rates of such shifts of demand would be to appreciate foreign currencies relative to the dollar, even if no price changes took place anywhere.

A similar analysis applies when productivity increases as a result of some technological improvements in one country, for such a structural change expresses itself in an increased demand for that country's cheaper and perhaps better exports. This is especially true of innovations in the export industry. Tariff changes and export subsidies would similarly influence exchange rates via their influence upon reciprocal demand quite independently of international price movements.

Y

CAPITAL MOVEMENTS

Capital movements are the other important influence that Keynes mentions. Although Keynes concentrates on short-term speculative capital movements, long-term capital movements may have an equally important effect on exchange rates, as will be shown presently. Short-term speculative capital movements, otherwise known as "capital flight," may arise from a desire to make a profit or avoid a loss on exchange fluctuations, as in the case of "hot money," or from a desire for safety and security, as in the case of "refugee capital." Let us see how movements of such short-term capital may affect exchange rates.

Suppose that the price of the pound on the New York sterling market falls from $4 to $3.80 and is in danger of falling still farther. This means that dealers and banks can get fewer dollars for their pounds, or, what amounts to the same thing, more pounds for their dollars. They therefore try to get out of dollars and into pounds to avoid a loss or to make a profit. As a consequence the demand for dollars falls and the supply of pounds increases, thereby tending to lower the price of the pound still farther. So much for the abstract. Let us now take a concrete example.

Assume that the exchange rate between the dollar and the pound on the New York sterling market is $4 = £1, while simultaneously the rate quoted on the London dollar market is $3.80 = £1. Seeing this discrepancy, dealers and banks will sell dollars for pounds in London to resell the pound proceeds in New York to make a profit of $0.20 per pound. In sending "hot" dollars to be sold in London, dealers and banks will increase the supply of dollars in the London dollar market, and thus cause the sterling price of the dollar to fall (i.e., to appreciate the pound sterling). Similarly, in sending equally "hot" pounds to be resold in New York, they will increase the supply of pounds in the New York sterling market, and thereby cause the dollar price of the pound to fall (i.e., to appreciate the dollar). These movements of "hot money" will go on until the discrepancy between the two markets is wiped out so as to render the "hot" pursuit of speculative happiness inexpedient. In the meantime the damage is done —to exchange stability as well as to the purchasing power parity theory. For, on the one hand, the price of the pound has fallen as a result of the increased supply of pounds so as to appreciate the dollar unwarrantedly, while, on the other hand, the new exchange rate between the dollar and the pound has nothing whatsoever to do with general price movements or changes in purchasing power parities.

The same analysis applies to an import of "refugee capital," whether due to political crises abroad or to safe investment opportunities here. It can be stated in general that an inflow of "hot money" or an import of "refugee capital" tends to raise the exchange value of the currency of the capital-receiving country and that a withdrawal of such capital will lower it. Thus an actual or expected change in the domestic price of a foreign currency may lead to an inflow or outflow of "hot money" to cause a further change in the exchange rate between any two currencies involved, without there being any price changes in either country. The appreciation of domestic currency due to an inflow of short-term capital of a speculative nature is utterly unrelated to current needs, and therefore tends to upset equilibrium in the balance of payments of the country whose currency has appreciated. This implies that speculative short-term capital movements will have to be controlled; otherwise they will cause countries to adjust their balance of payments via internal price deflation or inflation. But this is a secondary impact of exchange fluctuations.

As for the influence of *long-term* capital movements, the exchange rate between the dollar and the pound sterling, for instance, will be affected by whether it is the United States or Britain that does the lending on long term. That is to say, it is the one-sided movement of long-term capital that is relevant to the present analysis. Suppose that the United States, for example, decides to lend to Britain by buying long-term British securities or by getting British I.O.U.'s in exchange for long-term loans to Britain. The effect on the exchange rate between the dollar and the pound can be seen more easily if looked at from the British angle. Thus when Britain borrows from the United States, it acquires claims on dollars, and the supply of dollars on the London exchange market increases. Consequently the sterling price of the dollar goes down, making the external value of sterling higher relative to the dollar. If, for example, the sterling price of a dollar before the capital import was £.25 (reciprocal of $4 per pound quoted on the New York market), it must fall below that figure—say, for simplicity's sake, to £.20. This means that the pound has become more expensive relative to the dollar as a result of the capital import from the United States. Britain can now purchase in the United States more cheaply than before the appreciation of the pound, even though the prices of American export goods have not fallen at all. The reverse would be true if the United States imported long-term capital from Britain, that is, the appreciation of the dollar relative to sterling on the New York exchange market.

Thus we can generalize by stating that the one-sided *export* of capital tends to *raise* the external value of the capital-*importing* country's currency, and that the one-sided *import* of capital tends to *lower* the external value of the capital-*exporting* country's currency. These effects can readily be seen in the following diagrams.

The original equilibrium rate of exchange between the dollar and the pound is taken to be $4 per pound on the New York exchange market and £.25 per dollar on the London exchange market, since $4 is the reciprocal of £.25, or one-fourth. After the American loan (capital export) to Britain, the supply of dollar exchange increases, as shown by the leftward shift of the supply curve S_2, with the result that the sterling price of the dollar on the London dollar exchange market falls to £.20—an appreciation of sterling. This fall in the sterling price of the dollar is reflected in a rise in the dollar price of the pound on the New York sterling market—a depreciation of the dollar. When the pound becomes more expensive relative to the dollar, individuals and dealers try to get out of dollars and into pounds, as was explained in con-

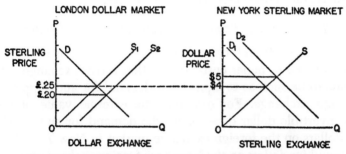

FIG. 31. EFFECTS OF LONG–TERM CAPITAL FROM THE UNITED STATES TO THE UNITED KINGDOM ON THE DOLLAR–STERLING EXCHANGE RATE

nection with "hot money." This means that the demand for sterling must rise as high as to equilibrate the dollar price of sterling and the sterling price of the dollar, or $5 = £1$ on the New York market and £.20 = $1 on the London market ($5 is the reciprocal of £.20, or one-fifth). The upward shift of the demand curve D_2 reflects the increased demand for pounds sterling on the New York sterling market.

There are many other criticisms of the purchasing power parity theory, both theoretical and practical,[2] but the fore-

[2]E.g., see G. H. Halm, *International Monetary Cooperation* (Univ. of North Carolina Press, 1945); G. Haberler, *International Trade* (Macmillan, New York, 1936); J. Viner, *Studies in the Theory of International Trade* (London, George Allen & Unwin Ltd., 1937); S. Enke and V. Salera, *International Economics* (Prentice–Hall, New York, 1947); L. A. Metzler, " Exchange Rates

going discussion of the basic defects of the parity theory suggested by Keynes, namely, the failures to consider the influence of reciprocal demand and to appreciate the independent role of capital movements, is sufficient to show that the determination of the external value of currencies depends not only on international price relations but on many other factors. We are now ready to discuss a more adequate explanation of the determination of foreign exchange rates, namely, the "balance-of-payments" theory.

The Balance-of-Payments Theory of Exchange Rates

The most satisfactory explanation of fluctuations in the external value of paper currencies is that a free exchange rate tends to be such as to equate the demand for and supply of foreign exchange. For example, the external value of the inconvertible dollar depends on the demand for and supply of dollars on the foreign exchange market in New York. *The demand for dollars on the New York foreign exchange market comes from people who offer foreign exchange in order to obtain dollars,* while *the supply of dollars comes from people offering dollars to obtain foreign exchange.* American exporters are an example of the first group, i.e., demanders, and American importers exemplify the second group, i.e., suppliers. Thus, for example, the *demand* for dollars by holders of pounds sterling constitutes the sterling-*supply* schedule, and the *supply* of dollars by those wanting pounds sterling constitutes the sterling-*demand* schedule. In other words, on the New York sterling market the demand for dollars is the same thing as the supply of pounds sterling, and the supply of dollars is another way of looking at the demand for pounds sterling. The intersection of the sterling-supply curve and the sterling-demand curve gives the equilibrium price of sterling that equates the amount of pounds sterling offered

---

and the International Monetary Fund," in *International Monetary Policies,* Federal Reserve Postwar Economic Studies, No. 7, Washington, 1947.

and the amount of pounds sterling demanded. If the equilibrium dollar price of sterling on the New York market happens to be $4 per pound, the equilibrium sterling price of the dollar on the London market tends to be £.25, which is the reciprocal of $4, or one-fourth, as was explained earlier.

Now the demand for foreign exchange arises from the debit items in the balance of payments, whereas the supply of foreign exchange arises from the credit items. "Debits" here refer to all payments made during a given period by residents to foreigners, and "credits" include all payments made during the period by foreigners to residents. If, for example, the United States has a net debit, its demand for foreign exchange—say, pounds sterling—must exceed its supply of pounds sterling, with the result that the dollar price of sterling will go up or, what amounts to the same thing, the external value of the dollar will go down relative to sterling. That is to say, the dollar becomes cheap in terms of sterling. Conversely, a net credit in the American balance of payments will lead to a drop in the dollar price of the pound, that is, to the higher external value of the dollar or the expensive dollar relative to the pound. We may write the causal relations among the demand for and supply of foreign exchange, the demand for and supply of dollars on the foreign exchange market, credits and debits in the balance of payments, and fluctuations in the exchange value of the dollar, as follows:

> Supply of foreign exchange = demand for dollars on the foreign exchange market (i.e., New York)
>
> Demand for foreign exchange = supply of dollars on the foreign exchange market
>
> Credits > debits on current account = increased supply of foreign exchange
>
> Debits < credits on current account = increased demand for foreign exchange
>
> Demand for foreign exchange > supply of foreign exchange = higher domestic price of a

foreign currency (i.e., the cheaper dollar relative to another currency)

Supply of foreign exchange > demand for foreign exchange = lower domestic price of a
foreign currency (i.e., the expensive dollar
relative to another currency)

Since the demand for and supply of dollars on the foreign
exchange market depends on the demand for and supply of
foreign exchange, it is useful to list the major factors responsible for changes in the demand for and supply of foreign exchange. It is well to recall, in this connection, that the demand
for and supply of foreign exchange is in the final analysis
nothing else than the demand for and supply of foreign goods
and services; the former is derived from the latter. As has already been stated, the supply of foreign exchange arises from
the "credit" items in the balance of payments, while the demand for foreign exchange results from the "debits." Therefore, to know what constitute "credits" and "debits" is to
know the sources of the demand and supply of foreign exchange, as shown in the following list.

Supply (credits)

1. Commodity exports.
2. Services rendered to foreigners (e.g., shipping and
   freight).
3. Travel expenditures by foreigners.
4. Interest and dividends on
   foreign securities owned
   here.
5. Remittances and charitable
   contributions by foreigners.
6. Government expenditures
   by foreign nations.
7. Imports of long-term capital (i.e., export of stocks
   and bonds to U.S. by for-

Demand (debits)

1. Commodity imports.
2. Services rendered by foreigners.
3. Travel expenditures by na-
   tionals abroad.
4. Interest and dividends on
   American securities owned
   by foreigners.
5. Remittances and charitable
   contributions by residents.
6. Government expenditures
   by the U.S.
7. Exports of long-term capital
   (i.e., import of foreign
   stocks and bonds, American
   direct investments abroad,

Supply (credits)
eigners, foreign direct investments here, and foreign loans to here).
8. Imports of short-term capital (i.e., increase of foreign-owned bank balances in the U.S.).
9. Gold exports.

Demand (debits)
and loans to foreigners).
8. Exports of short-term capital (i.e., increase of American bank balances abroad).
9. Gold imports.

It is customary to put 1, 2, 3, 4, 5, and 6 on both sides in the category of "current transactions," 7 and 8 in "capital movements," and 9 in "gold movements." By far the most significant item is represented by commodity exports and imports; it is usually the single largest source of the demand for and supply of foreign exchange. But the quantitative significance of any one item differs from country to country. If a country has a *deficit* in its current account (items from 1 to 6) as a result of an excess of visible and invisible imports over similar exports, it must experience an *adverse* balance of payments in the sense that it is paying off the debts by drawing on its foreign exchange reserves, by exporting gold, or by borrowing on short term from creditor countries—in short, *by giving foreigners claims on its currency.* Conversely, a *favorable* balance of payments means that a *surplus* country (on current account) must be *accumulating claims on foreign currencies.* It is not difficult, therefore, to see the relation between the balance of payments and the exchange rate.

Since *an increase in a country's claims on another country's currency means an increase in the supply of that currency on the first country's foreign exchange market,* the domestic price of that currency tends to decrease, thus appreciating the external value of the creditor country's currency. Suppose, for example, that the United States is accumulating more claims on the rest of the world than the world is on us. Assume the original exchange rate between the dollar and all foreign currencies to be $4 = £1$ (£ representing foreign currencies). Then the supply of foreign exchange on the New York exchange market must increase relative to demand and the new equilibrium rate of exchange must therefore fall below $4—say, to $3.80. This would make the dollar expensive relative to all other currencies and the United States a dear market in which to buy. Eventually American exports would decline. This would wipe out a favorable balance of payments in the United States, cheapen the dollar relative to other currencies, and so on—back to equilibrium. Conversely, a deficit country is likely to have a weak exchange-rate position, since *an increase in foreign claims on its currency means an increase in the demand for foreign exchange relative to supply to cause a decline in the external value of its currency.* But then the deficit country will be able to wipe out an adverse balance of payments by increasing exports, thanks to the depreciated external value of its currency. Therefore a deficit country's position may be weak with respect to the exchange rate but strong with respect to export advantages.

The advantage of the balance-of-payments theory of exchange rates is not difficult to see in the light of the above discussion. It is perhaps useful to make a few generalizations about this advantage. First, the explanation of the determination of exchange rates in terms of supply and demand forces facilitates equilibrium analysis, not to mention its consistency with common sense. Second, the theory is more realistic in that the domestic price of a foreign currency is seen as a function of many significant variables, not just purchasing power expressing general price levels. But the greatest practical significance of the balance-of-payments theory lies in the fact that it clearly shows the possibility of adjusting balances of payment disequilibria through exchange-rate adjustments rather than through internal price deflation or inflation as implied by the parity theory.

The Manipulation of Exchange Rates

EXCHANGE DEPRECIATION

How can a country with a net debit overcome its position of disequilibrium? Under the gold standard the answer was deflation, but under the paper standard it is usually exchange depreciation, though other methods are also available. The extent of exchange depreciation for equilibrium purposes depends on (a) the degree and duration of disequilibrium, and (b) the marginal propensity to import. If a country is confronted with a serious and continuous adverse balance of payments, an appreciable fall in the exchange rate is required to restrict imports significantly. The country's marginal propensity to import is likely to be high if its imports consist largely of foodstuffs, raw materials, and other necessities. When therefore the marginal propensity to import is high, the exchange rate will have to be brought down very low (e.g., from $4 = £1 down to $8 = £1, or a 100 per cent fall in the exchange value of the dollar). Conversely, if the country's imports consist mainly of luxuries, its marginal propensity to import is likely to be low and therefore a small fall in the exchange rate will be sufficient to correct an adverse balance of payments. The most effective way to decrease imports is of course to deflate the total money income of the country in question, as was customary under the gold standard. But there is no need for money incomes to be reduced if exchange depreciation does the trick just as well. In fact, it is largely to avoid a painful process of deflation that the method of letting the exchange rate depreciate has come to be adopted. The process of equilibrium adjustments via exchange depreciation may be described in the following sequence.

1. Disequilibrium—a net debit.
2. A reduction in American balances (i.e., foreign exchange reserves) held in foreign centers.

3. Exchange depreciation (i.e., a higher price for drafts on foreign centers).
4. Arrest of imports and other debit items and stimulation of exports.
5. An increase in the flow of foreign currencies into the balances held by American banks in foreign centers and a decrease in the flow of foreign currencies out of those balances.
6. Equilibrium in the American balance of payments.

Instead of allowing exchange rates to fluctuate naturally, the central bank may offer to buy foreign exchange at higher prices and thus bring about exchange depreciation. This is the familiar method of *competitive exchange depreciation.* As a means of gaining export advantages, exchange depreciation is a dangerous weapon, capable of destroying long-run international equilibrium.[3] But as a method of preserving internal stability, i.e., by maintaining equilibrium in the balance of payments, exchange depreciation deserves approval. For the stability of internal prices, credit, and employment is generally considered preferable to the stability of the exchange rates. Precisely because it is the line of least resistance, exchange depreciation is at once attractive and destructive. Competitive exchange depreciation not only wipes out temporary export advantages but also discourages international trade and investment in longer periods.[4] Exchange depreciation loses its chief justification if it stifles international trade to such an extent as to upset internal stability. This suggests that constructive use of exchange depreciation requires inter-

[3] For this reason the members of the International Monetary Fund are required not to engage in competitive currency depreciation. However, the Fund allows the downward adjustment of the par value of a member country's currency up to 10 per cent without prior approval, if and when necessary.

[4] Competitive exchange depreciation is not likely to be a serious problem when there are world-wide shortages of commodities, as during an immediate postwar period. (See R. F. Mikesell, "The Role of the International Monetary Agents in a World of Planned Economies," *Journal of Political Economy,* December, 1947.)

national co-operation with respect to the national efforts to stabilize income and employment. Such considerations as this prompted the establishment of the International Monetary Fund, the International Bank, and the International Trade Organization. More on this subject later.

EXCHANGE STABILIZATION

Exchange stabilization is an attempt to overcome the disadvantage of erratic movements in exchange rates without losing the advantage of free exchange markets. It is also an admission that *laissez faire* in international monetary matters does all concerned more harm than good. If exchange fluctuations according to the free play of supply and demand are deemed undesirable, a country may deliberately try to influence the demand for and supply of foreign exchange in order to stabilize exchange rates. A country may establish an *exchange stabilization fund,* as Britain did in 1932 or as the United States did in 1934 with resources of $2 billion in gold taken from the profit resulting from the devaluation of the dollar. An exchange stabilization fund is a device to prevent appreciation or depreciation of domestic currency relative to another currency.

To prevent the appreciation of the dollar on the foreign exchange market, for instance, the stabilization fund buys foreign exchange and gold to create an artificial demand for foreign exchange. Contrariwise, to prevent the depreciation of the dollar, the fund increases the supply of foreign exchange. The fund's supply of foreign exchange and therefore its ability to sell foreign exchange is definitely limited at any moment, since it may not possess sufficient foreign exchange as part of its assets. Of course the fund can always increase the demand, that is, buy foreign exchange with domestic currency, since the government can borrow from the banking system. Therefore it is easier to prevent the appreciation of the dollar than to prevent its depreciation.

Suppose that the government decides to stabilize the dollar-sterling rate at $4 = £1. Suppose, further, that the dollar has appreciated to $3.60 = £1 and is in danger of rising farther. In this case the stabilization fund will step into the foreign exchange market and buy enough sterling to offset the demand for dollars. This attempt to prevent the appreciation of the dollar is shown in Figure 32 (A). Figure 32 (B) shows a situation in which the fund has increased the supply of foreign exchange in order to prevent the depreciation of the dollar

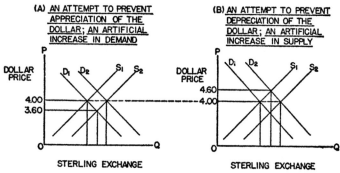

FIG. 32. OPERATIONS OF THE STABILIZATION
FUND

from $4 = £1 to, say, $4.60 = £1. In Figure 32 (A), the supply of sterling exchange increases due to, say, an American export surplus, from S_1 to S_2 and, the demand being equal, lowers the dollar price of sterling exchange (i.e., to raise the external value of the dollar) from $4 to $3.60. At this juncture the stabilization fund steps in and increases the demand for sterling exchange, that is, buys up sterling, until the original equilibrium rate of $4 is restored. The fund has in effect depreciated the dollar. Note that the demand has been increased by an amount equal to the increase in the supply, thus offsetting the appreciating effect of the latter. D_2 represents the artificially increased demand. Figure 32 (B) illustrates the opposite situation, namely, the restoration (or maintenance) of the equilibrium rate of $4 by increasing the supply of sterling exchange from S_1 to S_2 to offset an increase in the demand for sterling exchange from D_1 to D_2 due to, say, an import surplus. If the exchange rate had been left to the free play of market forces, it would have depreciated even beyond $4.60. The fund has, in effect, appreciated the dollar. In both cases, however, the fund has stabilized the external value of the dollar at $4 = £1.

EXCHANGE CONTROL

In contrast to mere intervention in the free foreign exchange market, exchange control represents the government monopoly of foreign exchange transactions. During the 1930's one country after another adopted exchange control, first as an emergency measure to arrest capital flight and then as a permanent measure to insulate itself from the adverse repercussions of a depression elsewhere. The orthodox method of coping with a flight of capital is the deflation of prices, incomes, and employment, since such a measure leads to high interest rates which deter capital from leaving. But this method presupposes a gold standard with all its disadvantages. A country confronted with capital flight and therefore with the depletion of central bank gold reserves could go off gold and let the exchange value of its currency depreciate low enough to reverse the process of a flight from domestic currency into foreign exchange. But such a course of action would be self-defeating, since the country in question would have to give up more of domestic currency for the same amount of foreign currencies. Devaluation is equally objectionable for the same reason. Under these circumstances a country facing capital flight would resort to exchange control in order to restrict the demand for foreign exchange and to increase its supply. This is precisely what Germany did, for example. Instead of going off gold, Germany adopted exchange control in 1931 after inordinate withdrawals of marks by foreign holders of mark balances (an increase in the demand for foreign exchange).

Germany controlled the demand for foreign exchange by forcing foreign creditors to agree not to withdraw their balances. The supply of foreign exchange was restricted by a permit system. The demand for foreign exchange was also cut down by import restrictions. The Nazis later allowed only imports deemed necessary for armaments, restricted luxury imports and general imports from unfriendly countries, and increased the supply of foreign exchange by forcing German holders of foreign securities and bank balances to sell them to the government authority for marks. It may be noted parenthetically that a successful program of exchange control requires vigilant supervision over all foreign exchange transactions, particularly "black market" transactions. For it is possible to evade exchange control by selling illegally the foreign exchange acquired, that is, at a rate higher than the officially pegged rate, or by quoting lower prices for exports than the prices actually paid and thus pocketing foreign exchange without the knowledge of the authority.

Exchange control sometimes takes the form of a *clearing agreement,* such as obtained between Germany and a host of other European countries during the 1930's. With such an agreement existing between, say, Britain and the United States, trade between them is merely a matter of bookkeeping. Suppose that the pound sterling is pegged at £.25 per dollar for clearing purposes. If an English importer buys $1,000 worth of goods from an American exporter, the English importer must under these arrangements pay into the Bank of England the equivalent of $1,000, or £250. The Bank of England then credits the United States with £250, and the United States government (or its fiscal agency, the Federal Reserve bank) in turn credits the American exporter in question with $1,000. An American importer does likewise with the United States government. Thus no direct transactions in foreign exchange are involved. Exports and imports tend in the long run to be equal, since balances accumulated in the clearing pool must be used to finance an equal amount of imports from the other party.

As an instrument of *bilateral finance,* a clearing agreement diverts foreign trade from the channels of multilateral trade by requiring a perfect balance between every pair of trading nations involved. But even as such, a clearing agreement is often defended on the ground that some trade is better than no trade at all, especially when it is difficult to export to free-currency areas or to import from countries which expect to be paid in free, convertible currencies. Stripped of its bilateral nature, a clearing agreement can promote multilateral trade, as Keynes' proposed "Clearing Union" based on international bank-money, called "bancor," clearly demonstrated a theoretical possibility of an international system of payments without the use of gold or foreign exchange.[5] A Keynesian "Clearing Union" may yet catch the imagination of the world economy troubled with a "chronic shortage of dollars."

Another version of exchange control is a *multiple exchange* system—a system which originated in Latin America during the Great Depression as part of the attempt to overcome a persistent tendency toward an adverse balance of payments. Under this system, the government fixes prices for foreign currencies, depending on the use to which foreign exchange is to be put or the source from which it is derived. For example, the government may set low prices (e.g., $3.50 per pound) to facilitate import of what it considers necessary and vital, while setting high prices (e.g., $4 per pound) for the purchase of foreign exchange arising from export of products which the government wishes to encourage. Thus the government in effect appreciates the external value of domestic currency to promote certain imports and depreciates it to stimulate particular exports. Generally speaking, high prices are paid per unit

[5] See *The Keynes Plan,* April 8, 1943.

z

for foreign exchange by importers of luxuries and low prices paid per unit for foreign exchange by importers of necessities. The government may also appreciate domestic currency to service external debts more cheaply by fixing low domestic prices for currencies of particular creditor countries. Thus a multiple exchange system discriminates against particular countries as well as against particular goods, whereas overall exchange depreciation or appreciation does not. For this reason it is outlawed by the International Monetary Fund.

While exchange control is far more effective than exchange stabilization in regulating fluctuations in the external value of currencies, it tends to restrict international trade and investment unduly. Exchange control is essentially an instrument of economic planning,[6] and is likely to be retained or adopted as long as capital flight and periodic depression plague nations. It is not without significance, therefore, that the Bretton Woods Agreements provide for permanent exchange control over autonomous short-term capital movements as well as for temporary exchange control under exceptional circumstances, as will be discussed in the next chapter.

[6] See H. S. Ellis, "Exchange Control and Discrimination," *American Economic Review,* December, 1947; for a sympathetic approach to the postwar problem of exchange control, see R. Triffin, "National Central Banking and the International Economy," in *International Monetary Policies,* Federal Reserve Postwar Economic Studies, No. 7, 1947.

19

The International Monetary
Fund—The Mixed Standard

THE INTERNATIONAL Monetary Fund as established by the Bretton Woods Agreements is a substitute for the old gold standard, and an alternative to both a system of completely free exchange rates and a system of extreme exchange control. In other words, the Fund is a mixed standard embodying within itself some features of the gold standard and the paper standard. It represents an attempt at "an improved system of International Currency," in Keynes' words. We are primarily interested in those aspects of the Fund which have a direct bearing upon the external value of currencies. In this chapter, therefore, we shall deal with the theoretical basis of the determination of exchange rates under the Fund, and with its practical implications for international currency relations and domestic welfare.

Keynes' Basic Proposals

Keynes' agenda for "an improved system of International Currency" serve as a useful starting point, since they clearly reveal what it is that distinguishes the International Monetary

Fund from the traditional systems of international currency. In the Keynes Plan, which Lord Keynes submitted (April 8, 1943) to the Bretton Woods Conference in behalf of his country, Keynes outlined the basic prerequisites of a sound system of international currency, as amplified below.

1. In place of a gold standard, which rigidly links the external value of a national currency to a fixed quantity of gold, and which ties the hands of the monetary authority of a gold standard country with respect to internal monetary policy, a new system must be established to use gold only as "a convenient common denominator by means of which the relative values of national currencies—these being free to change—are expressed from time to time." Thus Keynes advised nations to make gold a servant rather than a master. He considered gold useful, however, as "an uncontroversial standard of value for international purposes," as well as a store of value to satisfy the international speculative motive for liquidity, given the existing psychological-institutional complex. If Keynes defended gold as possessing "great psychological value which is not being diminished by current events," it may be presumed that his proposed nongold "bancor" (international bank money) would become a reality only when nations got out from under the spell of that black magic called gold. The important principle involved here, however, is that *there should be some new international currency the quantity of which is not determined accidentally or irrelevantly but can be adjusted deliberately according to fluctuations in "effective world demand."*

2. Another point of departure is Keynes' proposal that the relative exchange values of national currencies be determined by "an orderly and agreed method" in order to exclude such unilateral measures as internationally harmful competitive exchange depreciation. While, therefore, advocating exchange flexibility as a better alternative than exchange rigidity,

Keynes nevertheless considered it necessary for nations not to go to the extreme of depreciating the external value of their currencies to gain export advantages at the expense of one another. The principle to note here is that *nations should cooperate through some morally and legally binding international agreements in making such exchange-rate adjustments as are consistent with international price-cost structures and with balance-of-payments equilibrium positions.* This principle precludes the adjustment of exchange rates solely with reference to purchasing power parities or solely with a view to export advantages or import advantages, as the case may be.

3. Keynes further proposed the application of the insurance principle to the open system with foreign trade relations, that is, an international banking system analogous to the Federal Reserve System in the United States. Just as scattered reserves of individual banks are pooled together by the central bank in each country so that no one member bank need suffer for want of liquidity, so can each member-country be protected by a common pool of liquidity (i.e., gold or foreign exchange) against international liabilities and against balance-of-payment crises. Thus, by making international credit available to a deficit country, for example, an international banking system would help maintain that country's exchange-rate position, which might otherwise be weakened by a loss of scarce gold or foreign exchange (i.e., help minimize the depressing effect of an inevitable decrease in its supply of foreign exchange on the external value of its currency). The essential point is that *there should be an international central reserve system to serve as a common pool against exchange-reserve crises, so that no nation may, "for causes which are not of its own making," resort to discriminatory and restrictive measures of "self-protection from disruptive outside forces."*

These, then, are the major fundamental principles that Keynes outlined in his Plan as a basis for Bretton Woods monetary discussions and as a guide to the realization of "an improved system of International Currency." [1] It remains yet to be seen to what extent the International Monetary Fund as a going concern will live up to Keynes' expectations, for the Fund has accepted Keynes' basic ideas only in principle, along with many other ideas. We shall leave this matter to the future to decide.

The Fund and Exchange Rates

How are exchange rates to be determined under the International Monetary Fund? What are the criteria for determining "correct" exchange rates for member-countries? In what manner is a member-country supposed to adjust the external value of its currency? What provisions does the Fund have regarding exchange depreciation, exchange control, exchange convertibility, and other exchange problems? These are some of the vital questions that need to be answered, if we are to understand the advantages of the mixed standard over the gold standard or the paper standard.

1. The Fund requires that the par value of a member-country's currency be "expressed in terms of gold as a common denominator or in terms of the United States dollar of the weight and fineness in effect on July 1, 1944" (Article IV, Sec. 1). This requirement by itself gives the false impression that the external value of a national currency may be as fixed and rigid under the Fund as under the gold standard. It should

---

[1] The White Plan, the American counterpart of the Keynes Plan, was submitted a little later than the Keynes Plan (revised July 10, 1943) and embodies substantially the same principles. For controversial discussions on Anglo–American currency proposals, see, e.g., J. H. Williams, "Currency Stabilization: the Keynes and White Plans," *Foreign Affairs*, July, 1943; J. Viner, "Two Plans for International Monetary Stabilization," *Yale Review*, fall, 1943; F. A. Lutz, *International Monetary Mechanism. The Keynes and White Proposals* (Princeton, 1943); J. Robinson, "The International Currency Proposals," *op. cit.*; A. H. Hansen, *America's Role in the World Economy*; G. Halm, *International Monetary Cooperation*; H. D. White, "Postwar Currency Stabilization," *American Economic Review*, March, 1943; D. H. Robertson, "Post–War Monetary Plans," *Economic Journal*, December, 1943.

be observed at once that this requirement is *for accounting purposes,* not for the purpose of maintaining stable exchange rates, as under the gold standard. In other words, it is as a common unit of account, not as an instrument of an automatic specie-flow-price system, that gold is stressed here. For, as Keynes pointed out,[2] the external value of a currency under the Fund is expressed in terms of gold as a common denominator without being "rigidly tied to a fixed quantity of gold" or involving "a financial policy which compels the internal value of the domestic currency to conform to this external value as fixed in terms of gold." If, for example, the dollar-sterling exchange rate is fixed at $4.03 = £1 as an expression of the relative gold weights of the dollar (0.889 gram) and the pound (3.581 grams), as was initially set by the Fund, it by no means precludes the possibility that the rate may be altered as domestic and international conditions necessarily change.

2. In order to facilitate multilateral trade among member-countries the Fund bars "competitive exchange alterations," and requires each member-country to "maintain orderly exchange arrangements with other members." In other words, the Fund thereby hopes to avoid the disadvantage of a *laissez-faire* exchange-rate policy as well as the disadvantage of un-alterable exchange rates, in short, to achieve *managed* exchange stability. To implement this exchange management the Fund provides for a 10 per cent adjustment, upward or downward, in the external value of a member-country's currency without prior approval by the Fund, and for a more than 10 per cent adjustment with the Fund's consent—all for the express purpose of correcting a serious disequilibrium in a member-country's balance of payments. This is an important concession to exchange flexibility which is impossible under either the gold standard or the paper standard. For under the gold standard exchange flexibility of any kind is out of the

[2] Speech, House of Lords, May 23, 1944.

question, while under the paper standard exchange flexibility is in the habit of degenerating into disorderly, discriminatory competitive exchange depreciation.

Theoretically any member-country could devalue its currency by more than 10 per cent, but it is doubtful that the other member-countries would concur, since they are not interested in one country's export advantages. In other words, a member-country is supposed to resort to the downward adjustment of the par value of its currency only as a last resort. The important principle involved here, however, is that *a member-country is spared the necessity of deflating its internal prices, incomes, and employment to overcome an adverse balance of payments as long as it can devalue its currency by such a proportion as is necessary and as may be approved by the Fund.* Nevertheless, there is danger that the desire for exchange stability and against competitive exchange depreciation may get the upper hand of exchange flexibility so essential to the avoidance of deflation. Such a danger is implicit in a tendency to identify exchange *stability* with exchange *rigidity*.[3]

Although the prevention of competitive exchange depreciation is a great merit of the Fund, it is considered to be a serious weakness of the Fund that neither surplus countries nor deficit countries are required to make appropriate exchange-rate adjustments, namely, the appreciation of the former's currencies and the depreciation of the latter's currencies.[4] This absence of the power to require the appreciation of currencies on the part of surplus countries and the depreciation of currencies on the part of deficit countries is found objectionable for two reasons. First, if surplus countries are not required to appreciate their currencies, they are presum-

---

[3] A. P. Lerner properly criticizes this tendency, but his plea for flexible exchange rates on the basis of automatic forces cannot be accepted, if speculative and planless capital movements are to be avoided. See his article, in *Planning and Paying for Full Employment.*

[4] On this point see J. E. Meade, *op. cit.*, pp. 101–102.

ably free to depreciate their currencies, and so would prevent deficit countries from getting the full benefit of devaluation. If, for instance, a deficit Britain depreciated its currency by 20 per cent to overcome an adverse balance of payments and a surplus America depreciated its currency by 20 per cent, Britain would be unable to gain an export advantage over America and would fail to overcome that adverse balance. If, on the other hand, a surplus America had to appreciate the dollar, while a deficit Britain was depreciating the pound, the rest of the world would find the surplus country (U.S.) an expensive place in which to buy and the deficit country (U.K.) a cheap place in which to buy, and would therefore import more from Britain, to the benefit of the latter's balance of payments. Second, unless the surplus countries are required to appreciate their currencies simultaneously with the required depreciation of the deficit countries' currencies, the result would be to throw balanced countries out of balance. For the deficit countries would be able to undersell the balanced countries as well as the surplus countries and so throw the balanced countries into deficit and compel them to depreciate to the detriment of all, while the simultaneous appreciation of the surplus countries would enable both the deficit and balanced countries to undersell only the surplus countries.

3. Since a change in the par value of a member-country's currency is made to depend on the existence of "fundamental disequilibrium," it is necessary to clarify the concept involved. The Fund presumably concurs in a proposed change in the par value of a member-country's currency (beyond the 10 per cent limit) if and when, in the opinion of the Fund authorities, the member-country requesting the change is confronted with *a persistent deficit* in its current account (an excess of debits over credits in current-account transactions) *which is met by such a critical loss of exchange reserves or gold or by such short-term borrowing from foreigners*

(imports of short-term capital) *as to necessitate import restriction, aggressive export drives, or large-scale imports of long-term capital.* This is a useful definition of "fundamental disequilibrium" as a first approximation, but it requires some refinement.

First, the above notion of "fundamental disequilibrium" is based on the tacit assumption of full employment not only in the deficit country requesting the exchange adjustment but also in the rest of the world. For if the deficit country in question is at less than full employment, its income-demand for foreign as well as for domestic goods may be low enough to keep imports down and so to keep all debit items in balance with all credit items without the help of exchange depreciation or of import restriction. Similarly, at less than full employment the export prices of the deficit country, not to mention general prices, may be low enough to keep up exports, if not to expand them, and so to maintain equilibrium in its balance of payments without the benefit of exchange depreciation. If, on the other hand, the rest of the world is simultaneously at less than full employment, the world's demand for imports from the deficit country is low, to be sure, but its export prices may be low enough to enable the deficit country to buy from the rest of the world more cheaply and so to keep its import costs in line with export revenues without the stimulating effect on its exports of exchange depreciation. Thus it is conceivable that equilibrium in the balance of payment coexists with less than full employment, so that there may be no "fundamental disequilibrium" to require drastic exchange depreciation.

Second, what if the member-country requesting an exchange adjustment is experiencing an adverse balance of payments *coupled with chronic unemployment?* Such a situation is possible if the state of less than full employment fails, *in fact,* to bring about equilibrium in the member-country's balance of payments. For then the adverse balance of payments will have the effect of not only increasing domestic unemployment via the reverse operation of the foreign-trade multiplier but also of prolonging that unemployment. The Fund's attitude toward a situation of this sort is not very clear, probably because the Fund does not wish to give the impression that it is willing to allow exchange depreciation to be used as a means of overcoming domestic unemployment rather than just "fundamental disequilibrium." The Fund takes the general attitude, however, that it would rather see a member-country faced with chronic unemployment *due to* a persistent adverse balance of payment depreciate its currency than see that country adopt discriminatory trade practices or resort to classical deflation. To this extent the concept of "fundamental disequilibrium" based on balance-of-payment considerations alone has been modified, largely owing to Keynes' effort to impress on the Fund authorities a notion of the vital relation between the balance of payments and the levels of domestic employment in general and between a persistent adverse balance and chronic unemployment in particular.[5]

Thus we are left with two basic criteria of Fund exchange-rate policy, namely, (a) concurrence in exchange depreciation *when there is a persistent unfavorable balance of payments even in conditions of domestic full employment, and* (b) similar action *when there is chronic mass unemployment because of a persistent tendency toward an adverse balance of payments.* This latter circumstance is of particular significance for those member-countries which depend heavily on foreign trade for total national income and which, therefore, experience the full impact of a serious unfavorable balance of payments.

[5] In response to Keynes' request for clarification the Fund authorities concurred in his view that measures to minimize the chronically depressing impact of an adverse balance of payments on domestic employment may also be measures to correct a "fundamental disequilibrium." See *New York Times,* March 19, 1946.

The Fund and Exchange Control

Since the International Monetary Fund is interested "in the establishment of a multilateral system of payments in respect of current transactions between members and in the elimination of foreign exchange restrictions which hamper the growth of world trade" (Article I, iv), it is pertinent to know the Fund's concrete provisions and their implications. The Fund's policy with respect to exchange control may be divided into (a) postwar transition measures, (b) permanent measures, and (c) exceptions to the rule. Let us, then, analyze and appraise these measures and exceptions with a view to understanding how the Fund hopes to promote "a multilateral system of payments."

1. In recognition of many postwar currency and balance-of-payment difficulties the Fund permits member-countries to retain or adopt such "restrictions on payments and transfers for current international transactions" as circumstances may necessitate (Article XIV, Sec. 2) for five years after the Fund begins to operate (1946–51) and thereafter with the Fund's approval (Article XIV, Sec. 4). This provision applies to the retention or adoption, during the above period, of all forms of exchange control discussed earlier, including multiple currency practices, and other discriminatory currency practices generally disapproved by the Fund. It is to be emphasized that only those forms of exchange control which restrict *payments and transfers for current transactions* are at issue here. In other words, the control of the demand for and supply of foreign exchange to prevent payments and transfers unrelated to current transactions (e.g., speculative short-term capital movements) is permissible always and therefore does not depend on the above provision. The member-countries maintaining exchange control under this provision are expected to *remove it as soon as they are in a position to settle their balance of payments without depending on the Fund's foreign*

exchange or gold reserves, or, in the terminology of the Fund, settle the balance "in a manner which will not unduly encumber their access to the resources of the Fund" (Article XIV, Sec. 2). This means that if and when a member-country has accumulated enough claims on other countries to be able to meet a deficit in its current account without borrowing additional foreign exchange from the Fund, then such a member-country should remove all exchange restrictions except those designed to prevent speculative short-term capital movements.

To appreciate the significance of the above provision, let us take for example the form of exchange control known as "exchange inconvertibility." The Fund defines "convertible currencies" as those "holdings of other members which are not availing themselves of the transitional arrangements under Article XIV, Section 2." This means that a member-country has inconvertible currencies when it holds the currencies of other member-countries which do have exchange control permitted under Article XIV, Section 2. Thus India, for example, may hold inconvertible currency (in the form of, say, bank balances) in London, if the British government, by virtue of the above transition arrangements, decides to restrict the withdrawal of claims due to India, that is, to "freeze" India's claims on the British pound. Now Britain is said to operate on a system of "exchange inconvertibility" when it has *a policy of not buying balances of its currency held by another member which needs the conversion of those balances* (into India's currency or into gold) for current-transaction payments. Why should the Fund permit such exchange control during the transition period? The answer is that in our example Britain as the central bank for sterling-area countries must have sufficient gold or dollar reserves to meet deficits of all those countries—in short, "dollar shortages" which may arise not only from current deficits but from more fundamental causes, as will be discussed later. If, therefore, in the opinion of the

Fund, the balance-of-payment position of Great Britain has strategic significance for international trade and finance as a whole, then it is only proper that Britain should be permitted to retain "exchange inconvertibility" until fundamental trade relations change in such a way as to warrant currency convertibility.

2. Barring transitional exceptions and "a general scarcity of a particular currency" (a problem which will be discussed shortly), the Fund's *general rule with respect to exchange control* is that "no member shall, without the approval of the Fund, impose restrictions on the making of payments and transfers for current international transactions" (Article VIII, Sec. 2a). More specifically, the Fund *prohibits* (a) exchange restrictions on all current payments other than those designed to facilitate capital transfers to close deficit gaps, (b) multiple currency practices, and (c) avoidance of the conversion of foreign-held balances into gold or into the currency of another member-country holding those balances; but it *permits* (d) permanent exchange control necessary to "regulate international capital movements" (Article VI, Sec. 3), i.e., to prevent "capital flight" from upsetting both exchange stability and members' balance-of-payments positions.

To see the rationale of these specific provisions clearly, one need only imagine what would happen in their absence. In the absence of (a), countries would probably resort to bilateral clearing agreements and other ingenious devices, to the benefit of a pair of countries involved but to the detriment of multilateral finance and trade. Likewise, in the absence of (b), countries would doubtless discriminate against a particular currency and in favor of another for economic and possibly political reasons, the effectiveness of such discrimination depending largely on the elasticities of reciprocal demand. Internally, also, importers of particular foreign goods (e.g., necessities) might get a better price for the foreign exchange they would have to buy from the government (i.e., the lower domestic price of foreign exchange), while exporters of luxuries might get more domestic money in exchange for the foreign exchange which they would have to sell to the government; all other importers and exporters would be penalized by unfavorable exchange rates fixed by the government.

Absence of (c) would normally prevent the holders of otherwise "convertible currencies" not only from making current payments to others but from expanding exports to others who could otherwise have sufficient means of payment, while enabling countries of "exchange inconvertibility" to enjoy one-sided exchange stability and equilibrium which would otherwise be disturbed by withdrawals of foreign-held balances. Lastly, the absence of (d) would mean that member-countries had no effective control over that highly disequilibrating factor known as "capital flight," and therefore over exchange instability and "fundamental disequilibrium." It is necessary in this connection to stress that the control of exchange reserves involved in (d) does *not* pertain to the control of either *equilibrating* short-term capital movements necessary to bring current debit transactions into line with current credit transactions, or to similar long-term capital movements necessary to balance all debits and credits. In other words, the exchange control in question refers only to *autonomous short-term* capital movements unrelated to current transactions which, if uncontrolled, would jeopardize exchange stability as well as international balance-of-payments equilibrium.

Thus the Fund hopes to maintain exchange *stability* without exchange *rigidity* on the one hand and to promote exchange *flexibility* with some exchange *control* on the other. Here again, true to a mixed standard, the Fund is trying to avoid the inherent disadvantages and weakness of both an unalterable gold standard and an unregulated paper standard. Therefore the Fund's policy with respect to exchange control may be properly regarded as one of "managed flexibility."

Nevertheless there is perhaps this danger to be avoided: namely, of compelling member-countries to remove the existing exchange controls on too rigid grounds of principle or along too legalistic lines, without due regard to concrete problems confronting any particular one of those countries. For there is no wisdom in deciding such important matters on abstract grounds without reference to concrete circumstances and probable consequences for all concerned.

The Fund's Lending Operations

In line with its express object of promoting international equilibrium in general and "high levels of employment and real income" in member-countries in particular, the International Monetary Fund makes its resources available to its members, if and when necessary. The sequence of events which the Fund's short-term lending operations are designed to prevent is, to put it crudely, adverse balances of payments, exchange instability, greater risks in international trade and finance, reduced effective world demand, severe and sustained disequilibrium in the international balance of payments, and domestic unemployment. The Fund's resources consist of a common pool of gold and currencies, which in turn consist of an aggregate of "quotas" paid in or payable by its members presumably on the basis of the relative financial and trade positions of the respective members. Thus we find the United States assigned an initial quota equal to about $2.7 billion and the United Kingdom $1.3 billion, while at the other extreme Liberia and Panama are assigned $.5 million each. The Fund began its exchange transactions with initial reserves amounting to some $8.8 billion. So much for the preliminaries.

1. The Fund "lends" to a member-country at the initiative of the latter which is in need of short-term credit to settle a current deficit in its balance of payments. The deficit country "borrows" the necessary funds in exchange for its I.O.U.'s.

What this means in effect is simply that the deficit country *buys* the needed *foreign exchange* from the Fund *with its own currency*. Suppose that a member-country faces a serious disequilibrium in its balance of payments. The country in question may buy foreign exchange from the Fund up to an amount equal to 25 per cent of its quota in any given year. The Fund now has the member-country's original contribution, plus that country's additional currency equal to the amount of the foreign exchange sold to it. If the short-term credit thus acquired helps the deficit country to overcome its adverse balance of payments, the country is required to "repurchase" its own currency in exchange for gold or "convertible currencies" which it has acquired subsequently. Thus the Fund's foreign exchange balances increase and its resources in the form of the borrowing country's currency decrease back to normal. Since a member is allowed to use up only 25 per cent of its quota to purchase foreign exchange from the Fund in any one year, the Fund is protected against quick depletion of its scarce currencies (e.g., dollar resources), while any deficit member is thereby barred from excessive borrowing from the Fund, not to mention the restraining effect of service charges levied on "the average daily balances of its currency held by the Fund in excess of its quota."

2. But suppose that the demand for dollar exchange increases to such an extent that the Fund faces the possibility of exhausting its dollar holdings. In these circumstances, the Fund deals with the problem of dollar scarcity in two ways, namely, (a) by increasing its supply of dollar exchange through purchase of dollars with its gold, and (b) by declaring the dollar to be a "scarce" currency. If the Fund's gold assets are enough to buy all the dollars needed by deficit members, then the Fund will not have to ration its scarce dollar holdings among the dollar-needing members. Thus the extent to which the first method will prove helpful depends on the amount of gold held by the Fund, and on the degree

of disequilibrium in the balance of payments of dollar-needing members. As for the second method, it constitutes an authorization to impose restrictions on currency payments and transfers in the "scarce" currency—an exception to the general rule against exchange control mentioned earlier. Any deficit member is thereby authorized "to limit the demand for the scarce currency to the supply held by, or accruing to, the member in question," but is required to remove such exchange restrictions "as rapidly as conditions permit." (Article VII, Sec. 3b.) For example, suppose that Britain decides to take advantage of this provision. Britain may limit the demand for dollar exchange by (a) making dollar exchange unavailable to importers in sterling-area countries who may wish to import such goods and services from the nonsterling area as may be supplied within the sterling area, or by (b) making foreign-held sterling balances inconvertible into dollars or gold. The first would mean a direct saving in Britain's dollar exchange reserves and the second an indirect one.

Fundamentally, however, it is more important to correct a sustained disequilibrium between those members whose currencies are "scarce" and those whose currencies are not, for that is what gives rise to a general scarcity of the former's currencies. This suggests that the burden of responsibility should not rest on the shoulders of deficit countries alone. Should the dollar be declared scarce, for example, it might prove helpful for the United States to take steps to provide others with more dollar earnings, e.g., a reduction of tariffs, loans, and other measures necessary to increase imports from the rest of the world or to stimulate world exports to the United States. Otherwise deficit countries might find it necessary to do much more than restrict the demand for foreign exchange; they might be compelled to adopt discriminatory import restrictions, exchange depreciation, "beggar-my-neighbor" export stimulants, and, worst of all, deflationary internal measures. For the United States is likely to be accumulating more claims on the rest of the world than the other way around for many years to come.

3. Finally, it is interesting to observe the effects of the Fund's lending operations upon the credit conditions of member-countries. Suppose that a deficit country purchases foreign exchange from the Fund. The central bank of the buying country thereupon sells the foreign exchange so acquired to member banks. Then member banks' reserves with the central bank will decrease as they pay for the foreign exchange out of their excess reserves. Member banks turn around and sell the foreign exchange to their customers, e.g., importers. Thus member banks' demand deposits decrease as customers pay for the exchange with checks drawn against demand deposits. Member banks may have to contract credit, unless they happen to have large excess reserves or short-term securities to sell to the central bank to get additional reserves. Therefore, it is conceivable that the purchase of foreign exchange from the Fund will have the same deflationary effects on domestic credit, incomes, and prices as the loss of gold had on the gold-losing countries. Conversely, the sale to the central bank of foreign exchange resulting from net exports will increase member banks' reserves and demand deposits, and could conceivably cause credit expansion.

But there is no reason to suppose that member banks in the deficit country have not large excess reserves or that the central bank does not make additional reserves available. If so, credit contraction need not follow from the deficit country's purchase of foreign exchange from the Fund. Nor need a surplus country experience credit inflation as a result of its central bank's purchase of foreign exchange from member banks, since the central bank is capable of counterbalancing any excessive credit expansion that member banks may initiate. Thus there is no simple analogy between the loss of gold and the loss of foreign exchange (which necessitates the purchase of additional foreign exchange from the Fund) or between an inflow of gold and an inflow of foreign exchange (which is subsequently sold to the central bank). It seems much more fruitful to concentrate on the favorable effects of the Fund's lending operations on domestic income and employment *via their effects on the international balance of payments.*

The essential point of all these discussions about the International Monetary Fund is simply that as long as member-countries can overcome their unfavorable balance of payments by borrowing from the Fund the necessary short-term credit (in the shape of foreign exchange, against 25 per cent of their quotas in any one year), they do not have to resort to the otherwise necessary but disturbing deflation or devaluation. Thus the International Monetary Fund is in principle capable of helping to maintain not only the stability of the external values of national currencies but also internal economic stability in the member-countries.

20

Monetary Sovereignty and International Equilibrium

^^^

THE THEORY of monetary sovereignty, which Irving Fisher and J. M. Keynes developed in reaction against the international gold standard, served the purpose for which it was intended, namely, that of providing a theoretical basis for national monetary measures to avoid or minimize the impact of depressions in other countries. Since it has again become possible for nations to co-operate in monetary and other matters for the common objectives of full employment and multilateral trade, we shall examine the implications of the theory of monetary sovereignty in the light of a new world setting.

The Specialization vs. the Payment Approach

The classical theory of international trade was essentially concerned with the optimum division of labor among nations on the tacit assumption of full employment; it was mainly interested in the "specialization" effects of foreign trade and only incidentally in its "payment" effects. Moreover, the classical analysis supposed the optimum allocation of resources among nations to be automatically brought about by free-market forces in general and by the specie-price mechanism in particular. The former meant *laissez faire* and the latter the quantity theory of money as expressed in the international gold standard. By precluding the need for conscious international trade and monetary controls, the classical theory of international trade was unable to prevent "the disastrous consequences of a *laissez-faire* system" from nullifying "the advantages of freedom of commerce."[1] For *laissez faire*, as symbolized by the gold standard, paid "no direct regard to the preservation of equilibrium," and depended mainly "on the working-out of blind forces."[2]

It is a significant historical coincidence that the same country which produced Adam Smith, who preached the gospel of free trade, should also produce John Maynard Keynes, who preached a new gospel of implementing "the wisdom of Adam Smith" by conscious international credit and monetary controls, by "an international framework for the policy of full employment," and who advocated the marriage of the short-run expedients necessary for domestic full employment to the "wholesome long run, classical medicine."[3] Just as Keynes was instrumental in shifting the center of gravity in the domestic field from the analysis of the optimum allocation of a given volume of output and employment to that of the determination of the levels of output and employment itself, so was he responsible for the change in international economics from classical preoccupation with the international allocation of a given volume of trade to the new analysis of the determinants of the level of that trade itself. Owing to Keynes' persistent efforts, there is today a general recognition of the vital relation between domestic employment and

[1] J. M. Keynes, speech in the House of Lords, May 23, 1944.
[2] *Ibid.*
[3] Keynes, "The Balance of Payments of the United States," *Economic Journal*, June, 1946, p. 186, and also his speech in the House of Lords, May 23, 1944.

international trade. It is significant in this respect that the International Trade Organization calls itself an international organization for "trade *and* employment."

As long as full employment is assumed, it is logically valid to concentrate on the specialization effects of international trade, for, on the assumption of full employment, nations would have everything to gain from the unrestricted flow of goods and services and thus enjoy the fruits of the international division of labor. With all nations having full employment, no nation would be concerned with the adverse effects of its foreign trade on domestic income and employment, or find it necessary to stimulate exports in order to increase the volume of domestic employment. In other words, the balances of payments would not be a matter of serious concern to nations which, by hypothesis or in fact, had full employment through purely domestic policy.[4] On the tacit assumption of universal full employment, classical economists could cogently argue for free trade, just as they concentrated on *laissez faire* via the price system in the domestic field, that is, on the explanation of individual prices and quantities, taking output and employment as given.

It soon became clear that full employment could not simply be assumed away, and that free trade was seriously threatened in a world with less than full employment. The gold standard, with its inherent bias toward deflation, stood in the way of domestic full employment. Thus international trade became a desperate attempt to "export" unemployment from one nation to another,[5] and "beggar-my-neighbor" trade policies became the rule rather than the exception.[6] Under those circumstances it was but natural that nation after na-

---

[4] But a full-employment economy would consider the exports necessary to pay for imports as a sacrifice of *real* domestic income, i.e., output otherwise available for domestic consumption.

[5] *Cf.* Keynes, *The General Theory of Employment* (1936), pp. 382–383.

[6] See Joan Robinson, *Essays in the Theory of Employment* (Macmillan & Co., London, 1937).

tion should reject free trade as "a long-run platitude" and resort to short-run "expedients" to achieve export surpluses and so to increase domestic employment. "The practical men of affairs" vaguely sensed the unrealism of the classical assumption of full employment, and intuitively favored protective devices or any other measure of commercial policy which promised larger exports and smaller imports.

Knowing the unrealism of the classical assumption of full employment and being keenly conscious of the actual world of underemployment, Keynes was sympathetic toward the practical men of affairs and to all those who sought salvation in some form of economic nationalism. Contrary to the popular impression, however, Keynes was far from advocating autarchy as a permanent solution. To *understand* why nations confronted with underemployment must, under *laissez faire*, resort to a policy of self-sufficiency or to outright "beggar-my-neighbor" policies is not the same thing as to *justify* such a policy in order to perpetuate *laissez-faire* conditions. Rather, Keynes' point was that *laissez faire* should be superseded by such a conscious domestic full-employment policy as to render superfluous self-defeating economic nationalism and "beggar-my-neighbor" trade policies.[7] In the short run, in which an adequate domestic full-employment policy may be difficult of realization, it is but the part of practical wisdom, in Keynes' view, to allow nations to adopt or retain such external measures as will compensate for deficient domestic demand (e.g., exchange and import controls). It is not surprising, therefore, that his views on this and many other points have been incorporated into the Bretton Woods Agreements.

The Mechanism of the International Spread of Depression

To understand fully the rationale of monetary sovereignty, we must know the general process by which depressions are

[7] See Keynes, "National Self–Sufficiency," *Yale Review*, summer, 1933, and *General Theory*, pp. 382–383 and Chap. XXIII.

diffused through the world.[8] Keynes' balance of payments theory of exchange rates, multiplier analysis, and income-expenditure approach have done much to enrich our knowledge of this process. It is now a matter of history but still a matter of didactic significance that the Great Depression of the 1930's spared few countries.

There is no essential difference between the process of deflationary spreading in a closed economy and the international propagation of depression from one point of the open economy to another. In both cases the initiating factor is the change in income, consumption, and investment; and the multiplier mechanism is what transmits fluctuations in income and employment from one point to another. The main difference between them lies in the fact that the international spread of depression (or prosperity) is complicated by such peculiarities of international economic relations as greater labor immobility, autonomous currency systems, political sovereignties, different marginal propensities to import, time lags in the balance-of-payments adjustments, and radically different cost structures.[9] For the sake of simplicity, it may be well to ignore some of these complications and to give a simplified explanation of the mechanism of the international spread of depression.

Let us begin with the assumption that a major depression has occurred in one country. This depression will be transmitted to other countries having trade relations with that country through a resulting decrease in the latter's *imports*. From the standpoint of other countries this means that their income and employment will contract sharply via the backward or reverse operation of the foreign-trade multiplier, that is, through the downward effects of the initial decline

[8] *Cf.* J. Polak, "International Propagation of Business Cycles," *Review of Economic Studies*, February, 1939; O. Morgenstern, "On the International Spread of Business Cycles," *Journal of Political Economy*, LI, 1943, 287–309.

[9] *Cf.* League of Nations, *Economic Stability in the Postwar World* (Geneva, 1945), pp. 90–92.

in export revenues on consumption, investment, and aggregate income. The extent to which a depression in one country will affect the level of activity in another depends mainly on the former's marginal propensity to import. Although the United States, for example, has a small average propensity to import, it has a slightly larger marginal propensity to import, with the result that its income elasticity of demand for imports is believed to be greater than unity.[10] This is so because imports into the United States consist largely of industrial raw materials and luxuries, for which the demand is relatively elastic with respect to income. This means that a decrease in the money income of the United States will lead to a more than proportional decline in its import demand, and therefore to a corresponding decline in the exporting country's income and employment.

Therefore the international propagation of a depression in one country depends not only on the ratio of that country's imports to its income (i.e., the average propensity to import) but also on the increment or decrement of these imports *pari passu* with a given change in income (i.e., the marginal propensity to import). A nearly self-sufficient economy like that of the United States has a low average propensity to import; but it does not follow that a depression in such an economy will produce small repercussions elsewhere. On the contrary, unless America's income-elasticity of de-

---

[10] If, e.g., the average propensity to import is expressed as M/Y, where M stands for imports and Y for income, the marginal propensity to import can be expressed as dM/dY. The income elasticity of demand for imports can be obtained by dividing the marginal propensity to import by the average propensity to import, i.e., $(dM/dY)/(M/Y)$, or alternatively $(dM/M)/(dY/Y)$. If the national income is $200 billion and imports amount to $10 billion, the average propensity to import is 10/200, or 0.05. If, on the other hand, national income increases by $50 billion and imports increase by $4 billion, the marginal propensity to import is 4/50, or 0.08. The income elasticity of demand for imports, according to either of the above formulas, will be 1.6, which is greater than unity. This is approximately the recent trend in the United States. For further discussions see R. Nurkse, "Domestic and International Equilibrium," in *The New Economics* (Knopf, New York, 1948), pp. 270–272.

mand for imports is modified by changes in consumer tastes, tariffs, technical methods of production at home and abroad, and other trend forces, economic fluctuations in the United States are bound to exercise a much greater influence on other countries than the small ratio of foreign trade to its total trade would indicate.

On the other hand, a depression abroad is transmitted to the domestic economy through a decline of *exports* and the resulting multiple contraction of domestic money income. A decline in foreign expenditures for American exports, for example, will have a more depressing effect on domestic activity than might be expected of a country whose income from exports comprises but a small proportion of its national income. There are two reasons for such an effect. First, the "leakages" (i.e., the domestic marginal propensities to import and to save) associated with newly injected purchasing power are smaller in the United States than in other industrially advanced countries. This means that an initial decrease in foreign expenditures for American exports will lead to a larger decline in domestic income than if the foreign-trade multiplier were smaller due to larger marginal propensities to import and to save (i.e., a smaller marginal propensity to consume domestic products). Thus it can be stated that the smaller the domestic marginal propensities to save and to import, the greater the multiplier impact on domestic income of the decline (or the increase, for that matter) in exports. Second, American exports include a preponderance of durable commodities and capital investments for which the world demand is highly elastic with respect to income and frightfully uncertain, and which are usually the first targets of foreign restrictive policy.

Thus in an open system fluctuations in domestic income and employment spread to other countries through their effects on imports, while those in foreign income and employment are transmitted to the domestic economy through their effects on exports. The magnitude and intensity of international repercussions of a depression or a "boom" depend largely on different marginal propensities to import. *Monetary sovereignty is an attempt to insulate the domestic economy from adverse repercussions of a depression elsewhere.* When chronic shortages of dollars are added to the international spread of cyclical disturbances, it is not difficult to see why nations rebelled against the gold standard, adopted exchange stabilization or control, and finally built a framework of international monetary co-operation to supplement domestic full-employment policies.

A "Chronic Shortage of Dollars"—A Fundamental Disequilibrium

Apart from the international spread of cyclical depressions, with its attendant balance-of-payments difficulties, a fundamental disequilibrium [11] (i.e., a constant tendency toward an adverse balance of payments) is believed to loom large in the background. A "chronic shortage of dollars" is considered to be prima facie evidence of the existence of a fundamental disequilibrium.[12] The rest of the world, particularly Britain, seems to feel that a continuous net credit in the American balance of payments has the effect of keeping them in a perpetual disequilibrium from which it is difficult to escape and which upsets their domestic full-employment policies. The outside world therefore considers the unsolved problem of

[11] In contradistinction to domestic equilibrium, which exists when national income has no tendency toward inflation or deflation, external equilibrium is a situation where there is no tendency for a deterioration in the balance of payments to require persistent monetary "stop-gaps" or for an improvement to court increased foreign discriminatory monetary and trade policies.

[12] For controversial discussions see Keynes, "The Balance of Payments of the United States"; J. Robinson, "The International Currency Proposals," *Economic Journal*, June–September, 1943; Alvin Hansen, *America's Role in the World Economy* (London, George Allen & Unwin Ltd., 1945), Chap. XX; S. E. Harris, ed., *Postwar Economic Problems* (McGraw-Hill Book Co., New York, 1943), pp. 379–381; J. H. Williams, "Economic Lessons of Two World Wars," *Foreign Affairs*, October, 1947.

a chronic shortage of dollars as an additional reason for retaining a larger measure of monetary sovereignty.

For some long-run reasons the rest of the world is expected to be confronted with a chronic shortage of dollars, not mere temporary shortages due to cyclical or extraordinary circumstances (e.g., the world need for imports of American consumer goods and capital equipment during the postwar period). If so, one cannot look with optimism on the present world holdings of gold and dollar balances (excluding those arising from financial aid under the Marshall plan) amounting to some $18 billion, especially in view of the great inelasticity of world demand for American exports in the transition period. What, then, are some of these secular factors contributing to a chronic shortage of dollars?

1. One of the basic reasons for a chronic shortage of dollars lies in the difference in the average and marginal propensities to import between the United States and the rest of the world. While imports make up a small fraction of American national income (averaging from 5 to 10 per cent), the rest of the world depends much more on imports from the United States. This difference in the average propensity to import is due to the difference in the degree of industrial development and economic self-sufficiency. Moreover, the marginal propensity to import is much higher elsewhere than in the United States, indicating that a given increase in foreign income tends to stimulate American exports more than a similar increase in American income does foreign exports. In other words, the initial American expansion of imports, while causing a multiple expansion of foreign income, also causes others to increase their expenditures for American goods and services beyond the initial increase in American expenditures for foreign goods and services. Thus a higher marginal propensity to import elsewhere, imbedded as it is in less-developed industry and less abundance, tends to aggravate adverse balances of payments of others, particu-

larly in times of inflationary pressure and general economic
expansion.

2. A corollary to the first factor is the difference in comparative productivity advantage between the United States
and others. The United States has over time superseded all
others in the field of consumer durables and capital goods,
which enter into competitive international trade on an ever-
increasing scale. It happens that these goods are just what
the rest of the world most needs and wants. It should be noted
in this regard that an attempt to provide others with dollar
credits via foreign investment would not have permanently
beneficial effects on their balances of payments, if the dollar credits so provided merely expanded American exports
still further, since foreign investment usually leads to an expansion of foreign demand for American capital goods. It
is conceivable that America's productivity advantage may
be somewhat offset by a change in her cost structure. If, for
example, money wages in the export industries get out of
line, that is, pushed beyond productivity by, say, trade-
union action—exchange rates being equal—American export prices will rise to change the terms of trade against the
United States.[18] The odds, however, are on continued productivity advantage by the United States, judging from constant technological improvements of a cost-reducing nature.
There is no immediate prospect that the other industrial countries will achieve superior productivity advantage, even with
outside financial and technical aid for reconstruction and
development. Nor is there much hope that the backward
areas of the world will be able to industrialize so rapidly and
so completely as to achieve independence from American
capital goods. Thus the past and existing gaps between the
productive and exporting capacities of the United States and

---

[18] It was probably such a situation which Keynes envisaged when he spoke
of the United States as becoming a "high-cost" country (see his "The Balance,
etc.," *op. cit.*).

those of other countries contribute to a fundamental dis-equilibrium.

3. Another reason for a chronic shortage of dollars may be found in the persistent tendency of foreign capital to flow into the United States for reasons of safety and security. If political and economic uncertainties are the rule rather than the exception elsewhere, the United States will probably receive an excessive amount of long-term foreign capital (i.e., foreign "refugee funds" invested in American securities), as it did during the 1930's. Unless American lending exceeds this kind of "perverse" borrowing, other countries will merely drain their gold and dollar exchange by "lending" to the United States. Although most countries now have exchange control over a flight of short-term capital, it is not clear that the fear of devaluation or some political disturbance will not give rise to a wholesale flight of "hot money" to the United States in the future, as happened between 1934 and 1939. This kind of short-term capital movement is, of course, a disequilibrating factor, and merely intensifies a chronic shortage of dollars. A loss of gold or exchange reserves incident to capital flight is presumably made good, in time, by the rise in domestic interest rates which capital flight causes. But since the change in interest rates is no longer connected with gold movements, as it once was under the gold standard, and since "cheap-money policy" is a secular trend, everywhere (except of course during inflation), it is doubtful that liquid funds can be attracted into the countries losing gold or exchange reserves, thereby closing a gap in their balances of payments created by capital flight. To the extent, therefore, that long-term or short-term capital is allowed to flow into the United States, the rest of the world will be subject to a chronic shortage of dollars more than if capital movements were controlled domestically or internationally.

4. The last factor is a continuous export surplus on the part of the United States, whether due to "errors of policy"

or to the relatively low price elasticity of the world demand for American exports. Quite apart from the limit imposed on American imports by postwar world scarcity, the persistent excess of exports over imports that characterizes United States foreign trade may be due in part to myopia in commercial policy (e.g., a high-tariff policy). The basic explanation, however, seems to lie in the high degree of self-sufficiency and industrialization that gives rise to a relatively low marginal propensity to import. Hence, unless and until the rest of the world achieves the same degree of self-sufficiency and industrialization, which is doubtful in any foreseeable future, it will not have a lower marginal propensity to import than the United States. With the United States, economic self-sufficiency is a matter of natural endowment plus industrial efficiency, but for others to be economically self-sufficient it would be necessary not only to increase their industrial efficiency but to sacrifice the gains from comparative advantage in most lines of production. Thus it is not a simple question of developing a willingness on the part of the United States to increase imports, but a difficult question of fundamental structural adjustment in the world economy as a whole. In the meantime the United States is likely to maintain a continuous export surplus and therefore the position of a long-run creditor.

The general cure for a chronic shortage of dollars can be discussed more fruitfully in conjunction with the principles and instruments of monetary sovereignty which follow, although the foregoing analysis of the secular causes of a general shortage of dollars does suggest *ad hoc* correctives.

Principles and Instruments of Monetary Sovereignty

Some relevant principles and policy implications emerge from our discussions of the "payment" effects of international trade, the international propagation of depression, and a chronic shortage of dollars. These principles and policy implications form the basis of modern monetary sovereignty and international monetary co-operation.

1. In the absence of a system of stable international currency relations and in view of the political and psychological difficulty of co-ordinating national fiscal and monetary full-employment policies, it is necessary for each nation to preserve some freedom of action in monetary matters in order to insulate itself from the adverse effects of economic fluctuations elsewhere and to maintain its internal economic stability. In other words, no nation should be tied down to an international system of rigid exchange rates which imposes the alternatives of deflation and inflation on every adhering member-nation. The degree of monetary independence which is compatible with both internal and external equilibria includes (a) the right of each nation to adjust the par value of its currency (i.e., to revalue or devalue) or the domestic prices of foreign currencies (i.e., to depreciate or appreciate the exchange value of the domestic currency), not in order to achieve export advantages but to correct a persistent disequilibrium in its balance of payments; (b) the right of each nation to regulate the outflow or inflow of capital or gold, in order to have *complete* control over domestic interest rates and to stabilize long-term domestic investment; and (c) the right of each nation to pursue, without "outside dictation," such over-all fiscal-monetary policies as may be necessary to prevent the extremes of deflation and inflation and to maintain continuous full employment.

2. Monetary sovereignty further requires a measure of national freedom in commercial policy. "Beggar-my-neighbor" measures of commercial policy are clearly out of the question for obvious reasons. The kind of commercial policy that is required for the success of monetary sovereignty must be a flexible one compatible with the maintenance of equilibrium; it should be permitted if and when necessary and other-

wise forbidden.[14] Over-all import control is considered the most appropriate supplement to monetary and exchange control. It does not much matter whether import control is brought about by import quotas, exchange controls, or tariffs, as far as its effects on the balance of payments are concerned. Since the kind of import control that is contemplated here is expressly related only to a disequilibrium in the balance of payments, and not to the self-defeating purpose of achieving an export surplus, any particular type of import control chosen will not be subject to the usual criticisms of autarchy. The principle to be recognized here is that a nation confronted with a persistent adverse balance of payments should be permitted to adopt import quotas or any other suitable import restrictions, in addition to monetary measures, solely for the purpose of closing the deficit gap.[15] It follows that a nation enjoying a favorable balance of payments, if it adopted import control, would be condemned by world opinion as pursuing a "beggar-my-neighbor" policy. If a nation's balance of payments exhibits a persistent tendency toward a net credit, the relaxation of import restrictions and the revaluation or appreciation of its currency will correct this type of disequilibrium.

3. Given the necessary measure of monetary sovereignty and protective commercial policy, there is no plausible ground for an unwillingness to solve the problem of domestic employment by purely domestic policy. No nation can excuse its failure to maintain full employment by putting the blame on its balance-of-payments difficulties, for the simple reason that such difficulties need no longer be solved by a painful process of deflation.[16] If balance-of-payments difficulties can

[14] Keynes, speech in the House of Lords, December 18, 1945.

[15] On this point see Nurkse, *op. cit.*, and also R. Hinshaw, "Keynesian Commercial Policy," in *The New Economics*, pp. 315–322.

[16] On this point see Margaret F. W. Joseph, "Principles of Full Employment," in *Planning and Paying for Full Employment*, eds. Lerner and Graham (Princeton University Press, Princeton, 1946), p. 37.

be solved by methods which are not detrimental to income and employment at home or abroad (i.e., methods other than internal deflation and "beggar-my-neighbor" policies), nations will have the greater chance of maintaining full employment by domestic policy without being embarrassed by a depression elsewhere. This is the *raison d'être* of monetary sovereignty. The dispensability of the problem of balance-of-payments difficulties, via monetary sovereignty and its corollary flexible commercial policy, firmly establishes the principle that domestic policy (as distinguished from foreign trade policy) is primarily responsible for maintaining full employment at home. To the extent that nations learn and follow this principle, they will find it unnecessary to "export" unemployment to one another to the detriment of long-run international equilibrium, and will enjoy the fruits of free exchange of goods and services in the atmosphere of universal full employment and prosperity.[17]

4. The theory of monetary sovereignty does not preclude international monetary co-operation. For the solution of the problem of balance-of-payments difficulties will not by itself guarantee full employment; it merely supplements an inadequate solution of the problem of employment by purely domestic policy. Monetary sovereignty is neither a substitute for domestic full-employment policy nor an alternative to international co-operation for freer trade and fuller employment. The International Monetary Fund, the International Trade Organization, and other international economic agencies (U. N. affiliates) have incorporated a measure of monetary sovereignty and protective commercial policy in recognition of the need for some degree of "economic insularity." By outlawing "beggar-my-neighbor" policies on the one hand, and by permitting a measure of flexibility in exchange and import adjustments on the other, these international organizations have impressed upon each and every

[17] *Cf.* Keynes, *General Theory*, p. 282.

member-nation that the maintenance of full employment is primarily a national responsibility, and only secondarily a matter of joint international monetary and trade policy. If these international organizations succeed in providing a favorable international setting (i.e., currency stability and multilateral trade), member-nations will be, to that extent, encouraged to pursue a consistent full-employment policy at home. In Keynes' words, "it is as providing an international framework for the policy of full employment that these proposals (the Bretton Woods monetary and banking agreements) are to be welcomed." [18] It is useful in this regard to cite the purposes of the International Monetary Fund as the typical example of United Nations economic policy:

> (ii) To facilitate the expansion and balanced growth of international trade, and to contribute thereby to the promotion and maintenance of high levels of employment and real income and to the development of the productive resources of all members as primary objectives of economic policy.
>
> (iii) To promote exchange stability, to maintain orderly exchange arrangements among members, and to avoid competitive exchange depreciation.
>
> (iv) To assist in the establishment of a multilateral system of payments in respect of current transactions between members and in the elimination of foreign exchange restrictions which hamper the growth of world trade.[19]

5. The broad principle that emerges from our discussion of a chronic shortage of dollars is that the United States—the largest creditor nation—should minimize its internal economic fluctuations and maintain continuous full employment to expand its imports. This is not to put the entire responsi-

[18] Speech in the House of Lords, May 23, 1944.
[19] Art. 1, Annex A, Final Act.

bility on the United States, as some are inclined to suspect.[20] The debtor nations, for their part, will have to do more than maintain full employment—that is, to industrialize, to rationalize industry, to adopt a rigorous program of import austerity, and many other things—if they are to get out of a fundamental disequilibrium. But regardless of what others are doing, it is to the long-run interest of the United States and of the debtor nations that full employment should be maintained in this country. Such a policy is far more important than a stop-gap policy of foreign financial aid, however helpful the latter may be in the short run. That the maintenance of continuous full employment by the United States is a *sine qua non* of international stability may be appreciated when it is recalled that dollars supplied to the rest of the world (via imports and long-term foreign investment) by the United States dropped from $7,400 million in the "boom" year 1929 to $2,410 million in the depression year 1932, that is, by 67 per cent.[21] It is clear that the rest of the world will not accept such devastating effects of a depression in the United States by letting their gold or foreign exchange deplete or by deflating internal prices, incomes, and wages. It is even doubtful that the other countries will be able to minimize the impact of a serious depression in the United States by import restrictions, currency devaluation, and exchange depreciation. It is therefore a major responsibility of the United States to sustain full employment, and thus to contribute to long-run international equilibrium.[22]

[20] See, e.g., Williams, *op. cit.*

[21] *Cf.* United States Department of Commerce, *The United States in the World Economy* ("Economic Series," No. 23, Washington, D.C., 1943).

[22] For the responsibility of the United States in the world economy see *ibid.*; Hansen, *op. cit.*; B. Mitchell, "Full Employment and Foreign Trade," in *Planning and Paying for Full Employment*, pp. 147–153; League of Nations, *op. cit.*, pp. 244–245; Nurkse, *op. cit.*

21

Foreign Investment, the World Bank, and Employment

THE POSTWAR needs of the war-devastated and backward areas, and the fear of stagnation possibilities in the United States and other mature economies, lend strong support to the belief that foreign investment ought to be expanded to the concurrent benefit of international standards of living and domestic employment. We are now in a position to investigate the extent, if any, to which such a belief is justified. More specifically, we shall consider the role of foreign investment in general and that of the International Bank for Reconstruction and Development in particular in the national and international drive for full employment. It is convenient to divide our discussions into two sections: (a) a consideration of foreign investment as a palliative to cyclical unemployment, and (b) a similar consideration with respect to "secular stagnation."

Foreign Investment and Cyclical Unemployment

Foreign investment [1] is one way to offset a cyclical deficiency of aggregate domestic demand. In other words, it is

[1] By "foreign investment" we shall mean, for the purpose of the present

a method of increasing foreign expenditure for exports.[2] In so far as cyclical unemployment is concerned, the foreign demand for capital goods is crucial. Accordingly, foreign investment is an attempt to increase foreign expenditure largely for capital goods. It is generally assumed that reconstruction and development in the rest of the world will, if properly financed, give rise to increased foreign demand for capital goods, and therefore stimulate domestic employment in the United States when aggregate home demand begins to level off. The practical problem is to direct foreign demand toward capital goods at a time when the domestic capital-goods industries are at a low ebb. Obviously, unregulated private foreign investment cannot be expected to have that effect. Two other types of foreign investment are plausible in this respect: "tied loans" such as those made by the Export–Import Bank, and long-term loans such as those made by the International Bank for Reconstruction and Development.

Although the Export–Import Bank requires that the proceeds of its loans be spent in the United States,[3] it has little direct control over the time, volume, or manner of foreign spending. It is possible that the foreign borrowers may spend the proceeds for consumers' goods rather than for capital goods, and at a time when the stimulus of extra exports is not

---

discussion, intermediate and long-term loans to foreign countries needing capital to reconstruct their war-damaged economies or to develop their backward economies.

[2] An increase in the national income resulting from interest and amortization payments is left out of account for two reasons. One is that in the future foreign lending is likely to be expanded at "generous terms." The other is the likelihood that part of the multiplier effect of the increased national income on domestic employment will "leak out" to the benefit of employment elsewhere, since the increased national income gives rise to a higher domestic propensity to import and thus decreases the lending country's favorable foreign balance. On this point see J. M. Keynes, *General Theory*, p. 120.

[3] Bilateral finance is generally considered harmful to long-run international equilibrium. Thus we find Professor Jacob Viner recommending that "all new lending activities by the Export-Import Bank" be terminated because its bilateral requirement "clashes with the proclaimed policy of the United States in favor of multilateralism in trade" ("In Defense of 'Dollar Diplomacy,'" *New York Times Magazine*, March 23, 1947).

needed. Even though the bank had sufficient funds to lend, its tied loans might not find enough foreign applications. For the borrower would rather have the freedom to spend the proceeds of a loan where he pleased (i.e., in the cheapest market). In so far as American export prices are low relative to foreign export prices, given stable exchange rates, the bank's tied loans will attract foreign borrowers and thus provide the American export industries with a direct stimulus.

Long-term loans by or through the International Bank are required to be used for importing the essential materials for reconstruction and development. In view of America's exceptional capacity for production, there is little doubt that the requirement mentioned above will have the ultimate effect of increasing foreign expenditure for American exports, particularly capital goods. Now the question is whether the bank can plan its lending operations according to short-run business activity in, say, the United States. That is to say, can the bank lend liberally during the cyclical downswing and contract or discontinue lending during the upswing?

Some have expressed hope for the possibility of such timing.[4] On the other hand, it has been pointed out that the bank is likely to expand its lending operations at a time when the stimulus of extra exports is not needed to increase domestic employment.[5] Another has called attention to the fact that the ultimate initiative in bank operations lies with the borrowing countries.[6] There is also the constant danger that the

---

[4] E. Staley, *World Economic Development* (International Labour Office, Montreal, 1945), pp. 105–107; also H. B. Lary, "The Domestic Effects of Foreign Investment," *American Economic Review*, XXXVI, No. 2, May, 1946, 672–685.

[5] Viner, "International Finance in the Post–War World," *Lloyds Bank Review*, October, 1946, pp. 3–17; reprinted in *Journal of Political Economy*, LV, April, 1947, 97–107.

[6] A. I. Bloomfield, "Postwar Control of International Capital Movements," *American Economic Review*, XXXVI, No. 2, May, 1946, 687–709. Dean H. R. Bowen of the University of Illinois has privately expressed the view that it is possible that the International Bank will reserve some of its lending power for "hard times," although he concedes that during a world-wide depression the foreign demand for capital goods will be small.

International Bank will make loans on a political basis irrespective of employment conditions. The availability of multinational loans would then be unable to prevent economically poor and politically weak countries from going in for capital formation at the expense of consumption.[7] Under these circumstances, it is difficult to see how the International Bank can time its loans in such a way as to prevent or reduce cyclical unemployment.

Perhaps the most serious obstacle to the export of capital goods via foreign investment lies in the fact that major capital goods are incapable of entering international trade.[8] Building equipment and materials, which play the dominant role in gross capital formation in this country, have been cited as examples. Thus, even if we make the favorable assumption that foreign investment leads to the export of capital goods at the right time, we cannot be certain that sufficient capital goods will be exported to increase domestic employment significantly. The impossibility or difficulty of exporting critical capital goods is somewhat counterbalanced, however, by the feasibility of exporting other durable goods which have a strong "acceleration" effect on employment—for example, automobiles, refrigerators, washing machines, and radios.[9]

Crucial to cyclical unemployment though the foreign demand for capital goods may be, it is amiss to stress it at the expense of demand for consumers' goods, particularly con-

---

[7] Note, for instance, that the ten-year reconstruction plan of Java relies on national as well as foreign capital. (See *New York Times*, April 9, 1947.) This is a point which is often overlooked by advocates of private foreign investment. As backward areas become more conscious of the need for political independence and freedom, they will doubtless try to free themselves from foreign economic domination as well. To this extent, the export of capital will become more difficult, if not impossible.

[8] N. S. Buchanan, *International Investment and Domestic Welfare* (Henry Holt & Co., New York, 1945); also "American National Income and Foreign Investment," in *Planning and Paying for Full Employment* (Princeton University Press, Princeton, 1946).

[9] See A. H. Hansen, *America's Role in the World Economy* (London, George Allen & Unwin Ltd., 1945), p. 136.

378 *Monetary Theory and Public Policy*

sumers' durable goods. For the total effect of foreign investment on domestic employment can be measured satisfactorily only by referring to the total foreign demand. Whether foreign investment leads to the export of capital goods or to that of consumers' goods, it has the same multiplier effect on domestic incomes and employment as if new purchasing power were created through gold inflow [10] or through deficit spending (i.e., by borrowing from the banking system). The main justification for emphasizing demand for capital goods is, of course, that business fluctuations in this country are chiefly in the capital-goods industries. Another justification is the familiar fact that a new demand for capital goods, in addition to the normal replacement demand, leads to a manifold expansion of production and employment in the capital-goods industries. But it is more realistic to take into account the multiplier effect of the investment-fostered foreign demand on domestic employment as well as its acceleration effect.

As to the stimulating effect of foreign investment on the total volume of employment, it makes little difference whether it is regarded as a means of increasing aggregate investment or as "an expansion of consumer credit." [11] But it makes a significant difference to domestic employment policy which effect of foreign investment is stressed. If the anticipated foreign demand for capital goods is large, the main domestic effort will be to increase the propensity to consume in order to reach the desired level of employment. If, on the other hand, foreign investment is expected to lead largely to an increased demand for consumers' goods, it will be necessary to concentrate on the domestic measures to increase the propensity to invest. Contrariwise, foreign in-

[10] Strictly speaking, gold inflow would not lead to credit expansion if member-banks were indebted to the Federal Reserve banks, since they might use the new gold to pay debts rather than to extend new loans.

[11] See J. H. G. Pierson, *Full Employment* (Yale Univ. Press, New Haven, 1941), p. 191.

vestment may, as far as possible, be adjusted to conform to the relative strength of the propensities to invest and to consume at home.

Foreign Investment and Secular Stagnation

Large-scale, generous developmental foreign investment is considered by many as a *sine qua non* of sustaining continuous full employment in mature economies. Such investment, it is argued, would be a solution to the savings-investment problem and therefore a counteracting force to secular stagnation.

Prima facie, it would seem sensible to adjust the propensity to save (which is merely the propensity not to consume) in such a way as to conform to the propensity to invest, thereby solving the savings-investment problem. Indeed, there is increasing evidence that public policy in the more advanced countries, including the United States, is moving in that direction. Experience has shown that a progressive income tax, social security benefits, and low interest (long-term) go a long way toward increasing the propensity to consume, and therefore toward checking a constant tendency to oversave. Those measures, however, have a definite limit beyond which they cannot be continued without involving mature economies in an impasse. Such "central controls" as Keynes deemed necessary "to bring about an adjustment between the propensity to consume and the inducement to invest" [12] are suggestive of such an impasse. For it is quite possible that these central controls may go beyond the point of "securing an approximation to full employment." [13] Similarly, apprehensions about the disastrous effects of a zero rate of interest on "the continuation of our capitalistic system" [14]

[12] *Op. cit.*, p. 379.
[13] *Ibid.*, p. 378.
[14] H. C. Wallich, "The Changing Significance of the Interest Rate," *American Economic Review*, XXXVI, No. 5, December, 1936, pp. 761–787, esp. p. 785.

reflect the above-mentioned limit to "a guiding influence on the propensity to consume" which Keynes considered part of state responsibility.[15]

Realization of the limit to the public control of the propensity to save, among other difficulties, has doubtless influenced many to accept a high propensity to save as given and to turn to a consideration of politically feasible measures to increase the propensity to invest. In so far as it is politically feasible, large-scale foreign investment at generous terms finds its objective justification in institutional, technological, and psychological difficulties which stand in the way of adjusting the propensity to save to the propensity to invest for continuous full employment. Thus the inability or unwillingness to increase the marginal efficiency of capital via drastic compensatory measures at home leads mature economies to adopt a program of expansionist foreign investment as a matter of course. How far foreign investment, as such, will go toward solving the secular savings-investment problem in the postwar period depends mainly on the effectiveness of an international mechanism for expanding that investment.

An expansion of foreign investment for developmental purposes, and at generous terms, presupposes an international setting in which nations are willing to co-operate in trade and financial matters and a domestic setting in which enlightened self-interest prevails. The International Bank for Reconstruction and Development is the first attempt to regulate long-term capital movements among nations according to some preconceived long-range plans, including employment stabilization. The multinational character of its organization is a strong presumption against "beggar-my-neighbor" policy. The bank provides the lending countries with sufficient safeguards against default and the borrowing countries with liberal and flexible schedules of interest and amortization payments. As a nonprofit-making organiza-

[15] *Op. cit.*, p. 378.

tion, the bank is committed to a policy of making loans at low rates of interest. It also encourages private investors to participate in the multinational financing of world reconstruction and development.

In view of the increasing sensitiveness of backward areas to traditional private capital exports, and in the light of the disastrous results of private foreign investments in the past, the multinational lending of the International Bank may properly be regarded as the most effective, though not the exclusive, means of expanding foreign markets for American exports. In participating in multinational lending, the United States need not apologize for the fact that such participation does help improve domestic employment, for continuous full employment in America is bound to have favorable repercussions on the internal prosperity of the undeveloped areas. The potential demand for capital in these areas is so great that it appears as if multinational lending were an ultimate answer to stagnation possibilities.

Yet there are a number of considerations that preclude too optimistic conclusions with respect to the effectiveness of the International Bank as a counterstagnation agency. Attention has been called to the possibility that the bank may lend to the limit of its resources in the transition period "and then have to wait for earnings and repayments to flow in before it can again engage in large operations." [16] In other words, it is feared that the bank's resources are inadequate to maintain high levels of employment continuously. Although the bank can raise additional funds by issuing its own debentures in the private capital markets, it is prohibited from expanding loans and guaranties beyond 100 per cent of its capital equities. Therefore, even though the bank may thus add lendable funds to its capital stock, interest, and "commission charges," it has a definite limit beyond which it may not increase its liabilities in the form of loans and

[16] Viner, "International Finance in the Post–War World."

guaranties. Furthermore, despite the gilt-edged quality of its securities, the bank may fail to attract private investors if, for instance, the private capital markets are ill-disposed for economic or political reasons.

The second consideration has to do with the bank's lending policy. Even if we make the favorable assumption that the bank's resources are adequate at all times, strict adherence to the self-liquidating principle would definitely limit the volume of multinational lending. Operating on the basis of prudence, the bank would reject the applications for what it considered to be poor risks, and thus prevent unwittingly a potential increase in foreign expenditure for exports. Thus there is the danger that the desire to maintain the bank's capital position at a sound level might give rise to too conservative a lending policy to help prevent stagnation possibilities in mature economies. It is conceivable, though improbable, that the bank might deviate from the orthodox principle to adjust its lending activities to conform to the long-run employment requirements of both the lending and the borrowing countries. A deviation, if at all, is likely to eventuate on political grounds, however.

Apart from the bank's lending policy, it is not very certain that bank loans will result in the export of sufficient capital goods to balance a deficiency of home investment. It has been suggested, for instance, that—in so far as secular stagnation is due largely to the lack of "extensive investment"— the inability to export "construction" renders foreign investment rather ineffective in preventing that stagnation.[17]

---

[17] Buchanan, "American National Income and Foreign Investment," in *Planning and Paying for Full Employment*, pp. 161–162. If the inability to export building equipment and materials is offset by the ability to export other employment-generating durable goods in the short run, as shown already, such an offset is even more plausible for the long run, in which the mature economies can better adjust to the production of these latter goods. The tendency to identify secular stagnation with the lack of extensive investment is unfortunate, for it implies that mature economies stand or fall with their ability to counteract declining population growth or to discover

In other words, it is not only the volume of bank loans, but that of exports resulting from those loans, that determines the effectiveness of the bank as a counterstagnation agency. The bank, however, can hardly be blamed for the fact that construction is incapable of entering international trade.

Perhaps the most important consideration is the basic incompatibility of the bilateral tendencies of the major member nations with the multinational objectives of the bank. In an atmosphere of unyielding independent political sovereignty and in a typically underemployment world it is difficult to see how the bank can function multinationally in fact as well as in theory.[18] Should the bilateral tendencies dominate bank operations, multinational finance would be undermined to the detriment of employment stability. For bilateral lending, if guided by political or military considerations, would result neither in increased productivity in the undeveloped areas nor in increased employment in mature economies.[19]

For these reasons, it is doubtful that the International

---

new frontiers. The stagnation thesis has, however, made it clear that, given a deficiency of extensive investment, stagnation possibilities arise from uncertain and unpredictable intensive investment, or from a deficiency of public investment to supplement private investment, or from a combination of the two. It is no overstatement to say that stagnation is man-made, for the refusal to let public investment compensate for a deficiency of private investment, however caused, lies at the root of the matter.

[18] The first change in the bank's presidency was reportedly associated with its internal conflicts over the issue of economic versus political lending. The *New Republic* (March 24, 1947), p. 6, for instance, considered an appointment of a "Wall Street lawyer" as "a victory for the private bankers." This is obviously a half-truth, the other half being "a victory" for bilateralistically minded "diplomats." Viner makes the observation in this regard that "the bankers, instead of being the prime movers, are the instruments, sometimes willing, often reluctant and insubordinate, of the diplomats" ("In Defense of 'Dollar Diplomacy'"). The whole truth that emerges from these observations is that a shift of emphasis from economic to political lending, and a political reaction against multinational lending, reflect a more fundamental conflict between the system of free-market economies and that of state-controlled economies.

[19] In this connection, former Secretary of the Treasury Henry A. Morgenthau, Jr., warned the Senate Banking Committee, June 12, 1945, that if the bank made loans on a political basis "this could only mean the rule of power politics in international relations."

Bank can be counted upon to serve as an effective counter-stagnation agency. To the extent, however, that the industrial-ization of the backward areas is promoted by genuinely multinational loans, the bank will make a contribution to the solution of the secular savings-investment problem.

Conclusions

As far as cyclical unemployment is concerned, foreign in-vestment is not only an unreliable but an undesirable means of increasing domestic employment. While it is capable of increasing foreign expenditure for exports, foreign invest-ment cannot be planned in such a way as to provide just the kind of stimulus that is needed to maintain full employment at home. It is undesirable because it tends to justify and per-petuate the inability or unwillingness to solve the problem of cyclical unemployment by purely domestic policy.

Reliance upon foreign investment, however unjustified, serves to emphasize the stubborn reality of psychological resistance and political impediments to the necessary eco-nomic reforms for full employment. As long as cyclical dis-turbances remain intact for lack of effective countercyclical measures, so long will there remain a temptation to use foreign investment to get extra exports needed to increase domestic employment. This temptation often expresses itself in a sophisticated but nonetheless "beggar-my-neighbor" pol-icy, for the emphasis is always on export surpluses at all costs rather than on more imports at full employment.

Stagnation possibilities present a more powerful case for foreign investment. The case is reinforced by the obvious benefits to the undeveloped areas of developmental loans. On the one hand, a high propensity to save feeds on existing accumulations without proportional investment. On the other hand, the outlook on intensive investment, not to mention extensive investment, is gloomy indeed, partly due to in-creasing cost rigidities and partly due to resistance to con-

tinuous large-scale public investment. Thus foreign investment comes to the rescue of the savings-investment problem,
whose solution within the national borders and within the
framework of a free-market economy is clearly difficult. It is
therefore no accident that Keynes and others saw in developmental foreign investment a hopeful offset to a deficiency of
home investment.

Rising nationalism in backward areas and the past record
of unregulated private investments are a presumption in
favor of multinational lending at generous terms and on a
purely economic basis. Multinational lending, as such, is
capable of making a significant contribution to the solution
of the secular savings-investment problem, and yet there are
numerous difficulties in the way—underemployment equilibrium and independent political sovereignty itself being among
the most formidable. Nevertheless, the International Bank
is a hopeful step in the direction of effective international employment stabilization.

The mature economies that have not learned "to provide
themselves with full employment by their domestic policy" [20]
are in no position to dismiss foreign investment as "a marginal
factor." The United States, no less than Britain, which must
"export or expire," [21] "cannot expect to build up the volume
of exports required to help absorb the output of our greatly
expanded industrial plant" without "an increasing volume of
foreign investment." [22] Thus, with all its limitation, foreign
investment is bound to play an ever-growing part in the
national drive for full employment.

[20] Keynes, *op. cit.*, p. 382.
[21] Chancellor of the Exchequer Hugh Dalton. (See *New York Times*, April
20, 1947.)
[22] United States Treasury, *The Bretton Woods Proposals: Fund and Bank*
(Washington, D.C., 1945).

Index

387

For Product Safety Concerns and Information please contact our EU
representative GPSR@taylorandfrancis.com Taylor & Francis Verlag GmbH,
Kaufingerstraße 24, 80331 München, Germany

Printed and bound by CPI Group (UK) Ltd, Croydon, CR0 4YY
08/05/2025
01864342-0001